Behind the Diversity Numbers

Behind the Diversity Numbers

Achieving Racial Equity on Campus

W. Carson Byrd

HARVARD EDUCATION PRESS
CAMBRIDGE, MASSACHUSETTS

Paperback ISBN 978-1-68253-632-2
Library Edition ISBN 978-1-68253-633-9

Library of Congress Cataloging-in-Publication Data is on file.

Published by Harvard Education Press,
an imprint of the Harvard Education Publishing Group
Harvard Education Press
8 Story Street
Cambridge, MA 02138

Cover Design: Ciano Design
Cover Image: Hill Street Studios/DigitalVision via Getty Images

The typefaces in this book are Adobe Garamond Pro and Gill Sans.

Contents

Foreword

Walter R. Allen, University of California, Los Angeles, November 9, 2020

As I write, Americans are exercising their franchise in unprecedented numbers in national elections to decide who will lead the country in this moment of crisis. The vote is a referendum on the crises of a COVID-19 pandemic, mass protests against police violence, and extreme economic disruption and disparities. In a larger sense, the body politic will express its ideals and visions for the future. Ultimately, the election and discourse around enduring inequities by race, gender, and class speaks to the unfulfilled promise of the American Dream.

This important book arrives at a pivotal moment in history when the United States continues to be ruptured by mass protests. The public lynching of George Floyd and the clandestine murder of Breonna Taylor compromised our nation's conscience, ideals, and core institutions. A national movement for social justice, driven by widespread condemnation of wanton police violence and brutality against Black people, has shaken the very foundations of our nation.

The COVID-19 pandemic has also massively disrupted life in our society. This scourge leaves no one untouched, even as it exacts the greatest toll on those who are most vulnerable and marginalized. It is difficult to turn a blind eye, to make excuses, to quietly accept the status quo when the tragedies are no longer restricted to Black, Brown, poor, women, and others who live at the intersection of multiple disadvantages. As these threats to "domestic tranquility" loom, even the most taken-for-granted pleasures and routines have been compromised. Everyday life in America will never be the same.

Behind the Diversity Numbers astutely connects higher education—colleges and universities—to these larger, expansive social dramas. Carson Byrd highlights high-profile court cases where competing visions and facts for elite colleges and universities are being contested. The root question is, who will have access, success, and legitimacy in these hallowed spaces? The stakes extend beyond diversity on college campuses to determine individual and group position in the American economic hierarchy (and, by association, in the racial hierarchy). Certainly, the value of a college education—whether at an elite or a lower-ranked institution—cannot be minimized. A college degree enhances life chances, experiences, and outcomes exponentially; over a lifetime, college graduates earn a million dollars more than do high school graduates.

Racial inequality is expressed not only in educational disadvantage but also in threads across rampant police violence, health crises, and diminished quality of life. Byrd persuasively ties higher education to the systemic racism that degrades, blocks opportunity, and then penalizes Blacks and other victims of the nation's racial caste system. A college degree sets the course of life chances and life outcomes, thus helping to ultimately decide "winners" and "losers." Byrd argues that despite claims to meritocracy, the college attainment game is rigged.

This book challenges status quo defenders, who, when faced with the dilemma of explaining persistent racial inequality in US higher education (and in the larger society), prefer to emphasize individual differences over structural or organizational patterns. Treating the system of meritocracy as sacrosanct, they argue that success or failure is personally determined (blaming the victims of racism, discrimination, and inequality). Are we to believe everyone has an equal chance to achieve the American Dream? Karen and Barbara Fields reject notions of "*the* American meritocracy," pointing out, "If admission to the ranks is skewed and manipulated, then its members are not a meritocracy in the first place; they are a self- perpetuating oligarchy, even if they imagine themselves the best and the brightest."

Byrd boldly charges into the center of existential debates over equity, diversity, and inclusion in higher education. Using recent court cases about race-conscious admissions at Harvard University, the University of North Carolina at Chapel Hill, and the University of Texas at Austin as the lever, he skillfully connects systemic racial inequity in the larger society to major institutions like colleges and universities and to individual life experiences and outcomes. Yet, as he wryly observes, the primary focus in these complex, polarizing "lawsuits against colleges around one of the most debated set of policies in the last fifty years" centers on narrow, decontextualized statistical analyses. Byrd cautions that "the way institutions quantify and analyze diversity, equity, and inclusion may reflect other related issues shaping how we understand these important aspects of college life and how we address inequity and injustice in higher education" (see the introduction).

Behind the Diversity Numbers offers an instructive reflection on the "raced" origins and implications of quantification, including statistical analyses, in higher education research. Using QuantCrit (derived from critical race theory, or CRT), Byrd presents a conceptually elegant, theoretically rich, and empirically rigorous critique. He forcefully rejects the idea that the statistical concepts, theory, methods, and perspectives commonly seen in educational research are neutral. The book provides an excellent tutorial, based on a fully formed, mixed-methods research perspective. He persuasively argues how quantitative science can combine with CRT to achieve complex, "thick" descriptions of key macro-, meso- and micro-level factors underlying privilege or disadvantage. He clearly recognizes the assets and liabilities of quantification in the study of higher education. Rejecting the idea that one size fits all, he instead embraces the imperative that research methods and statistical analyses should be chosen to match the research questions at hand. He scrupulously rejects the illogic of using only quantitative methods when qualitative methods are better suited ("quantitative mismatch"). Hammers are excellent tools when one wants to drive a nail but poor choices when the goal is to crack an egg. Put another way, it is ridiculous to search for a quarter you lost on Twelfth Street, over on Fifth Street because the light is better there.

Byrd discusses the unintended, sometimes negative consequences of quantification in the study of equity, diversity, and inclusion in higher education. These approaches suffer from a failure to consider the larger historical, systemic, and organizational circumstances that individuals contend with. Quantification summarizes widely dispersed observations and recognizes explanatory patterns in the data. In this way, the method minimizes the noise and messiness of on-the-ground reality in favor of a bird's-eye view with neatly ordered categories. Quantification is the appropriate standard when the

primary goal is to enumerate, summarize, and generalize individual characteristics across the larger sample or population. It aims to combine individual,
idiosyncratic, particularistic traits into general characteristics or categories.

Paradoxically, quantification can in fact ignore context, nuance, and
granular variation while claiming to statistically weigh these factors. For example, statistical controls hold other variables constant to examine a specific
bivariate relationship. However, such manipulations do not necessarily remove the cumulative direct and indirect consequences of mismeasured or
unmeasured factors. Witness the joke about a statistician who stumbles on a
student's corpse but who concludes that "holding all things constant" (body
temperature, respiration rate, heartbeat, etc.), there is no cause for concern;
the student is just fine. After all, the student is on campus that day. An absurd
formulation, to be sure, but this book challenges equally absurd research that
expresses surprise over the predictable educational underachievement of college students who, during their K–12 education, were condemned to failing
schools, unqualified teachers, substandard books, deficient labs, and stomachs
growling from hunger. Similarly, Shaun Harper notes that research tends to
focus on academic failure among Black male college students, rather than on
their academic success. Perhaps this imbalance reveals more about the society
(and the researchers) than it reveals about the students.

Quantification often ignores the nuance, richness, and "thickness" of
everyday life, opting instead for more distant abstraction. This approach can
miss the lived experiences bound up in a particular Black college student's
truth, in a particular university, at a particular time. Statistical and mathematical manipulations, like regression to the mean, are valuable when the primary
goal is to summarize variation across large numbers of individuals and answer
questions like "Does high school GPA predict college GPA?" The resultant
single or average measure can then be attributed with some precision to *all*
individuals in the sample or population. However, individuals who don't fit
the normed group reality or, better still, the stereotypes are most often—and
most easily—dismissed as outliers. Interestingly, Sigmund Freud's emphasis
on the outlier, or "single case," produced rich theories of social organization
and behavior writ large. Similarly, great informational, theoretical, policy, and
even methodological value has resulted in fields that prioritize the case: law,
business, and medicine.

We are reminded that statistical significance does not necessarily equate to substantive validity. For instance, individual traits like GPA or test scores are known to be highly correlated with admission to highly selective colleges. Research confirms this "empirical fact," which incidentally rests on the American cultural belief that "people rise and fall on their own efforts, intelligence and academic merits" (chapter 1). The fact that college GPA varies across major, institution type, gender, social class, and race is consequential. More to the point, racial discrimination determines educational opportunities and outcomes from the womb for a child who is born poor, Black, and female.

Behind the Diversity Numbers cautions against uncritical acceptance of quantitative measures as undisputed fact. Statistics do not "speak for themselves." Instead, what matters is *who* measures, *what* is measured, *how* statistics are interpreted, and the *consequences* associated with the findings. Yes, statistical measures are seemingly objective abstractions, but they are also social products rooted in the society's historical, political-economic, and racial system. Byrd notes that the power to determine who speaks and who will be heard is strongly determinative. Who dominates the mic determines whether a conversation about race and the achievement gap will compare white students with Black students *or* will compare white students with Asian American students. Again, the numbers and statistics do not speak for themselves.

Behind the Diversity Numbers points to recurrent themes in higher education discourse and research—questions such as "Who is on campus?" and "What are they learning?" Meanwhile, significant normative, structural, and organizational questions like "Why?" are overlooked. Byrd creatively extends the assessment of campus racial climate to focus on campus microclimates, like the experiences of a Black, lesbian, poor, first-generation student who is at the intersection of multiple hierarchical identities. Byrd provides an action agenda for change, advocating the need to "recognize that a true transformation of colleges and universities to promote diversity, equity, and inclusion and not reinforce racial inequalities requires that the institutions refrain from dumping into the laps of individuals the responsibility for organizational change. Universities, as racialized organizations, can create and maintain racial inequalities without individual malice and even with people's best intentions" (chapter 4).

This book offers a penetrating interrogation of how statistics are used in the Harvard University affirmative action case. Since statistical analyses center individuals (aggregated to categories), the broader conceptual, sociohistorical, and organizational contexts that drive persistent racial disparities are ignored. Diversity becomes a numerical "problem" for study, with statistics as the best (only) tools, and the primary goal is to reach set categorical benchmarks rather than reduce or eliminate inequality. Byrd examines how campuses' "history of racial exclusion," their organizational approach to diversity and inclusion, and indeed the very notion of diversity itself require more scrutiny to establish "what disparities on campus mean and what should be done about them" (introduction). It is sobering to be reminded how earlier goals of "race and restorative justice" were compromised by the *diversity rationale*. In a profound shift, the original emphasis on aiding students who were targets of racial bias, harassment, or discrimination was replaced by an emphasis on using their limited presence in "white spaces" to benefit the majority, for example, to prepare white students for diverse workplaces. Derrick Bell's "interest convergence theory" anticipates this shift when he argues that racial "remedies if granted, will secure, advance, or at least not harm societal interests deemed important by middle and upper class whites." In a society founded on white supremacy, the cultural, ideational, organizational, economic, political, and educational systems cooperate in the goal of maintaining a rigid hierarchy where white people are at the pinnacle and Black people are at the bottom. *Behind the Diversity Numbers* reminds readers that some of our most beloved social institutions—our schools and colleges—contribute to unequal experiences and outcomes. And what's more, our understanding of these institutions may be distorted by the way they are quantified and analyzed, leading to benefits accruing for some, to the detriment of many.

Post Script

All votes have been cast and counted in a national election with record-setting participation. Yet some see fit to dispute the empirical, statistical, and mathematical evidence of this referendum. Their challenges mostly question the legitimacy of votes from largely Black, urban areas. This week, Harvard successfully defended its race-conscious admissions policy in the First Circuit Court of Appeals. The ruling upheld judgements from numerous prior cases that had tried and confirmed similar elements. One wonders why it was necessary to revisit this well-trod legal ground—even as another court challenge to race-conscious admissions at the University of North Carolina at Chapel Hill is currently underway. Widespread national protests supported the Black Lives Matter movement against police violence. Nevertheless, Black and Brown people continue to die in disproportionate numbers by the hands of police. The conundrum connecting these seemingly disparate events has to do with how racial mythology dismisses or reframes the reality of racial oppression. In each instance, we see how racial projects systematically reinforce and defend the notion of white superiority—even to the point of rejecting indisputable empirical evidence to the contrary. These racial projects make you question not only which numbers matter but also which lives matter.

Behind the Diversity Numbers interrogates the use, misuse, and dismissal of empirical evidence in the quantification of diversity and merit in higher education research. Byrd tells universities seeking truly diverse, inclusive campuses that given the persistent, stubbornly rooted reality of racial inequity, "neither quantifying nor dequantifying diversity will save you" (chapter 4). He warns, "Excluding race and ethnicity from these policies does not mean that race is still not a factor in who is admitted to a university . . . [C]olor-blind approaches allow other structural inequalities that shape students' lives to take precedence and continue to privilege white students" (chapter 1). Derrick Bell offered a similarly pessimistic assessment of racial gains and prospects after the US Supreme Court case *Brown v. Board of Education of Topeka* (1954), which outlawed racial segregation. In his *And We Are Not Saved: The Elusive Quest for Racial Justice*, Bell declares, "On the agenda of unfinished business, America's continuing commitment to white domination looms especially large for those citizens of color whose lives are little less circumscribed than were those of their slave forebears."

Over sixty-five years later, our pursuit of racial equity and justice in higher education, and society as a whole, is still unfinished business. *Behind the Diversity Numbers* provides a compelling argument for why we must stop blaming the so-called bad apples and focus on what our universities, as complex organizations, must do to change their orientations toward racial equity efforts that matter for who and how they are counted. Universities must examine how racialized experiences and outcomes are analyzed and monitored and identify what can be done now and in the future to undercut a racially unjust and inequitable system.

INTRODUCTION

Following the Numbers to Diversity and Inclusivity

A SERIES OF MAJOR COURT CASES reaching the US Supreme Court docket in the last several years highlights the seemingly rigid political dividing lines in society on issues that can affect our everyday lives. The court is examining gerrymandering, the provisions of the Voting Rights Act, marriage equality, expanding health care, and other important issues of our times. These cases often involve a wide range of experts and organizations and have become serious topics of conversations around the United States, including discussions in the news and around family dinner tables. Yet, when people think of some of these high-profile court cases, do they envision two economics professors as the star witnesses? Most likely not. People would no doubt joke about what two economists arguing in court would look like, perhaps comparing the hypothetical arguments to those of the famed lawyer Johnnie Cochran: "If the model doesn't fit, you must acquit, and rerun your analyses with a larger sample size and cluster your standard errors!" Certainly, most disagreements between academics are benign exchanges about small details, but in a series of recent lawsuits against colleges both sides have made professors and their analyses vital to their arguments. The cases have centered around a set of policies hotly debated since the 1970s.

Consider a recent Q&A session about an economist's analysis of the admissions policy at a highly selective university. During the session, another economist noted that "the statistical evidence does not support the claim" made by his peer and that the analyses seemed "nonsensical to me."[1] Although you might expect that this discussion was happening at some idyllic college campus or at a national economics conference, the Q&A occurred in a Boston courtroom during the fall of 2018. How did two economists and their statistical analyses find themselves at the center of a legal battle followed closely across the United States?

These economists were in the midst of the polarizing debate on affirmative action. University of California economist David Card disputed the findings of Duke University economist Peter Arcidiacono in the recently argued case brought against a university's race-conscious admissions policy. Card, a hired expert witness for Harvard University, presented critiques and counteranalyses on behalf of the university, which was the defendant in the case *Students for Fair Admissions, Inc. v. President and Fellows of Harvard College* (commonly referred to as *SFFA v. Harvard*). The charges levied against Harvard included the argument that its admissions office was biased against Asian American applicants, effectively placing a cap or an illegal quota on how many Asian American applicants were admitted each year for a new cohort of students. Late in October 2018, Card testified that Arcidiacono, the Students for Fair Admissions expert, failed to clearly show that the university's admissions process penalized Asian American applicants because of their ethnicity. Further, he argued, no evidence supported the assertion of a yearly cap on the number of Asian Americans admitted to Harvard each year. The reason for the disagreement was the methodological approach and statistical analyses of how the applicants were scored on a range of background, academic, and social indicators. Depending on how each economist conducted the quantitative analysis, the results differed on how students fared in the review of their applications.

The economists' statistical analyses and expert testimonies dominated the legal arguments for both sides. The case clearly hinged on the number-crunching abilities of the economists. Only once did the expert testimonies not come from current or former university administrators or the economists. As one story noted, the "statistics [gave] way to personal stories about diversity" as Harvard called to the stand a handful of students and alumni, all of whom were people of color, to describe their experiences with, and the importance of, diversity in higher education.[2] The university and its supporters argued that the educational and social benefits of diversity were threatened by the Students for Fair Admissions lawsuit. Harvard argued that losing the case would dismantle the university's ability to consider race and racism in an applicant's life experiences and perspectives they could bring to campus as a potential student.

Although the context of the case helps reveal how diversity, equity, and inclusion are constructed in higher education, an important question remains and affects both sides of the legal arguments. Why was it seen as odd for Harvard to have students and alumni as witnesses in a legal case about how students benefit from elite colleges and the diversity they cultivate through admissions practices? Put another way, why did a conversation about a highly selective university's admissions policy hinge on the quantification of people's experiences and backgrounds? Recent lawsuits against colleges' race-conscious admissions policies have shed light on the battle for exclusive opportunities and resources at many selective US colleges and universities. In their efforts to combat threats to race-conscious admissions policies, universities tout the educational benefits of diversity. They back their arguments with thirty years of social science research and data collected from millions of students nationwide. The research shows a strong connection between racial diversity and the learning and social outcomes of college students.

I challenge us to think deeply about how the common approaches to analyze and promote diversity, equity, and inclusion in higher education may thwart these aims in different circumstances. This book describes how quantifying diversity and inclusion to create or modify policies and programs in higher education can have latent consequences not easily foreseen. To this end, I use a wide range of institutional data, including recent lawsuits against colleges operating race-conscious admissions policies, and examine the important research on campus climates. Quantitative approaches often fail to recognize that racial inequality relates to people's lived experiences, not just outcomes, and can lead administrators and policy makers to ignore the important details that can better inform their decisions. Further, the way institutions quantify and analyze diversity, equity, and inclusion may reflect other related issues shaping how we understand these important aspects of college life and how we address inequity and injustice in higher education.

I examine how organizational logic and routines encourage the quantification of diversity and inclusion. Such a focus on numbers shifts our perspective of what disparities on campus mean and what should be done about them. Diversity becomes a "problem" to be studied, and quantitative approaches are framed as the best tools to study it, given the organizational logic of higher education.[3] Numbers-driven approaches thus create metrics out of people and establish goals for universities to attain. This organizational approach to diversity and inclusion orients people's view to obtaining certain numbers, or benchmarks, rather than reducing inequality on their campuses.[4] This book discusses how most universities doggedly pursue quantitative approaches to diversity and inclusion, despite research showing that these approaches conflict with the true goals of higher education. One shortcoming of these methodological approaches is that they focus on how white students, as well as faculty and staff, benefit from diversity without adequately addressing power, injustice, and marginalization on campus. To understand this shortcoming in quantitative approaches and possibly others, we must examine the history and organizational contexts of colleges and universities.

Rethinking "Normal" Colleges

Colleges and universities throughout the United States have unique histories detailing their purpose and evolution, which provide windows into how higher education has played an important part in racializing bodies, numbers, and perspectives of inequality. Many of the earliest colleges were founded to educate only a small segment of the population. Throughout history, higher education simultaneously educated and excluded many groups in society, in this way becoming major actors in producing or maintaining racial stratification and inequality. An awareness of this history helps us reconsider how our supposedly normal colleges operate as racialized organizations.[5] Additionally, by recognizing that race, racism, and higher education are interconnected in US history, we can see that colleges and universities are not benign organizations. This viewpoint prevents us from glossing over the processes of racial stratification and inequality embedded in colleges' everyday functions, including their research methods for diversity and inclusion.

Overview of Race in the Development of American Higher Education

As American higher education evolved, it affected and reflected the racial era of the time. Much has been written about the early years of American higher education and its exclusivity for young white men from well-connected, wealthy families.[6] During the colonial period, colleges supported the violent seizure of land and resources in the expanding territory from Indigenous communities and enslaving many people of African descent to build these institutions of higher learning. Recent in-depth histories describe how white people not only used enslaved Black men and women to build campuses but also based new legal codes, medical practices, and social sciences (e.g., anthropology, psychology, and sociology) on colonial views of non-European communities.[7] These academic offerings also included the development of new quantitative methodologies for statistics and applied them for the construction of racial differences that shaped public policy and the perception of race and inequality.[8] By the end of the nineteenth century, the walls and knowledge of American colleges and universities were influenced by race and racism in many ways.

From the emancipation of enslaved people at the end of the Civil War in the 1860s to the early 1970s, Black, Native American, Latinx, and Asian and Pacific Islander communities were effectively excluded from a majority of colleges and universities. These educational opportunities were mostly reserved for white men.[9] Even with the expansion of women's higher education opportunities, college attendance was still mainly enjoyed only by wealthy white people. Only a few institutions, such as Oberlin College and Berea College, attempted to provide integrated higher education options in the depth of the Jim Crow era.[10] Despite the founding of institutions with the explicit purpose of training Black teachers and offering vocational training, these institutions were structured as underfunded, educationally inferior options to reinforce the racial inequality across the nation.[11] Nonetheless, despite their many obstacles, these colleges developed into pivotal organizations in communities, survived, and continue to disproportionally serve students of color well into the twenty-first century.[12] Even though higher education expanded during the mid-twentieth century, particularly after World War II, when the GI Bill encouraged college attendance by veterans, higher education remained highly segregated. During this time, older institutions accumulated higher status and more resources to buoy the positions of their mostly wealthy and white students across generations.[13]

Accompanying the expanding higher education system was the creation of standardized admissions tests to preserve the racial exclusivity of these increasingly high-status institutions and their resources in the face of increased immigration during the Jim Crow era. Universities, particularly those associated with the Ivy League, sought testing approaches that supported narrow definitions of intelligence and merit while applying versions of "geographical affirmative action" for white men from outside the legacy families and communities from which these institutions pulled most of their students in the Northeast.[14] Soon, high test scores were signs of the "best and brightest" among white students, given their access to these resources and educational opportunities. Simultaneously, the creation of eugenic perspectives and policies to reinforce racial stratification and inequality in broader society also emanated from these institutions. For example, the creation and measurement of racial differences still in use today were originally developed to justify social Darwinism.[15] Thus, universities were producing research and policies to support racial inequality and exclusion on and off campus.

The struggle to desegregate campuses with a long history of educating only, or mostly, white students continues well into the twenty-first century. Few higher education institutions desegregated willingly, let alone quickly, though some in the Northeast did develop race-conscious admissions and desegregation policies earlier rather than responding to the national protests of the civil rights and Black Power movements of the 1950s to 1970s.[16] The push for increased student and faculty representation, particularly by Black students, and the expansion of the curriculum beyond its Eurocentric focus catalyzed a slow, difficult evolution of who was on campus and what they were learning.[17] Desegregation and shifts in the inclusiveness on college campuses with such policies as affirmative action in college admissions were often met with crystalized resentment of these changes along with stereotyping of Black students entering these colleges.[18] Despite historic increases in both college attendance overall and for students of color today, universities remain rigid in their racial attitudes. Race supposedly enters an institution but is not a central feature of the institution, according to these common perspectives.

The long-fought battle to desegregate college campuses and create learning environments that are more inclusive led to a contentious set of policies around race-conscious admissions, often referred to as affirmative action. Beginning with the 1978 *Regents of the University of California v. Allan Bakke* decision, which outlawed the use of racial quotas to reserve seats according to applicants' race or ethnicity for an entering college class, numerous cases have been brought to the courts to redefine access and opportunity in higher education.[19] Central components of these cases include the construction of difference and diversity, how universities can shape access and opportunity for students, and how these conversations and related policies tie to the missions and goals of universities as educational organizations. The legal and social science case for race-conscious admissions policies hinges on an argument for the educational benefits of diversity. According to this perspective, increased racial and ethnic diversity (and, as more recently argued, socioeconomic diversity) on campuses can benefit students both academically and socially.[20] However, as described in subsequent chapters, we must carefully consider how institutional situations reflect popular legal and social science arguments that frame who benefits from this diversity. These arguments can inadvertently lead to racial stratification and inequality on college campuses.[21]

Higher education has a racialized history that shaped many of the early functions, policies, and everyday interactions on college campuses. And unfortunately, many of these foundational aspects of higher education persist today. Contrary to popular belief, universities are not color-blind, race-neutral, meritocratic educational organizations; nor were they ever founded to be that way. Instead, these organizations generally supported different processes to produce or reproduce racial stratification and inequality in society through higher education.[22] These processes include many seemingly objective and systematic approaches such as documenting, measuring, and interpreting diversity and inclusion with the goal of fighting inequality. However, by more holistically framing how race is interwoven into different aspects of colleges, we can identify how even the best-laid plans to combat racial inequality may actually lead to its reification and reproduction in the future.

Colleges as Racialized Organizations

As the preceding discussion shows, the history of higher education and the organizational trajectories of institutions also reflect the development of racial categories, stratification of resources, and persistent inequality known as racial formation.[23] Colleges and universities stratify resources and opportunities by race and ethnicity at the organizational level.[24] By recognizing the American higher education system as racialized, given this history of racial stratification and inequality, we can better examine what diversity and inclusion policies and evaluations can accomplish in the future.

Even identifying institutions by demographics and their noted missions takes on new meanings when they are considered critically. The US Department of Education identifies approximately one hundred institutions as historically black colleges or universities (HBCUs) and identifies others as tribal colleges, Asian American and Native American Pacific Islander–serving institutions (AANPISIs), or Hispanic- or Latinx-serving institutions (HSIs). If an institution lacks one of these identifiers, what type of college is it, exactly? How do we compare these specially identified institutions with one another as well as with nonlabeled institutions? Sociologist Eduardo Bonilla-Silva suggests that identifiers such as HBCU operate as a "racial tag" that associates stereotypical views of who these institutions serve and what their academic and social offerings may be for students.[25] That is, these institutional identifiers reveal how the American higher education system operates in relation to, and influences, racial inequality in educational opportunities and resources.[26] Further, as higher education scholar Gina Garcia notes, among institutions identified as HSIs, the faculty, staff, and administrators do not embrace this identification in the same way and sometimes denigrate it. Their attitude, she says, reflects another aspect of racializing universities: the tendency to see value in some institutions over others and to normalize the status distinctions that rely on race.[27] If an institution has no racial identifier, then most people will describe it as "just a college" and leave unquestioned how a college operates as a racialized organization that influences access to resources and opportunities.

Considering educational resources and opportunities, HBCUs have endured the long-held societal stigma as derivative and inferior educational spaces for Black and other students of color. Such perspectives allow universities not racially identified to operate as normalized white institutions.[28] These nonlabeled institutions can also offer a greater variety of academic and social opportunities, including the important aspect of financial sustainability, than racially identified organizations can offer.[29] Organizations, much like individuals, can take for granted their unmarked whiteness, that is, the racialized aspects of everyday life that benefits white people. How people navigate this unmarked whiteness on the campuses of Harvard, Princeton, the University of Michigan, and the University of North Carolina, for example, justifies a pernicious understanding of these organizations as places that are more racially equitable than not.[30] Missing is the recognition that racial advantages and disadvantages are relational and woven into the processes and policies of universities. Our approaches to issues of diversity and inclusion in higher education frequently ignore the multidimensional aspects of racial inequality on our campuses. This limitation muddies how race-related distinctions within and between universities can reflect people's views of racial inequality, its causes, and how higher education and society "launder racial domination by obscuring or legitimating unequal processes."[31]

How Racialized Organizations of Higher Education Work

By recognizing not only that some colleges and universities have a history and an organizational life tied to race and racism but also that the entire system of US higher education does, we can better examine the racial disparities interwoven in our institutions. This book stitches together several streams of research to explore how diversity and inclusion policies that rely heavily on quantitative data can warp our interpretations of people's experiences on campus and might perpetuate racial inequality in higher education. To understand how racial stratification and inequality are embedded in organizational life, we must open up the proverbial black box to identify how the different components of universities interrelate. We must clarify how a university operates as, to use sociologist Victor Ray's term, "racialized organizations."[32]

Organizations are guided by schemata that are effectively the unconscious and unwritten rules, or "common sense," shaping people's thoughts about what organizations should be doing and their own roles in organizations.[33] Once these rules are attached to the distribution of resources and opportunities, the underlying and unwritten logic establishes durable structures for people to navigate.[34]

For a simple example of how these unwritten ideas and rules manifest themselves in higher education, let's consider faculty members. Faculty are generally evaluated for their contributions to three areas: research, teaching, and service. The weight given to each of these three areas depends on the type of institution a person may work in (e.g., a research-intensive institution versus a small liberal arts college) and other internal differences such as having a graduate program that promotes research activities. All faculty members are supposed to provide service in various forms to their departments, institutions, professions, and the community. Service work is typically the least recognized aspect of faculty work. Despite these broad guidelines, faculty members of color, especially women, perform much more service work than do their white, particularly male, colleagues. The first-mentioned group of faculty members is overwhelmed with requests to mentor students of color, work with different campus organizations, serve on search committees to increase diversity, sit on community panels, and take on other activities that make other tasks such as conducting research and publishing much more difficult.[35]

This taxation of faculty of color extends to their teaching, as education scholar Gloria Ladson-Billings found in her examination of African American faculty in teacher education programs across the nation. She found that these faculty members are disproportionately asked (and often "strongly suggested") to teach the diversity courses in their departments.[36] These classes take faculty away from their areas of expertise and rely on the stereotypical assumption that, as faculty of color, they should be able to teach courses about diversity in education.

As just described, the organizational schema among universities suggests that faculty members are evaluated by their research, teaching, and service and that it is up to each individual faculty member to meet these general expectations. However, most universities unwittingly include a racialized aspect in this guideline. They are slow to recognize that faculty of color are performing much more service work than their white colleagues are, and these efforts are systematically overlooked in their evaluations. Thus, as white colleagues are publishing and teaching courses in their areas with less taxation of service work, their faculty colleagues of color have the opposite experience. The oft-stated solution "Protect your time by just saying no" to students and other service requirements may align with the common ideas in an organization, but this advice ignores the campus inequalities. It aims instead to change the faculty members of color, not the policies and processes that advantage their white colleagues' careers. Persistent racial disparities and their connections to university policies and processes may not catch people's attention and register as inequality or unfair evaluations. But the seemingly clear disparities in duties between faculty of color and white faculty begs the question: how could someone *not* recognize the unequal circumstances a colleague may be facing and not judge the colleague as a poor performer if the evaluator were sitting on a promotion and tenure committee?

Racial inequality on campuses and in the larger society is not relegated to outcomes; it also reflects people's experiences and understandings of those outcomes. To understand why organizations such as universities might not change to promote more diversity, equity, and inclusion, we must consider how people make sense of the unequal distribution of opportunities and resources around them. These perspectives about racial inequality are a feature of people's racial ideologies, or the frameworks people use to rationalize the racial inequality around them.[37] Racial ideology reinforces the unwritten ideas and rules of an organization for how and why it functions in particular ways. As demonstrated by those who, to rationalize a university's racialized policies, suggest that it's up to individual faculty of color to protect their own time, not everyone perceives racial inequality as a structural issue. Some see it more as an individual issue that people should work hard to overcome.[38] This rationalization for why we have racial inequality in society and on college campuses in particular can shape what is viewed as the "appropriate" solution to address inequality, if inequality is viewed as a problem at all. Through everyday organizational routines such as considering an applicant for admission to a university, racial schemata connect to resources, and a bureaucracy stratifies people's access to these resources and opportunities.[39] The legitimation of unequal outcomes and processes through organizational norms can mask how racial inequality is reproduced through organizational actions, establishing patterns across the sum of individual actions.[40]

Organizations are framed as race-neutral and color-blind, and changes to their policies and processes can be seen as "illegitimate intrusions into the normal, meritocratic, neutral function of organizations."[41] Yet people's mental gymnastics to justify racial inequality and the belief that organizations are race-neutral hint at the importance of race in many organizational functions, particularly for colleges and universities. A poignant example of this situation involves people's perspectives about race-conscious admissions policies in higher education. People believe that these policies disrupt the seemingly meritocratic functions of the unlabeled racialized organizations of higher education. In an intriguing study by sociologist Frank Samson, white people reported that a person's grades should take higher importance for Black applicants for college admissions than the grades should count for Asian American or Pacific Islander applicants.[42] The white respondents' stereotypes about groups merge with their perceptions of possible threats to their group's resources to reinforce how they believe universities, as racialized organizations, should function as a more or less rigid meritocracy. These findings also suggest how white people's different emphases of grades in college admissions means they will overwhelmingly benefit from these admissions policies and practices behind seemingly race-neutral organizational functions. Thus, as Ray points out, by linking race and resources in the organizational processes and polices affecting college admissions, affirmative action policies are "battle-ground policies" of racial politics because they can change organizational structure and challenge assumptions of color-blindness.[43] Especially for college admissions, an increasing awareness that the organization is racialized can challenge the organization's assertion of race neutrality and the norms that shape racial inequality. Clearly, higher education needs additional changes—beyond mere tokenism disguised as a serious effort—to pursue more equitable and just actions.[44]

Other Organizational Components That Can Reinforce Racial Inequality

Important aspects of everyday life at universities—beyond their formal policies and organizational schemata—can also reinforce racial stratification and inequality. For example, a university's history, demographics, curricula, and culture, including its symbols and traditions, can play important roles.[45] Each of these components interacts to shape the opportunities that people can un-earth within places marked by, and normalizing, whiteness.[46] As explained earlier, most colleges and universities were founded for and by white people while excluding and often using people of color for white educational and career advancement.[47] Although many institutions can have similar histories, these similarities should not overshadow particular insights into how each university individually supported and was part of the larger racial structure to survive and thrive throughout history.

Recently, universities began acknowledging through deep historical exca-vation their connections to slavery. One institution, Georgetown University, enacted a reconciliation and atonement project after finding that past admin-istrators sold 272 enslaved people in 1838 to gain financial stability when the university was facing possible closure, leading to its survival and development into the elite institution it is today.[48] Although Georgetown's actions occurred over 180 years ago, organizations have, throughout all US history, supported the various iterations of racial stratification and inequality within the legal codes and, importantly, following the norms of the time.[49] Thus, the current era is continuously marked by racial inequality in and through organizations such as colleges and universities, suggesting that these organizations are work-ing within the current cultural and structural realities to perpetuate these processes (racial stratification) and outcomes (racial inequalities) as they had done decades and even centuries ago. These actions should not be reduced to whether something is a deliberate act to produce or sustain racial inequality; they simply reflect how racialized organizations function in society.

Perhaps one of the most discussed integral components of universities is the demography of campuses. The representation of different racial and ethnic groups on campus provides intriguing information about how people under-stand educational opportunities and, more perniciously, how race influences ideas of merit, diversity, inclusion, and equality. When institutions are referred to as "normal colleges" or "just a college," their demographic composition of students leads people to think of *a predominantly white institution*. This term uses the literal faces of those on campus to prevent deeper consideration of the college's processes that shape racial inequality. Returning to segregation in higher education as a fixture of racialized organizations, we must recognize that "segregation, by design, limits access to organizational resources" that are informed and "historically enforced through custom, policy, and law."[50] This book explores how segregation in higher education can be perceived differently through categorization and policy analyses that can hide racial stratification in plain sight and legitimate it as a normal function of universities. Segregation cannot be untangled from resources and opportunities on campus.

A university's symbols, traditions, and broader campus culture can also amplify the unwritten ideas and rules guiding different organizational processes that support racial stratification and inequality. These aspects of campuses provide physical and ideological glue for legitimating a legacy of racial exclusion. Although the evolution of organizations seems more inclusive than in the past, they can still reinforce racial stratification and inequality. For example, it is easy for a college to point out that it has a more diverse student body or has promoted equality through increased graduation rates for underrepresented groups when none of these students were allowed to enroll at the institution until fifty or sixty years ago. Universities present their campuses as racially neutral spaces in most respects, particularly compared with the past. They brandish antidiscrimination and equal opportunity policies as signs of improvement and declare their institution racially progressive.[51] But an institution's space is not equally available to all. Students of color face many problems as they pursue their degrees, and faculty of color must work around challenges each day.[52] If colleges operate as racialized organizations, as argued, they must recognize how the methodological approaches of researchers influence the colleges' assessment of their own racialization and how they propose to eliminate this inequality.[53]

Finally, colleges and universities do not simply influence those who enter their campuses; they also have an impact on broader society. Racialized organizations are not disconnected from the structural and cultural realities of society, and in many ways, they work to support mechanisms of racial stratification and inequality. As the recent reconciliation and atonement project of Georgetown University attests, people struggle to publicly acknowledge that beloved colleges can buttress racism through their everyday organizational routines and goals across history. When institutions do acknowledge these connections, people tend to rationalize these instances as bad apples or historical relics rather than acknowledge that most institutions reinforce racial inequality; they continually want to identify racists in a land where racism supposedly no longer exists.[54] Racialized organizations such as universities sometimes distance themselves from present-day effects of racism in the organization by placing them in the past. Because charges of current racism can injure the organization's reputation, universities' automatic defense is often to showcase their diversity-promoting efforts on campus as proof that racism cannot have such negative effects if they are showing some commitment to overcoming it and are becoming more inclusive.[55] These efforts shape inequality off campus as well in communities that rely on institutions to educate and employ them, but the broader effects of inequality are seldom considered in studies of diversity in universities. I take up some of these connections later, in chapter 4.

The current study of diversity work, particularly how researchers and policy makers analyze and interpret diversity, equity, and inclusion in higher education, provides an intriguing look at what happens when we shed the view of organizations as color-blind and race-neutral to focus on the influence of the underlying ideas and unwritten rules guiding organizations and their routines about diversity and inclusion that initially conflict with this color-blind perspective.[56] A racialized organization approach of colleges "centers the role of human agency in generating new mechanisms while also explaining the stability of organizational inequality."[57] This reframing of colleges as racialized organizations allows us to ask, what challenges exist in universities' efforts to promote, measure, and analyze diversity and inclusion in higher education through quantitative approaches? This book will show that common quantitative approaches to assess diversity and inclusion in higher education may actually perpetuate inequality at an organizational level.

Quantifying Diversity

To understand how the numbers-driven approaches gained center stage in the diversity, equity, and inclusion policy conversations of higher education, we have to recognize why people adhere to quantitative approaches in general. Numbers have power in society. And in recent decades, many aspects of our everyday lives have been quantified. We quantify different features of the progress of the economy, for example, and more personally, we use such quantifications as college rankings to understand our options and opportunities.[58] Quantitative methods provide researchers, administrators, policy makers, and the public with a numeric representation of different experiences, groups, and social phenomena. The use of numbers in relation to diversity and inclusion in higher education is a contentious issue on some fronts but not on others. Before tackling the arguments around the quantification of diversity, equity, and inclusion, we should first understand quantification.

In quantification, researchers create a numeric representation of a social phenomenon and communicate it across different areas of society for use in decision-making.[59] A social scientific approach to quantification aims to improve decision-making and inferences about social phenomena by simplifying complex aspects of society to manageable and observable units for hypothesis testing.[60] The reliance on quantification as the best scientific measurement and analysis method puts great power in quantification to inform decisions in organizations such as universities. Because people presume that quantitative approaches are more rational and objective, they put much faith in how authoritative such analyses and subsequent decisions are for policy.[61] By understanding how something such as diversity is quantified for decision-making purposes, we can identify the potential pitfalls of such approaches for addressing the very issues these approaches aim to tackle through policies and different initiatives. Sociologists Wendy Espeland and Michael Sauder describe the quantification of college characteristics into rankings: "As a new idea or technology becomes available, and as new groups begin to use it, the meaning of the innovation changes, including the nature of the problems it is designed to solve."[62] In light of their observation, one aim of this book is to identify how our problems have changed as diversity and inclusion became more quantified.

The degree of quantification can vary in research. Sociologists Daniel Hirschman, Ellen Berrey, and Fiona Rose-Greenland explain that the levels can range from not quantified at all, with decisions made through holistic and judgmental processes, to wholly quantified, whereby decisions are made through a mechanical and seemingly objective process.[63] Hirschman and his colleagues identify and describe four steps of quantification: (1) categorization, (2) classification, (3) enumeration, and (4) valuation. *Categorization* establishes a system of groupings for different aspects of society, which are often "discrete, bounded bins" that can be coded for analyses. The next step, *classification*, establishes rules or guidelines for assigning people or phenomena to categories. *Enumeration*, the counting of these categories, soon leads to *valuation*, or the assigning of a numeric value to a category. When connected together, these steps form a system of quantification with guidelines for categorizing, classifying, and assigning numeric values to phenomena.

Organizations can also conduct a dequantification process. In dequantification, an organization's quantitative routine is eliminated or modified in favor of a qualitative routine.[64] The use of quantification and dequantification can vary in organizations and notably can simultaneously exist in collaboration with other variations of quantification.

College admissions policies are one example of these multiple forms of quantification. In their examination of affirmative action at the University of Michigan, Hirschman, Berrey, and Rose-Greenland describe how quantification and dequantification can work together in an organization's decisions.[65] Information about grades and standardized test scores increased in how rigid they were measured quantitatively for use in admissions decisions. But this same quantitative information is linked to dequantified information about the racial or socioeconomic background of an applicant to make a singular decision (i.e., a variation of admission or rejection to an institution).

Given the complexity of our social world, quantification can simplify large amounts of information so that it can be analyzed more efficiently.[66] However, quantification also promotes commensuration to condense this information into manageable and simple metrics, essentially creating a bottom line for us to consider in the midst of a complex social world. Metrics merge social phenomena into a numeric value that is often interpreted as being more or less instead of a different kind of phenomenon altogether.[67]

For example, the College Board recently created an "adversity index" that quantified the school and neighborhood environments of individual applicants for college admissions. Poverty in schools and neighborhoods, average college-going rates and college entrance test scores, and other aspects of students' schools and communities were initially merged into a singular measure for admissions staff to interpret how much "adversity" a student faced despite the many differences in the forms of adversity present and how they influence students with different backgrounds. After a backlash to this quantification of a complex set of circumstances, the College Board backed off somewhat from this approach. The organization aimed to produce a series of measures that can tap into potential obstacles (i.e., adversity) that students must overcome in their pursuit of a college degree.[68] As noted in chapter 1, college admissions policies well illustrate how people can accept quantification for one aspect of the social world yet contest its use for another aspect when considering racism and inequality due to organizational norms.

The continual reliance on quantitative approaches to measure and analyze aspects of society can be a double-edged sword over time. On the one hand, refined quantitative measures of racial inequalities in student support services can influence campus leaders' decisions, for example. On the other hand, continuously relying on quantitative approaches to identify racial inequalities can establish a difficult structure to change or disassemble when quantification is considered the best way to document such inequalities.[69] Conversations about the quantitative measurement and analyses of diversity and inclusion in higher education have many layers. We must understand how using quantitative methodologies to examine colleges' diversity and inclusion efforts are distinctly about people represented by the numbers, not the numbers themselves. The quantification of diversity and inclusion in higher education can dehumanize people for the sake of supporting organizational logics. Organizations want to appear as if they are supporting diversity and inclusion by creating documents, measures, and language about diversity and inclusion.[70] Like the colleges we study and work with to help them become more diverse, equitable, and inclusive, we have to understand the depth and power of the organizational norms informed by the underlying and unwritten ideas that can lead us to misuse and misinterpret certain quantitative approaches in the pursuits of these goals. Further, we must recognize when our ideologies can shape our explanations of racialized organizational processes that cause everyday inequality. Similar to the Harvard college admissions court cases noted at the beginning of this introduction, we need to focus on how increasing enrollments of different student groups rather than helping students enter and thrive on our college campuses became a central facet of diversity, equity, and inclusion work in higher education.

Quantification as Racialization in Universities

The creation and use of so-called diversity numbers shows how racialization at an organizational level occurs through quantification. One way that quantification racializes people is by categorizing and assigning different meanings of race. The process then attaches these meanings to people, cultural objects, material resources, and opportunities.[71] The categorization of humans into races and ethnicities is a macro-level (i.e., societal) racial practice. It links many organizations and infuses them with racial schemata (organizational logics) and ideology (individual and collective racial beliefs). For example, the United States has a long history of creating race and ethnicity as measurable categories with differing meanings and stratifying resources using these categories; the US Census is one such example of this history.[72] Through the everyday use of race and racial categories by individuals and organizations, these categories gain an air of objectivity and legitimacy and reinforce unequal structures for people to navigate.[73] The rearticulation of diversity through measurement, analysis, and policy in higher education showcases how universities perpetuate and shift the racialization of bodies and dissemination of resources and opportunities according to the organization's purposes.

Falling into an early pitfall of quantitative approaches to diversity and inclusion, researchers leave unquestioned the racial categories of data and how race permeates an organization such as a college. Social science's reliance on quantitative methodologies in their analyses of diversity and inclusion limits what can be measured and counted, resulting in reductionism.[74] Additionally, "this problem is amplified when the measure is taken to be the phenomenon it represents."[75] Higher education scholar Benjamin Baez points out that when researchers reduce race to the categories given, they wind up naturalizing these categories in their efforts to understand diversity and inclusion.[76] Instead of further examining how race can manifest itself as a social fact, researchers shift their focus on how to best operationalize diversity on college campuses, measuring, monitoring, and comparing racial groups and their associated outcomes.

The messiness of trying to quantify the unquantifiable was notable in a previous study I conducted with two colleagues using large data sets collected and managed by the federal government.[77] We compared the racial and ethnic categories of the Integrated Postsecondary Education Data System (IPEDS), which is the main higher education data set collected by the US Department of Education, with the American Community Survey, an annual survey by the US Census Bureau. Our aim was to examine how the IPEDS categories may misconstrue the racial and ethnic diversity on college campuses and who earns particular degrees. We found that an IPEDS category for "nonresident alien" students was used as a sort of overarching group that collapsed all students from outside the United States into one category, regardless of how they racially identified.[78] If two students from a different nation attended the same US institution for their undergraduate degrees—one who identified as white and the other Black—the IPEDS approach would group both students as "nonresident alien" students, precluding any further information about how non-US students experience higher education once they arrive on campus. Citizenship and immigration status intersect with race and ethnicity in many ways that can influence student experiences and outcomes, but these interactions can be missed through these coarse quantification processes.[79]

As I will elaborate throughout this book, racial and ethnic categories are used in higher education for different purposes, including diversity work to create a more equitable and inclusive campus. These categories persist, despite their contested boundaries as student groups fight for recognition of who they are and what they experience.[80] Yet universities reporting to the federal government must use some sort of quantification to formulate a manageable understanding of who is pursuing postsecondary education in the United States and their experiences. Thus, quantification lends further credence to these racial categories and numbers because they are presumed to be objective metrics for analysis and decision-making.[81] These categories can then shape our interpretations of racial stratification and inequality in higher education research. As Baez poignantly states, "Such research that begins with unquestioned ideas about difference fails to shed light on why and in what ways those differences, and the oppression that result from them, are created in the first place."[82] The organization is reconstructed as a color-blind, race-neutral entity, and quantification decouples how organizational norms help produce racial stratification and inequality in higher education.

Researchers can easily reduce individuals to a simplified measure (i.e., a racial category) of "what individuals *are*, how they *think*, and what they *do*" without considering how the creation and use of categories is related to people's access to resources and opportunities.[83] Within academia, the production and communication of knowledge is a cornerstone of its existence. In the study of diversity and inclusion, we must not overlook how our knowledge of differences—be it about a specific outcome or experience—gains meaning through organizational practices and is represented by metrics.[84] Social science research provides important knowledge about differences; this information shapes the higher education and public discourse on issues such as race-conscious admissions policies, graduation disparities, and other related academic and social issues on college campuses. This type of knowledge is part of a normalized organizational mindset that can perpetuate the view that students of color—rather than the organizational processes and policies that lead to racial disparities—are what need to be examined.[85]

If organizational schemata encourage quantification that racializes individuals, knowledge, and the organization itself, then the study of diversity and inclusion in higher education must be understood within the cultural, political, and historical contexts informing the researcher, the perspectives and methods utilized for studies, and the organizations the researchers inhabit.[86] This basic understanding of quantification's influence on higher education policy is missing from many current discussions asserting that solid methods can overcome flawed theoretical frameworks.[87] For example, assumptions of student or faculty merit, and organizational influences on these assumptions, can hide how higher education perpetuates racial stratification and inequality.[88] I return to this specific example in chapter 1 to shed light on how racialization of seemingly objective academic measures can shift our understanding of admissions policies and the continuation of racial inequality. The cultural, political, and historical contexts are critical for the study of diversity, equity, and inclusion and indicate how analyzing diversity, equity, and inclusion may be "implicated in power when it makes the lives of historically subordinated individuals the subject of social science with all of its arbitrary classifications and latent hierarchies."[89]

A central issue with the quantitative study of diversity and inclusion in higher education is social science's framing of diversity as a problem to be studied. When diversity is framed as a problem, quantitative methods are privileged as the best tools to study it, given the underlying ideas among colleges and universities and the assumptions incorporated into the advanced training of, and embedded in, a majority of researchers' ideologies.[90] This approach echoes many other examples of how quantification creates metrics that are to be monitored and establish goals to attain; thus, the problem becomes whether certain numbers are obtained, not necessarily whether inequality is reduced.[91] Despite an increasing incorporation of more qualitative approaches to the study of diversity, equity, and inclusion, Baez builds on the work of sociologist Pierre Bourdieu to suggest how organizational norms influence social science research, even for researchers attuned to these issues: "But even when social scientists adopt the particular representations offered by those who have suffered discrimination, if they fail to describe the game in which representations, and the beliefs underlying them, are produced, then they have invoked one among many contributions to the creation of beliefs whose foundations and social effects should be described."[92]

In this book, I focus on how quantification has become the dominant tool for examining and explaining diversity, equity, and inclusion in higher education. If we take the recent research on the racialization of higher education, how diversity efforts in higher education can reproduce inequalities, and the internal and external forces that can influence our interpretation of this research, we must also understand the effects of quantification on these issues. Such an understanding helps us grasp the "social operations of comparisons and classifications" that "structure the world" and higher education in particular.[93] Throughout this book, I elaborate on how—because of organizational thinking—quantification and the policy analyses conducted to improve diversity can reinforce or at least misconstrue the racial inequality they seek to address. As will be seen, the overuse of quantification in higher education not only can reinforce racial stratification and inequality but also, more importantly, can obscure why racial inequality persists on campus as part of the university's programming, policies, and organizational processes. Without such in-depth attention, higher education is likely to be doomed to reproduce racial inequalities, and campus leaders will further absolve universities of their complicity in these inequalities.

Outline of the Book

The rest of this book examines how diversity, equity, and inclusion are quantified for varying university purposes. As part of universities' operation as racialized organizations, the circumstances surrounding the quantification of diversity may sometimes lead to the devaluing and undercutting of efforts to address racial inequality on college campuses. Each chapter relates quantification to the organizational schemata informing different areas of diversity work among universities. The chapters focus on several important areas of higher education, including college admissions policies, the measurement of diversity and representation on college campuses, and the important area of campus climate research often at the heart of promoting more equitable and just campus communities. I provide perspective on how organizational norms shape the use of quantification, and research in general, in the areas that reflect forms of racialization in light of sociopolitical contexts. Additionally, I articulate how people's racial ideology rationalizes the use of quantification for diversity work, given organizational and broader sociopolitical contexts. We learn how and why diversity, equity, and inclusion in varying quantified forms matter for higher education.

Chapter 1 examines the contentious discussion around affirmative action and college admissions. Critics argue that the "best and brightest" students should be admitted for their academic merits and that no other information should be considered in rendering these admissions decisions. Attempting to avoid the contentious conversation about race, an increasingly dangerous extension of these arguments focuses on socioeconomic status as a proximate measure of racial inequality. Yet, race and class operate in interconnecting ways that produce different realities for students. We need to consider these interactions and avoid simply replacing one characteristic for another in admissions considerations. This chapter explores recent lawsuits and research to uncover the organizational culture shaping perspectives of campus representation and racial inequalities in higher education. The quantification and methodological approaches that college admissions take to address diversity and merit present administrators and policy makers with a difficult situation. They need to understand the constant evolution of how these concepts are applied in reflection of organizational processes and policies. That is, these access-related issues set a tone for other discussions of how diversity and inclusion are pursued at individual universities and across higher education.

Chapter 2 tackles a common misconception about universities. The misconception relates to the representation of different racial and ethnic groups on campus and the ability to claim equity and inclusion because of these numbers. How can focusing on student demographics hide racial inequality on campuses? Additionally, how could universities enroll racially diverse student bodies yet simultaneously operate as segregated campuses? Building on the resurgent focus of critical quantitative work, the chapter first explores the perspective of racial and ethnic categories used in organizational analyses and decision-making. In light of common misconceptions of these groups and their histories in relation to higher education, universities use these categories without fully considering who is included or excluded. From this discussion, readers will learn how administrators, researchers, and policy makers can misinterpret even simple analyses of campus demographics and how this misinterpretation can undercut the clear identification of race-related issues on campus and potential solutions to them.

This chapter also examines data about faculty, staff, and student representation beginning in 1990. I describe the patterns of segregation on campus to provide a comprehensive picture of how the oft-used label of *predominately white institution* shortchanges consideration of other circumstances shaping the demographic realities of higher education. These circumstances include the existence of multiple layers of segregation that influences students' resources and opportunities. This discussion provides general approaches for universities and others to apply to their own data and to analyze racial segregation and inequality across the nation. These patterns of segregation and inequality hidden by narrow uses of quantification for policy and institutional change can overshadow and possibly discount the lived experiences of marginalization on college campuses captured by qualitative and mixed-methods approaches to decision-making.

Chapter 3 explores a popular research topic that forms the backbone of the narrative about the educational benefits of diversity and informs the design of higher education policies to promote equity and inclusion: the campus climate. Since the integration efforts in the 1960s and 1970s, a large segment of research developed to examine campus climates; the explicit purpose was to identify approaches to make campuses more inclusive for underrepresented student groups. This research area increased in importance beginning in the 1990s as new theoretical and methodological approaches were applied to the study of race on campus, while institutions were simultaneously pushed to justify their ongoing diversity and inclusion efforts in light of anti-affirmative-action and discrimination lawsuits against them.

Using a unique analysis of published scholarship on campus climates from 1992 to 2019, this chapter elaborates on what this other "climate science" finds to be the main obstacles to equity and inclusion efforts. The chapter also explores how policy suggestions garnered from this research may present additional obstacles to racial-equality efforts on college campuses because the policies focus on individuals rather than on organizational-level processes. Integral to this chapter's discussion is how to avoid confusing data, processes, and outcomes from this highly important research area. Misinterpretation can erroneously attribute a campus's racial climate to a person's actions instead of focusing on how universities can create and sustain more inclusive learning environments. Readers will gain insights on how to better apply this research to make organizational changes that affect students, faculty, and staff.

Chapter 4 brings together the main findings from the previous chapters to propose several approaches to combat racial inequality in higher education. It includes in its synthesis the effects of the recent coronavirus (COVID-19) pandemic and the resurgence of racial justice movements across the United States. My proposed approaches focus on different levels and areas of universities in an effort to promote organizational change that supports racial diversity, equity, and inclusion. In this final chapter, we consider how higher education's uses of quantification can help identify which problems need resolution. The approaches emphasize the use of multiple forms of data to better inform decisions that support the institution's stated missions of diversity and inclusion while further incorporating equity and justice.

This chapter also explains that higher education may not operate as a public good for everyone when a racial justice and equity lens is applied. We must move beyond the limited view of colleges as a public good for economic expansion or simply as a private good for individual students and their families to benefit from in the future. At the heart of this issue is the question, how do we make racial equality and justice a central feature of higher education rather than merely promoting individualized approaches that leave universities off the hook for pursuing racial equity and justice in the future? This chapter aims to be a springboard for institutional change. Its goal is to encourage higher education institutions to identify good leadership practices and policies that can address racial inequality and to institutionalize racial equity as an everyday component of organizational life in a postpandemic society.

28

The fixation on getting
resources and advantag
competitive system
use their socio
illegally.⁵ F
famili

CH

Transfoı
into Dive ᴀᴛ ᴛʜᴇ
College Gates

I N MARCH 2019, a scandal blanketed news media across the United States
and captivated the American public for weeks. A Justice Department investigation uncovered an elaborate scheme to assist children from wealthy
families in unfairly gaining admission to highly selective colleges and universities such as Wake Forest, Yale, Stanford, and the University of Southern
California through so-called side doors. These approaches, led by admissions
consultant and business owner William Singer, included bribing college admissions officials and athletics coaches, photoshopping pictures, lying on
college applications, pretending that students were of different races and ethnicities, and taking advantage of disability services for standardized tests, and
other schemes.[1] Most of the students involved apparently did not know what
their parents were doing to gain them advantages in the college admissions
game.[2] The participation of celebrity parents such as Felicity Huffman and
Lori Loughlin underscored the power of privilege in elite college admissions.[3]
Coaches and other personnel involved in the scandal were quickly fired; a few
parents were charged with crimes, including fraud; and some students linked
to the scandal had their admissions either investigated or revoked.[4]

their children into elite colleges known for their
ges is seen as a marker of good parenting in a highly
. The families identified in the scandal sought ways to
economic advantage unfairly, though, for the most part, not
owever, the admissions scandal reflects a broader issue of wealthy
s' ability to enjoy advantages in highly selective college admissions that
ve existed since the initial years of the first colleges and universities in the
United States.[6] In light of the weight that degrees awarded from prestigious
institutions carry in both social areas and the labor market, wealthy families
continue to seek new ways to gain advantages in these high-status institutions.[7] In the whirlwind of news coverage of the admissions scandal, another
important story floated in the background: a judge in Boston was set to rule
whether Harvard had discriminated against Asian American applicants in
college admissions in the *Students for Fair Admissions, Inc. v. Harvard College
(SFFA v. Harvard)* case noted in the introduction.

While many people followed the sensational story of the admissions scandal, the affirmative action case and its relationship to the scandal illustrate
how diversity, and particularly race and ethnicity, is framed as an attribute
that competes with merit in college admissions decisions. The case was based
on this assumption of competition, despite analyses suggesting that affirmative action policies do not harm the chances of white students, regardless of
college selectivity level.[8] As broader society continues to face constrained economic prospects, which disproportionately impinge on the lives of people of
color, more students are applying to highly selective institutions to try to avoid
a possible unstable financial future.[9] The hypercompetitive admissions game
at these institutions puts affirmative action policies in the political crosshairs,
given the long history of framing these policies as an unfair leg up for students
of color seeking to secure educational resources and opportunities. While
celebrity parents are seen as partly undercutting the supposed meritocracy of
college admissions, considerations of race and ethnicity at any point in admissions decisions at a prestigious institution are viewed as a much larger problem. As people fight for admission to Harvard and other elite schools, higher
education policies and processes clearly work to support racial inequality and
to perpetuate racial advantages and disadvantages for groups of people.[10]

In this chapter, I focus on the long-standing tension of including race and ethnicity in college admissions decision-making. The politics surrounding college admissions, and affirmative action policies in particular, greatly influence how race and ethnicity are incorporated into, or ignored by, reviews of applicants. First, I briefly explore which factors a holistic admissions review considers today and the approximate use of race in such reviews across the nation. Far from being a determining factor in admissions decisions today, the inclusion of race and ethnicity has drastically decreased since the 1990s. I describe how race was previously included in college admission reviews but has been transformed under quantification to a broader concept of diversity, to deflect political and legal challenges. I also highlight one of the newest uses of quantification: to try to improve the information admissions staff have on hand when they are reviewing applicants. I note how this approach may further remove race from admissions decisions despite its importance to the conversations about what obstacles students may face before applying to colleges and how higher education institutions can move closer toward racial equity.

This chapter also explores the ideology that informs how universities, particularly through their admissions offices, operate as racialized organizations that shape inequality. I elaborate on the dominant racial ideology's argument, which promotes the removal of race and ethnicity in college admissions because racial and ethnic considerations do not conform to the supposed rigor or objectivity of quantitative metrics of academic merit. Nor does the argument reflect the desire to be color-blind and disavow the taboo subject of race and racism. Finally, I summarize what happens in college admissions by using an increasingly popular color-blind approach emphasizing socioeconomic diversity. Not a harbinger of progress, this admissions approach can have dire consequences for efforts to reduce racial inequality in college admissions and socioeconomic inequality as well. Quantification, as this chapter shows, is not a straightforward, depoliticized process. But neither are college admissions, which are layered with both historical and current political contexts.

Holistic College Admissions

Most universities review applicants for admissions by considering a wide range of information that reflects an ever-evolving approach. Holistic admissions review includes different forms of information, including grades, coursework, test scores, and essays about how an applicant is contributing, or could contribute, to diversity on campus and in life; holistic applications often provide space for applicants to describe their skills and viewpoints on social issues and experiences.[11] This type of application is not new in college admissions; it is only an evolved form reflecting a contentious history of excluding different student groups such as women, Jewish students, and students of color more generally. Admissions reviews designed to exclude particular groups used a mix of "personality scores" and tests that originally homed in on the life and curriculum of boarding schools in the Northeast to perpetuate an exclusive form of higher education for white students of elite backgrounds.[12] Here, we can already catch a glimpse of the organizational norms reflecting unwritten ideas and rules informing admissions review throughout much of American higher education history. The presumption that only white students from middle- and upper-class backgrounds, particularly and almost exclusively men well into the twentieth century, were worthy students of admission oriented colleges to either completely exclude other students or to devalue their educational backgrounds as lesser than those of the white students who always had access to higher education, especially highly selective institutions.[13]

Nonacademic factors are a long-standing form of information included in admissions reviews, gaining popularity in recent decades as admissions offices seek to broaden the types of students on their campuses. However, this application information is not without controversy. The ability to use information about student backgrounds and experiences beyond their academics is seen as undercutting the objectivity of admissions review, and most of the disagreement surrounding the inclusion of this information is about race. The conflict is especially vulnerable to political and legal challenges such as in *SFFA v. Harvard*. In this legal case, critics call into question how Asian American applicants were stereotyped and were possibly downgraded in their scores.[14] Simultaneously, a growing test-optional movement has also shaped many college admissions offices, given the criticism of standardized admissions tests such as the SAT and ACT for their limited contribution to demonstrating a student's preparation, potential, and future performance on campus.[15] This movement asserts that although nonacademic factors are frequently criticized, the academic criteria included in admissions reviews are not without their flaws as well. Taken together, these ongoing political tensions suggest that holistic admissions, an ever-changing set of processes and policies to evaluate applicants, are constrained by organizational goals and the sociopolitical landscape.

Balancing the abundance of academic and nonacademic information is not an easy task for admissions staff as they review the many applications submitted to their institution. Most staff members describe their work as not so much an exact science as an art because of the multiple areas of a student's life, work, and potential that factor into their decisions to admit, wait-list, or reject the applicant for an entering class.[16] College admissions staff take different perspectives on holistic admissions. The administrators vary on how these processes and policies operate in admissions. Higher education scholar Michael Bastedo and his colleagues used a mixed-methods approach to study how college admissions officers define and apply holistic admissions review. The researchers found that the staff members define holistic review in one of three ways: (1) whole file, (2) whole person, or (3) whole context. Approaching admissions from the whole-file approach means that staff would read an applicant's entire file and not weigh one attribute more than another when rendering a decision. Staff who used the whole-person approach would use an applicant's materials to "get to know them as a person" and not relegate who the person is to only certain features of individual character. Using a whole-context approach in admissions, staff consider the family, school, and community situation of an applicant in addition to other materials to better understand where the applicant came from and what opportunities and obstacles the person experienced before admission.[17] Although the three types of approaches overlap, their differences can change who is admitted to a university.

The differences in holistic admissions approaches can have particular importance in terms of applicants' socioeconomic position. Bastedo and his colleagues found that a whole-context approach to college admissions increased the likelihood that staff would admit applicants from lower socioeconomic positions. This finding was more pronounced for highly selective universities. In a related study, with findings similar to those of Bastedo and associates, Don Hossler and his colleagues found that admissions staff employ a wide range of information beyond the academic factors in holistic reviews. For example, staff examine performance and attitudinal measures and look deeper into applicants' circumstances.[18] Although academic factors were still the most important consideration in admissions decisions, these studies suggest how more contextual information about applicants could be included to increase the inclusion of students from lower socioeconomic backgrounds. However, these studies overlooked perhaps the most contentious characteristic of student applicants: their race and ethnicity. The use of race-conscious admissions policies (i.e., considering race as one of many factors in admissions reviews) is not out of line with holistic review. In fact, with the inclusion of the applicant's racial and ethnic background, such policies add only one more piece of information about to a holistic review. Despite the slight difference between race-conscious and holistic approaches, the recurring misconception about the inclusion of race in admissions reflects the competition for admissions to highly selective universities.

Countering the popular narrative that admission to colleges and universities has become increasingly more difficult than in years past, most four-year institutions grant admission to a majority of students who apply each year.[19] As noted earlier, this belief is driven by the growing competition for the limited spots at prestigious universities, which are subsequently targeted by most legal challenges to their admissions processes.[20] Although most institutions use holistic admission review, people often assume that race can be the deciding factor for admission, regardless of the applicant's submitted material. In fact, the odds of Black and Latinx students gaining admission to selective colleges and universities has declined in comparison with white and Asian American students since 1972.[21] Also, the use of race in college admissions has decreased since the 1990s among a large segment of selective universities. Approximately only 35 percent of these universities consider race at all in their evaluation of applicants.[22] These decreases notably occurred for public and less selective institutions, where a majority of college students already enroll. These changes correspond to less racial and ethnic diversity at public selective institutions as well.[23] Additionally, because most people attend college close to their homes (on average no more than fifty miles away for all students and no more than twenty for public college students), their chances of attending highly selective universities are slimmer.[24] Since many highly selective institutions that practice race-conscious admissions are located in particular regions and metropolitan areas, the limited average distance traveled to college suggests that applicants rarely encounter such admissions policies.

Digging a bit deeper into the rarity of applying to a university that considers race in college admission reviews today, let's consider how selectivity relates to the use of race in holistic admissions review. There are approximately 2,330 four-year, not-for-profit US institutions that range from highly selective universities like Harvard to less selective universities such as Bridgewater State University in Massachusetts and the University of Central Oklahoma. This number includes specialized schools such as the Savannah College of Art and Design in Georgia. If we consider race-conscious admissions policies, only 352 institutions (15.1 percent of all four-year institutions) consider race at some point in the evaluation of applicants. Drilling down to the most selective institutions—those at the center of many popular discussions of how difficult it is to get into a "good college" these days and those featured in many lawsuits—only 124 institutions consider race in admissions and are "highly selective."[25] That means approximately 5.3 percent of all four-year institutions both are difficult to get into and consider race at all. That's it: just 5.3 percent of colleges are involved in the ongoing debate about affirmative action in college admissions. These statistics suggest that most people applying to college, including white applicants and, increasingly, segments of Asian Americans who spearhead the fight against affirmative action in college admissions, will rarely face highly selective admissions reviews, including those that consider race and ethnicity.[26]

Despite how seldom universities include race at any point during their holistic reviews, most people are unaware of how this information was used in the past, let alone today. If we consider one university's development of holistic admissions review and the use of race and ethnicity, we can pinpoint different ways that underlying ideas about the relationship of race and merit inform organizational cultures and reflect these political tensions around race in higher education and society more broadly. The University of Michigan's development of its holistic admissions approach and the inclusion of race exemplifies how quantification aligned with organizational schemata. Quantification has the power to transform specific concepts into broader ideas, accommodating the political challenges of including race in college admissions policies. Moreover, as the organization shifts its focus from race and ethnicity to "diversity," how racial information is included in holistic review processes changes as well.

Quantification and the Use of Race

Holistic admissions review often contains a diverging use of quantification for academic merit and dequantification of race and ethnicity. This divergence reflects how *resources* can be racialized as universities shift their policies and processes in pursuit of educational goals while simultaneously reacting to political and legal challenges to how they operate. College admissions can be understood as a process for gaining access to the opportunities and resources of a university and as key site where the political and legal challenges are balanced using different forms of data. As noted in the introduction, quantification is a process in which a complex attribute of an individual or organization becomes more or less quantified, that is, simplified into a numeric representation.[27] College admissions is diverging in two directions. Assessment of academic merit is using a more rigid and quantified set of metrics, while race and ethnicity assessment is becoming dequantified, or more qualitative, and embedded within a broader concept of diversity. The race and ethnicity changes are responses to the verdicts in affirmative action cases, most often at the hands of the Supreme Court.[28] This divergence also hints at how an organization's underlying ideas and rules informing their processes are shaped by collective and individual ideologies about the differences between diversity and merit—ideologies that I discuss later in this chapter.

Sociologists Dan Hirschman, Ellen Berrey, and Fiona Rose-Greenland elaborate on the diverging quantification processes they notably found when examining the University of Michigan's evolving admissions criteria and decision-making from 1964 to 2004 (2004 being one year after the *Grutter v. Bollinger* and *Gratz v. Bollinger* admissions cases involving the University of Michigan). In their longitudinal evaluation of how admissions criteria changed, the researchers found that the underlying ideas of the organizational norms informing the review process framed academic merit as strict, objective measures, and these features of an applicant were often left unquestioned because of their highly quantified form.[29] A student's test scores or grades were considered the culmination of individual intellect and work ethic. The grades were viewed as solely what that student had accomplished, but administrators did not fully consider how those individual outcomes were the result of organizational influences. However, academic criteria are not strictly objective metrics, despite their current usage in college admissions and in later assessments of students' careers, such as during internship evaluations.[30]

As they examined the University of Michigan's admissions evolution, Hirschman and his colleagues also found how race transformed into diversity.[31] The admissions staff initially used a grid system to group applicants by whether an applicant was a member of an underrepresented minority group (i.e., African American, Latinx, Native American) or not (i.e., white and Asian American). In 1978, the ruling in *Regents of the University of California v. Allan Bakke* ordered college admissions offices to meet a higher bar of strict scrutiny to ensure that race was "narrowly tailored" not to be a deciding factor of whether someone was admitted to an institution.[32] Then, after the 1996 *Hopwood v. University of Texas Law School* decision that challenged whether diversity was a compelling state interest, the University of Michigan changed to a points system for applicants. Called the Selection Index, the system awarded up to 150 points to applicants, 75 of which were from academic criteria, and admitted applicants to the university if they received 100 total points.[33] There also existed a so-called miscellaneous category that could award students up to 20 points if they were a member of an underrepresented racial or ethnic group, socioeconomically disadvantaged, or a scholarship athlete. Rather than consider race alone in this category, race was merged with low socioeconomic status and athletic prowess to create a more "diverse" applicant category.

As Hirschman and his colleagues note, the separation of diversity and merit was not argued by either side or the judges in the *Grutter* and *Gratz* cases in 2003, further crystallizing merit as a presumably objective measure of students' capabilities and transforming race into a broader conception of diversity.[34] After the ruling in *Gratz* (the undergraduate case), the University of Michigan was forced to dequantify diversity in its admissions policies and processes.[35] While academic merit was still quantified for use in admissions decisions, nonacademic attributes of applicants were now under a new version of holistic review. In the University of Michigan's case, two or three admissions staff would read an application and assign it a rating (poor to outstanding), and all the applications and their assigned grades would be considered by a full enrollment group in the admissions office.[36]

The dequantifying of diversity meant the further embedding of race into a politically palatable form of cultural diversity along with other individual nonacademic attributes. This highly individualized form of diversity allows for a vague understanding and use of the concept in both college admissions and broader society. As sociologist Shamus Khan describes in his ethnography of an elite boarding school, the transformation of race into diversity since the peak of the civil rights movement allows people to claim diversity without the taboo of race. Everyone becomes diverse; you only need to note in your application materials which form of diversity you hold for admissions personnel to consider.[37]

The resulting divergence of admissions criteria into academic measures (objective) and nonacademic ones (subjective) required the transformation of not only the holistic review process but also the admissions office itself. For example, the University of Michigan's admissions office was restructured to accommodate this reformulated admissions process; among other steps, the office hired additional staff and developed new manuals to guide staff through the lengthier review process.[38]

For the purposes of our discussion, the changes in the organization of the admissions office meant that the consideration of an applicant's race was moved from a specific category that operated as selection device in previous admissions processes (i.e., either to exclude or admit) to a set of categories for grouping applicants, forming a diversity category that was awarded points. Finally, race was treated as an individual attribute that could be elaborated on by the applicants in nonquantified ways through additional essays and information provided in the holistic review.[39] Reflecting that universities were operating as racialized organizations, the organizational view of race had morphed. No longer was race a distinctive feature that should be included through specific processes in college admissions. It was now one of many features contributing to diversity on campus and influencing the official "rules" for the admissions process.[40] Race was and continues to be a part of organizational policies and processes of universities as they adjust to the ever-changing political terrain and pivot toward promoting a broader mission of creating a diverse student body, which is not defined solely by race and ethnicity.

Michigan is not alone in its shifts to holistic review processes and the reasoning behind them. The use of a broader and vaguer conception of diversity for institutional and individual benefits continued in recent Supreme Court cases against the University of Texas in *Fisher I* (2013) and *Fisher II* (2016) and the ongoing battle *SFFA v. Harvard*.[41] In the *Fisher* cases, scholars found that a selective use of research, particularly quantitative studies, to argue for or against race-conscious admissions policies highlights how racial ideology can inform organizational thinking.[42] For example, opponents of race-conscious admissions policies note that diversity is beneficial in general but that college admissions should be color-blind and not rely on race to decide who could contribute to that campus diversity. They argue that race-conscious policies will take away resources from "deserving applicants." These arguments place admission to highly selective universities as a competitive resource bestowed by universities that themselves are racialized organizations.[43]

Although the recent cases against Harvard University, the University of North Carolina, and Princeton University are pitched as concerning the outcomes of Asian American students, the arguments made by the plaintiffs center on the positioning of white students.[44] Through these cases, universities and researchers have sought other approaches to provide more context about students' backgrounds—factors that could increase diversity without specifically relying on race, thus preserving the ongoing calls for color-blindness and legal precedents.[45] However, given the large amounts of information that could be included, condensing the complex reality surrounding each applicant into digestible, quantified forms for use in admissions is difficult. One recent approach, however, provides insight into the organizational norms shaping the quantification of inequalities for admissions decisions.

Quantification of Adversity

Beginning in 2017, the College Board set out to create a tool that summarizes for admissions staff the contextual information about the communities and schools of applicants. More specifically, the organization rolled out what was touted as a measure encompassing the adversity college applicants faced in their lives—adversity not easily accounted for in application information. Referred to as the *adversity index* in the media, the quantitative tool is officially known as Landscape (previously called the Environmental Context

Dashboard). It was developed across several years of research by the organization in light of other scholars' work on college access and admissions.[46] In line with many purposes of quantifying the social world, Landscape aimed to simplify contextual information about the different resources and opportunities applicants may or may not have had while pursuing their education.[47] Regarding the high-school-specific information, Landscape includes the size of the senior class, the average test scores at the school, the percentage of students on free or reduced-price lunch, the average SAT scores of students who attend college from the high school, and Advanced Placement (AP) participation and performance at the school. The tool also includes information about the applicant's community such as the probability that a person from the community will attend college; household structures in the community; median family income in a community; housing stability, including rental and homeownership rates; and community education and crime rates.[48] Not included in Landscape is any mention of the racial or ethnic diversity or related aspects of the applicant's high school or community.

Obviously, this type of background information could help admissions staff evaluate applicants who may be overlooked in traditional holistic admissions review. Bastedo and colleagues found that providing more information about applicants can increase the number of low-socioeconomic students admitted to selective institutions.[49] The College Board's Landscape is useful in many ways because applicants' socioeconomic circumstances can influence the educational and community resources available to them. Moreover, Landscape can be utilized by universities in states that ban considerations of race in college admissions such as Michigan since 2014. An earlier iteration of Landscape provided a single score of the extent of adversity an applicant faced in school and in the community. However, separate scores for adversity in an applicant's high school and community are now provided after the College Board reflected on critical feedback from the previous version of Landscape.[50]

Although a large literature documents how socioeconomic advantage can shape the education of children, additional research shows that such advantages do not cut neatly across race and ethnicity; nor do they remove racial and ethnic discrimination and inequality.[51] Thus, ignoring the intersection of race and class hinders our understanding of how adversity affects the lives of students applying to college. Even if students are financially secure, systemic racism can place obstacles in their paths toward college degrees; money doesn't necessarily shield a person from this sort of adversity. Approaches ignoring such intersections relate to the individual and collective racial ideologies that inform how universities and other organizations develop policies and processes to improve college access and diversity despite the decreased attention to race at all. We must further consider how racial ideology from inside a university and outside it can shape college admissions.

Complex Beliefs About Race, Merit, and College Admissions

People often subscribe to narrow perspectives of race and inequality, focusing on individual efforts in an unequal society. The continuous debate and legal battles around race-conscious admissions policies following the general forced desegregation of higher education are part of the collective dominant racial ideology that informs our conversation today about why race matters for educational opportunities.[52] Although many people argue that diversity and racial equality are generally important for society, they seldom support the mechanisms for pursuing these societal goals such as affirmative action in college admissions. This divergence in public opinion is known as the *principle–policy paradox*.[53] College admissions is a central feature of these debates. One side often argues that colleges should not consider race and ethnicity in admissions because of the need for solely merit-based standards. This group asserts that college admissions should operate as a meritocracy. In this section, we consider the complex relationship between people's beliefs about race and their support for merit-based standards, and we apply these observations to college admissions discussions.

The American public may not use the term *meritocracy* explicitly, but research shows that most Americans believe that people rise and fall on their own efforts, intelligence, and academic merits. Well into the twenty-first century, these beliefs in turn heavily influence people's views of why racial inequality persists.[54] As the reasoning goes, if a person does not gain entry to a university, the individual probably did not work hard enough or is not smart enough. Similar views are found among the students at highly selective universities; white students hold most strongly to these views compared with their Black, Latinx, and, to a certain extent, Asian American peers.[55] These individualistic beliefs are not applied evenly to people of different races and ethnicities, as people may consider circumstances more often for one group than they do for another when contemplating why someone failed to gain admission to a university, for example. Thus, people do not strictly follow their own beliefs about the importance of individual efforts and merits. Their beliefs are racialized to help them explain away inequality, and its associated advantages and disadvantages for different groups, as a normal feature of society. Such a racialized view is arguably found in the previously mentioned admissions changes as the relationship between merit and race was decoupled through diverging quantification processes.

Transformations of the underlying ideas and unwritten rules informing organizational policies and processes including the use of quantification for college admissions are catalyzed by dominant racial ideologies.[56] Americans' racialized ideas about merit and inequality in college admissions have been demonstrated in research. Sociologist Frank Samson found that white respondents were likely to support the strict use of academic criteria for college admission decisions when considering Black applicants but downplayed the importance of these same criteria when considering Asian American applicants.[57] This differential application of merit builds on the denigrating model-minority stereotypes of Asian Americans. These stereotypes, which also came into play in the *Fisher* affirmative action cases, purport that Asian American students are overrepresented and highly successful despite facing racial discrimination and underrepresentation across higher education.[58] Sociologists Jennifer Lee and Van Tran extend these findings, demonstrating that the mention of different racial groups as victims of discrimination can influence the support for race-conscious admissions policies. When Black and Asian Americans are framed as victims of discrimination, both white people and Asian Americans are less opposed to race-conscious admissions policies than they would be if only Black Americans are noted as victims of discrimination. Their study touches on the complex relationship of discrimination faced by different groups and how policies such as race-conscious admissions can influence opportunities and resources for these groups.[59] This relationship can also shape whether universities consider race important for admissions decisions.

Another aspect of the current dominant racial ideology is highlighted by social psychological research by Maureen Craig and Jennifer Richeson.

In their studies of how people perceive changes in US demographics, white people perceive increasing racial diversity in the nation as an indication that antiwhite discrimination is on the rise while discrimination against communities of color is on the decline.[60] Therefore, besides supporting simplified quantitative approaches to academic merit devoid of context about applicants for college admissions decisions, white people may view the increasing diversity on college campuses, not only in the nation as a whole, as a threat to resources. They might seek to protect their own racial advantages through different policies as they view some groups (e.g., Asian Americans) as bearers of more merit while holding others (e.g., African Americans) to a higher standard for why merit matters. Admissions to elite universities is one of the perennial subjects of debates about where meritocracy should be implemented in a color-blind fashion. The color-blind argument proposes that because these universities have high prestige in society, with exclusive resources and opportunities, admissions slots should be awarded to only the "best and brightest," or those considered the most meritorious, regardless of social background.[61] The earlier noted diverging quantification processes in college admissions reinforce the view that academic merit is the most objective criteria, despite its many flaws.[62]

The Racial Privilege of Merit and the Whitening of Diversity

While an academic meritocracy sounds good in theory, what constitutes merit has changed over time, and the opportunities to cultivate such academic characteristics are not readily available everywhere in society.[63] Most people agree that an applicant's grades and test scores are the standard-bearers for what constitutes merit in college admissions.[64] As discussed earlier, these academic characteristics are quantified to appear as objective measures of merit and potential.[65]

However, a cursory examination of the educational literature refutes such meritocratic beliefs. The influence of racialization on academic outcomes is revealed in many obvious ways. For example, this influence is evident in who is more likely to be sent to the principal's office for acting out in class and how these behaviors are interpreted by teachers. The influence is also revealed in who the teachers view as more deserving of placement in honors and AP classes. Even the sense of freedom to move around a school building reveals the influence of racialization. A final example is the systematic underfunding and segregation of schools.[66]

According to a racialized organizational perspective, schools overwhelmingly bequeath racial advantages to white students over students of color, perpetuating a practice that challenges the common belief that education functions as a meritocracy. Therefore, the purported objectivity of academic merit is actually the result of a highly racialized and unequal education system that cannot be considered solely the result of individual intelligence, talents, and work ethic. As the recent admissions scandal showed, even if you cannot attain more merit through the school, wealthy white parents can buy more points on tests through the prolific test-prep industry.[67]

Beyond grades and test scores, other attributes considered in admissions can literally be bought by wealthy families. Such a reality raises questions about the other supposedly tried-and-true measures for nonacademic potential often included in college admissions reviews. For example, applicants can exhibit leadership skills in numerous extracurricular activities, adding another layer of influence on college admissions. Although a consideration of extracurriculars can appear objective and meritorious, it also reflects structural inequality in society and can leave out many students from full consideration in these situations.[68] Not every high school offers debate teams or multiple arts, music, and athletic teams, among many other extracurricular options, for students to show their leadership capabilities. Affluent parents can either support these activities in the schools or seek out other opportunities for their children outside the school to provide evidence, come college application season, of the student's leadership abilities.[69] Thus, the assumption that students' tests scores, grades, and, by extension, other highly valued skills are completely objective measures of merit is disingenuous. Suffice it to say that although people strongly believe in meritocracy for college admissions, how objective these measures are and what constitutes merit are not static; nor do the measures provide easy interpretation of a student's abilities.

Despite the noted flaws of academic merit, people suggest that for college admissions, merit is a worthier aspect of a student's profile than is diversity. The political battles around race-conscious admissions followed a trajectory from the original use of such policies for racial redress to an emphasis on the importance of diversity for educational benefits and global competition. According to the newly framed race-conscious policies, the cultivation of a racially diverse student body is needed not for equity and justice but for competition and further advantages of the graduates of selective universities and their predominately white student bodies.[70] Today, however, the term *diversity* does not simply indicate race and ethnicity. Rather, it represents a broad cultural identity that spans racial and ethnic groups and includes other cultural features.[71] As sociologist Natasha Warikoo's study of elite college students found, diversity is framed as a "cultural identity that shapes individuals' worldviews and cultural practices."[72]

Before the University of Michigan affirmative action cases in 2003, to say that the student body was not diverse meant that there was an abundance of whiteness and a dearth of other racial and ethnic representation on campus. Today, because of further litigation and the banning of affirmative action in different states, a lack of diversity suggests that the student body does not represent the wide range of cultural characteristics of the nation; the definition now inserts white students into what counts as diversity.[73] Although much of the empirical research focuses on the educational and social benefits of racial and ethnic diversity among students, the discourse around diversity has shifted to promote a wide range of cultural diversity among the student body to cultivate these benefits, but with a slight twist. These efforts are described as promoting diversity without diluting the excellence or academic quality of universities while simultaneously providing students with marketable skills and experiences for a globally competitive labor market.[74] Subversively, these perspectives suggest that merit is not equally spread across racial and ethnicity groups, and the broadened diversity to include whiteness allows universities to describe diversity as a feature that also increases academic quality. This framing of broadened diversity and merit subtly reinforces a myth that increasing diversity means to reduce academic quality in higher education.

The persistent myth that promoting diversity in college admissions waters down academic standards presents an intriguing look at which people are thought to hold certain degrees of merit and which people presumably hold more of it.[75] Again, the quantification of merit is a key aspect of how people emphasize a few applicant attributes to rationalize racial inequality in higher education. Further, these views can suggest how people may recognize that admissions offices can distribute resources and opportunities that reproduce racial advantages and disadvantages in a competitive society, and rely on arguments about a color-blind meritocracy as the seemingly fairest approach for college admissions.[76] Although this perspective is not usually stated explicitly, the framing of race-conscious admissions policies as an unfair racial advantage for students of color that does not uphold the academic standards of a university reinforces a pernicious stereotype. The implication is that white students are inherently smarter, better prepared academically for life at elite institutions, and therefore are presumably the bearers of merit.[77] The preference then is for color-blind, race-neutral approaches to college admissions as reflected in each challenge to the legality of race-conscious admissions since the 1970s. These preferences emphasize the quantified form of merit that white students are consistently the most likely to attain in society.[78]

In a nod to the resource distribution power of universities, Warikoo found that white students in particular were more than willing to accept race-conscious admissions policies as long as the policies were constructed to value the white students' particular contributions to diversity. This attitude presents a *diversity bargain* by white people as they wrangle for a policy originally created for opening the doors for students of color formerly excluded throughout higher education.[79] The long battle around race-conscious admissions policies has witnessed an increasingly difficult bar that universities must meet to justify their use of race in admissions. If white applicants are not allowed to be fully considered under a policy or if the policy is presumed to reduce the academic excellence of an institution that favors an applicant because of race or ethnicity, then people argue that the policy must be changed to a color-blind, race-neutral approach.[80]

The recent lawsuits against Harvard University and the University of North Carolina, among others, arguably reflect a broader use of universities as racialized organizations and their quantitative analyses as a way to effectively transform higher education into a mechanism of social closure to protect white advantages. Through the two-pronged process of social closure, a group holding power and resources finds ways to (1) exclude or deny consideration of minority groups' access, and (2) usurp or take away the ability to challenge this exclusion.[81] The legal battles to slowly remove the consideration of race and ethnicity in many states and the continuing narrowly tailoring of these approaches clearly hinge on organizational policies and processes in highly selective universities. Seldom challenged is the construction of merit and how structural inequality can influence who is viewed as more meritorious in college admissions.

With this in mind, we can ask if some approach could help admissions staff consider race without necessarily relying on past approaches. While some researchers and organizations such as the College Board work to include additional consideration of applicants' socioeconomic backgrounds, others propose a more wholesale approach to race-conscious admissions in a politically contentious era: removing the consideration of race and ethnicity altogether.

Isn't There Another Way to Support Racial Diversity Without Race?

The desire to move beyond race and take color-blind approaches for college admissions has led to a few alternative strategies at state and university levels. For example, Texas implemented a plan that admitted applicants from the state to the University of Texas system if they graduated in the top 10 percent of their class (the cutoff has now been amended to the top 7 percent of a graduating class). But an increasingly popular argument recommends considering the socioeconomic position of an applicant as a substitute for race and ethnicity.[82]

Would this approach, to fully operationalize a color-blind and race-neutral review, assist universities with promoting racial diversity through college admissions more than the current holistic review that considers race? No, it would not. In fact, proponents for considering the socioeconomic background and the need to counter the overwhelming admission of wealthy students to prestigious universities would find that such an approach would undercut their own goals.

Why would people believe that a student's socioeconomic background would be a good proximate measure for race and ethnicity in college admissions, anyway? There exist a few arguments for such approaches. I will touch on two groups: the reverse-discrimination critics and what I identify as the widened-diversity critics. Both groups reflect the multiple forms of racial ideology to rationalize why race should or should not be considered in college admissions today.

Some critics of race-conscious admissions argue that considering race in admission evaluations is tantamount to reverse discrimination against white applicants. The assumption behind these critiques hinges on the belief that students of color are given exorbitant consideration, including points that can make race a deciding factor in admissions decisions.[83] In these critics' view, exorbitant consideration means any consideration of race and ethnicity at all. Such attention is termed a "plus factor" in admissions review; the simple consideration of race, regardless of how it factors into a holistic review process, is too much in this view. These critics also believe that the consideration of race in college admissions is discriminatory against white applicants. Generally, discrimination is the negative treatment of a person on account of a specific characteristic such as race or ethnicity. If discrimination could occur between two people in any direction, how then, could discrimination be reverse? The term *reverse discrimination* somewhat acknowledges the long history of white people's practice of discrimination, lawfully or not. [84] Reverse-discrimination arguments reflect an entrenched belief that the history of racial discrimination warrants the complete disavowal of any race-related policies in favor of color-blind policies, despite their deleterious impact on communities of color through past and current legal codes.[85] Thus, policies aiming for racial equality coupled with the illegality of racial discrimination today are interpreted by these critics, explicitly or not, as a forced approach toward equality. This interpretation exemplifies the previously noted principle–policy paradox.[86]

Critics think that the consideration of race in admissions is the opposite of the consideration of true merit. Race-conscious policies are not viewed as a form of equal opportunity. Arguably, the detractors of race-conscious approaches view the more equitable consideration of formerly excluded student groups as a threat to the long-held admissions advantages of white families and their children at highly selective universities. Thus, the framing of race-conscious admissions policies as reverse discrimination calls attention to an embedded organizational norm informing policy in higher education, particularly among prestigious universities, that promotes the education and well-being of white students over students of color. Without race-conscious policies, the normal processes and policies of university admissions offices would default to admitting many of the same students the institutions were founded to serve decades or even centuries ago.

A second group criticizing race-conscious admissions originates from across the political spectrum. This group often argues that promoting socioeconomic diversity is important for countering the wealthy elite people who have advantages in college admissions at highly selective universities. These critics also focus on how the legacy status of some applicants gives them advantages in the admissions process. Many universities have institutionalized preferences for students whose close family members attended the university in the past. As author and socioeconomic diversity advocate Richard Kahlenberg and others note, the preference for legacy students is often based on universities' philanthropic desires: to have families donate more money to the university. However, research finds that once a legacy student is admitted to a highly selective university, the donations decrease.[87] Why? Another generation has gained access to the resources and opportunities of the university and can begin to reap the benefits. The family has done its job at that stage of parenting. In light of the recent college admissions scandal discussed at the beginning of this chapter, legacy families will pay for admissions advantages for their children, and then this responsibility will fall on their children when they raise their own families. This part of intergenerational wealth transmission is what sociologist Robert Merton describes as the *Matthew effect*; families pass on advantages throughout history to shape the future, and the rich get richer.[88]

This second group of critics also views the political fighting around race-conscious admissions policies as an avenue to expand diversity with the inclusion of socioeconomic status. Such perspectives of widening diversity extends from the elite people's desire to co-opt diversity to be more inclusive for their own interests and to preserve their advantages generally and in higher education specifically. Sociologists Shamus Kahn and Lauren Rivera show that diversity is seen as an amorphous attribute that can be constructed to include even the most advantaged students as diverse.[89] Advantaged students' attempts to portray themselves as the "right kind of diverse" that aligns with the elite group's interests and tastes pinpoints another aspect of how universities operate as racialized organizations around college admissions.

Despite the increasing racial and ethnic diversity of elite people around the world, most of these people are identified as white and hold substantial power across sectors of society.[90] Aligning diversity with the interests and tastes of this privileged group is to align it with the most advantaged form of whiteness.[91] Diversity is moved from the realm of race and ethnicity to other realms that are more inclusive of white people, who already hold racial advantages. This shift in the meaning of diversity helps solidify these advantages by using the heated debates around race-conscious admissions to argue for a "less divisive" approach to diversity in college admissions: socioeconomic diversity.[92] Socioeconomic conditions extend across race and ethnicity, and critics argue that to promote more diversity, we should focus on the financial circumstances of applicants because "money is green, regardless of your race." Universities have adopted this approach of widening the meaning of diversity by incorporating low socioeconomic status and first-generation status (i.e., being the first in a person's family to attend college) in the definition. Thus, the political arguments around the inclusion of race have influenced not only the organizational principles of institutions but also their admissions processes. Hirschman and colleagues' examination of the University of Michigan's admissions process and policies found this shift in the university's definition of diversity. Race was embedded within a diversity category that now includes multiple attributes given equal weight, diluting the importance of race in holistic admissions review.[93]

Do Race-Neutral Approaches Work for Increasing Racial Diversity?

Regardless of the arguments for a socioeconomic diversity approach for college admissions to replace race-conscious approaches, the recent affirmative action court cases include a consistent stream of arguments and analyses about race-conscious policies and what they may achieve. Research supports a central feature of most proponents for socioeconomic diversity: that low-socioeconomic students face more disadvantages in college admissions and on campus than do wealthy students, especially legacy students and children of donors.[94] As noted previously, economist David Card, a key witness for Harvard in the ongoing court case against the university's admissions office, pointed out the flaws in the critics' analyses of who benefits and who doesn't in admissions reviews. Part of Card's argument described how racial and ethnic diversity would precipitously decline under race-neutral, socioeconomic-only approaches.[95]

In a similar analysis, education sociologist Sean Reardon and his colleagues note that universities can increase their racial diversity *more* by considering both race and class in college admissions. The authors reach this conclusion through a simulation analysis of student enrollments under different admissions scenarios. Reardon and his coauthors also found that when admissions only consider applicants' socioeconomic background, the university would have difficulty increasing racial diversity and even socioeconomic diversity on campus.[96] We also have "natural experiments" showing the downsides of ignoring race and ethnicity in college admissions. Currently, among states banning affirmative action in higher education, analyses suggest similar declines in the enrollment of students of color, a finding echoing Reardon and his colleagues' simulations in both undergraduate and medical school admissions.[97]

These studies demonstrate why consideration of both race and socioeconomic status matters. People have complex identities that include different forms of privilege and disadvantage. Intersectionality suggests that people and society cannot be reduced to mere binaries. Instead, continua are more in line with how society is organized and how groups relate to one another.[98] For example, proponents of socioeconomic approaches in college admissions could easily conclude that because white applicants on average have greater economic advantages than do applicants of color, then focusing on low socioeconomic backgrounds would automatically increase racial diversity. However, these same critics of race-conscious admissions policies readily agree that not everyone is wealthy, including white people. Yet, their arguments for why socioeconomic approaches are needed to increase racial diversity in college admissions rely on similar binary racial thinking: that being nonwhite means to be poor. As higher education scholar Julie Park concisely demonstrates, in line with some of the previously mentioned analyses, the complex intersection of race and socioeconomic position renders the reliance on only one aspect of identity embedded within broader social inequalities insufficient.[99] To promote diversity, we need more dynamic approaches to college admission, not simpler ones.

Entering a Racialized Organization Through the College Gates

When taken together, the increasing pressure to either ban race-conscious admissions policies or to substitute a purportedly less divisive race-neutral, socioeconomic-only approach couples with the conflicting constructions and uses of diversity. In this way, college admissions processes and policies constitute an integral part of the university as a racialized organization. Even if we think about why students may or may not apply to a college, admissions offices' responses or nonresponses to students matter. In an audit study using different forms of emails sent to white college admissions counselors from fictitious Black students, sociologist Ted Thornhill found that the counselors would weed out students seemingly "too concerned" with race and racism, not responding to these students or discouraging them from applying.[100]

Also, the antecedents of affirmative action bans by states shed light on the connections between racial advantages and college admissions offices. Education scholar Dominique Baker examined the enrollment patterns for the public institutions, including flagship institutions (i.e., well-funded and often selective public institutions), in forty-seven states, eight of which had affirmative action bans in place from 1995 to 2012. Baker's longitudinal analysis found an interesting connection between white student enrollment and affirmative action bans: states whose campuses, particularly flagship campuses, witnessed declining white student enrollment were more likely to witness voter support of affirmative action bans. These findings suggest that such bans—and probably the accompanying pressure to adopt race-neutral, socioeconomic-only admissions policies—relate to white students' access to coveted higher education opportunities and resources.[101] These possibilities are also expressed in qualitative studies of the anti-affirmative action movement. Sociologists Amaka Okechukwu and Ellen Berrey emphasize the underlying, and sometimes explicit, battles for retaining racial advantages in higher education by white critics of affirmative action in college admissions.[102]

How do the numbers-driven approaches to diversity and inclusion create tension with, and possibly hinder, university efforts to promote these organizational goals on campus? The battles around race-conscious policies and the search for race-neutral alternatives, particularly in states that ban affirmative action, have positioned racial diversity as an attainable goal of universities. That is, in the defense of diversity, universities must rely on such quantifiable outcomes as the demographics of the student body to monitor progress. Although I will discuss campus demographics in more depth in chapter 2, we need to remember that the promotion of diversity as a campus reality begins with college admissions and the selection of students who complement the university mission of diversity and inclusion. However, diversity can become reduced to a numeric representation on campus or a marketable symbol of an institution's prestige and educational value, rendering students into commodities, whether intentionally or not.[103] This unfortunate transformation often occurs with quantification, as pressure for university accountability turns some metrics into targeted outcomes, as Wendy Espeland and Michael Sauder's work on law school rankings attests.[104] The continual legal challenges to the use of race and ethnicity in college admissions also reflects a major pressure on higher education to be accountable.

Steps to Rethink Race and College Admissions

Universities and policy makers can take some initial steps to rethink how race and ethnicity are used in college admissions. First, they can avoid one of the more insidious ways that the definition of racial and ethnic diversity is affected by the debates about college admission policies. Specifically, we must carefully consider how critical mass, a central feature of legal arguments surrounding race-conscious admissions, is determined and used for higher education policies.[105] Generally, critical mass refers to the approximate amount of student diversity needed to cultivate the educational and social benefits of diversity on college campuses.[106] But as educational scholars Liliana Garces and Uma Jayakumar explain, critical mass must be considered in relation to the circumstances of each university. It cannot be quantified as a singular number to aim for across higher education.[107]

Proponents and researchers of different admission policies, whether they consider race and ethnicity to some degree or not, consistently discuss how policy changes may shape student demographics. In particular, they describe how the changes could lead to "comparable diversity" reported under current or past admissions policies. Ignoring Garces and Jayakumar's warning that critical mass is unique to time and circumstances, such framing fails to recognize that only a few colleges and universities are overrepresented by students of color or have equitable representation on campus. Also under this framing, what is an "acceptable" or "appropriate" level of diversity remains unclear. By aiming for so-called comparable levels of diversity, universities can maintain an underrepresentation of groups. These institutions might never reach a level of student diversity that, because of the opportunities, resources, and history of the institution, could promote the benefits of diversity. The benchmark of past diversity levels becomes the goal of institutional policies and efforts instead of stronger, healthier, and productive relationships among students from different backgrounds on campus.

As a second step to rethinking college admissions policies, we should recognize that excluding race and ethnicity from these policies does not mean that race is still not a factor in who is admitted to a university. As described earlier, color-blind approaches allow other structural inequalities that shape students' lives to take precedence and continue to privilege white students in college admissions discussions. There is no proximate measure or substitute for race in society. Socioeconomic status may be highly correlated with a person's race or ethnicity, but being poor does not automatically mean that the person is of a certain race. To fully capture the complexity of racial diversity, we must consider how race and ethnicity work in society and how they reflect differential access to opportunities and resources that can shape applicants' educational trajectories by the time their applications land in the admissions office.

Third, we must understand that merit is racialized. It reflects the structural inequalities of society and is not wholly objective. Perhaps one of the most difficult perspectives to grasp is that an A in a class does not necessarily correspond with a person's understanding of the material or good performance as much as we would think. Because of racial biases in schools, teachers might gently bump up grades for some students while not giving the same benefit of the doubt for others. When these biases in grading are added to differences in students' opportunities for extra credit, their opportunities to participate in extracurricular activities, and the amount of policing they receive in school hallways, we can see how the cumulative differences over nearly thirteen years of education produce the large racial disparities found in schools and colleges today.[108]

Fourth, if grades are racialized features of students' educational portfolios, then should these measures be quantified and weighed as heavily as they are, or should they be dequantified?[109] The short answer is yes, grades should be dequantified to some degree. But to do so, we must completely retrain college admission staff to revamp their review processes and policies, and universities need to explicitly discuss how much grades and test scores matter for admissions decisions. The College Board's development of a dashboard of adversity measures and contextual information, noted earlier and guided by Bastedo's important work, is a step in the right direction for giving admissions staff the data and tools to think deeper when completing holistic reviews of applications.[110] However, to fully consider how bias and structural inequality could shape an applicant's materials, particularly grades, admissions staff must be better trained to use this contextual information in their reviews. Such a change will not be easy, to say the least.

The admissions staff at the University of Michigan received nearly sixty-five thousand applications for the entering class of 2019.[111] This massive number of applications surpasses the number applying to many other colleges and universities, but the magnitude of reviewing thousands of applications in a short period should not be lost on anyone. In situations like at the University of Michigan, the quantification of such aspects of applicant's materials as grades and test scores is supposed to shorten the time to review, weigh important characteristics, and better inform decisions.[112] However, grades and test scores are not as straightforward as they seem. Nor do people believe that a 4.0 grade point average for one applicant is the same for another student from a different school. Context matters. Yet, admissions staff face pressure to make review decisions quickly but also to build more competitive entering cohorts of students. The staff must also balance donor and alumni demands and handle many other pressures that can influence rankings, future resources, future applications, and, ultimately, their own work as admissions staff members.[113] We need to further consider how to effectively consider the contexts of student grades and coursework to reduce the racial and socioeconomic biases that influence admissions decisions.

And finally, admissions needs to consider test scores that are noted for racial biases and other similarly concerning disparities. As many colleges are going test-optional, and as the COVID-19 pandemic forced institutions to at least suspend their usage of test scores in many regards for admissions decisions, these questions must take precedence if we are to make serious efforts toward equity and inclusion through college admissions.[114] A somewhat mixed bag of research suggests that test-optional policies benefit student diversity, although these policies can enhance perceptions of an institution's prestige as well.[115] Importantly, while a university may go test-optional for college admissions, they seldom go test-optional for institutional financial aid. If a student wants to be fully considered for scholarships and grants from an institution, test scores may be required. If an institution is to identify the long-held biases of standardized testing and choose to avoid them in admissions review, then it must also carry this policy forward in financial aid offices as well.

These are not the only steps that campus leaders and policy makers can take in college admissions. But these approaches provide a helpful starting point toward cultivating more diversity, equity, and inclusion in the policies and processes of universities around college admissions. The COVID-19 pandemic led to much uncertainty in society, and in higher education particularly, and changed the way people approached different aspects of their lives and how organizations operated. Perhaps these changes could also lead to more equitable college admissions practices across the nation.

Conclusion

How race, diversity, and merit in college admissions are framed clearly creates a challenge for considering who warrants admission and what the use of quantitative data can mean for both admissions decisions and monitoring racial equity. The ongoing political and legal wrangling around affirmative action in college admissions showcases how and why numbers can matter for questions of racial inequality—especially underrepresentation and student disparities—in higher education. As the brief discussion of critical mass notes, who is on campus, how they are counted, and what this information means for diversity and inclusion in higher education can shift which policies may be needed to support these institutional goals. These racial equity considerations all reflect the shifting organizational schemata and routines that shape racial inequality in higher education. I take up these diversity numbers of student demographics in the next chapter to better show how attempts to quantify diversity and use it in arguments for or against race-conscious admissions policies can further distort what we know about our students, faculty, and staff and their experiences on campus.

CHAPTER 2

Beyond
Predominately White

How Numbers Describe Racialized Campus Life

ONVERSATIONS ABOUT RACE and higher education often focus on college admissions. Attention to this aspect of higher education makes sense in many ways, particularly considering the weight society places on going to college—a college-for-all mindset. As journalist Paul Tough recently documented in *The Years That Matter Most*, parents, their children, college leaders and administrators, and a whole "admissions industrial complex" continuously discuss the importance of getting into the right college, its affordability, a college's place in the rankings, and other high-stakes pressures that keep everyone on their toes and anxious.[1] College access and affordability is undeniably an important issue, and people's views on race and inequality shape what solutions to stagnating or decreasing campus diversity can mean for future admissions policies and recruitment strategies. Chapter 1 provided insight into how universities can operate as racialized organizations through their admissions policies and how universities use diversity numbers in this aspect of higher education. But what about when the students arrive on campus to pursue their degrees?

Campus representation and student experiences are reciprocally related to college admissions practices. Conversations about a critical mass of students from different backgrounds to promote the educational and social benefits of diversity and the need to consider race in holistic admissions review provide a clear connection between these different aspects of organizational life in higher education.[2] To cultivate the benefits of diversity, universities need some level of student representation to promote interactions in a variety of campus forums, both formal and informal. However, what constitutes critical mass for campuses is not an easily attainable number.[3] Universities must aim for a more dynamic, fluid understanding of how diversity can promote educational and social benefits.[4] Unfortunately, discussions about what constitutes critical mass do emphasize concrete numbers about student representation on campus and, by extension, faculty diversity. Both critics of and proponents for affirmative action in college admissions use these numbers to support their arguments. Not only does quantification simplify complex social realities, but its outcomes also become organizational goals and benchmarks, heuristics, or cognitive shortcuts for understanding higher education inequality, such as the availability of resources and opportunities to racial and ethnic groups.[5]

This chapter elaborates on what racial inequality on our campuses looks like, specifically in relation to representation of groups in different positions, in an effort to improve how we interpret frequently constructed diversity numbers and to better understand racial inequalities on our campuses. Before we examine how the demographics of campuses may not necessarily be as straightforward as they appear, I suggest an emerging lens that can provide better information for examining quantitative data on diversity, equity, and inclusion-related efforts in higher education. This lens, known as critical quantitative work, or *QuantCrit*, provides a theoretically deeper methodological approach to analyze and interpret data.

Along a similar line, we must reconsider the racial and ethnic categories often used to describe campus diversity. We need to consider who is included in a group, and why, within a sociohistorical context of higher education. Generally, we have to ask, What's in a name? Racial and ethnic categories serve important organizational purposes and provide one point of tension when institutions try to clarify what campus diversity looks like, what counts as underrepresented, and why current classifications can contribute to, and do not necessarily reduce, racial inequality.

After discussing which racial and ethnic categories exist, the chapter looks at how institutions use these categories in their assessments of campus demography. Using examples of student, faculty, and the often-ignored staff of college campuses, I describe how universities may present themselves as racially diverse in some ways but may not operate to support the educational and social benefits of diversity. Further, segregation can exist on campuses but be hidden under the diversity umbrella. For example, the label of a diverse campus suggests that certain groups participate in different academic programs, but one ethnic or racial group's participation might overshadow the underrepresentation of another group, depending on what categories are used to summarize student representation in those programs.

Segregation is a structural feature of college campuses, aided by organizational policies and processes; it should not be described as the result of individual decisions, which have long been used for victim blaming, the impugning of marginalized groups for the inequalities they face each day.[6] Further, perceptions that students of color self-segregate on college campuses often miss that these students navigate an already-unequal space that privileges white students' perspectives.[7] The possibility of segregation hiding under a thin veil of campus diversity can shape how we understand who graduates from colleges and what their academic and future career pursuits may be and why. While campus diversity can signal equity and inclusion in some ways, the diversity label is not interchangeable with equity and inclusion; racial diversity cannot be the only outcome to monitor. The quantification of diversity can help answer certain questions, but it can also further complicate which solutions we may seek to promote equity and inclusion on campus.

As I discuss later in this chapter, we need to reconsider different aspects of advanced statistical analyses, the assumptions behind these models, and the importance of incorporating qualitative and mixed-methods approaches to get behind the diversity numbers for promoting equity and inclusion in higher education. Qualitative and mixed-methods projects provide the needed context for what we see in spreadsheets, graphs, and statistical models. A wealth of research exists to promote better monitoring of diversity and inclusion on college campuses and to show which pursuits can provide a more holistic view of campus diversity, its changes, and its contributions to the lives of students, faculty, and staff members. Finally, I challenge us to reconsider questions such as "What makes a campus too white?" if our goals are equity and inclusion in higher education, not simply increasing representation.

Adding Depth to Shallow Numbers to Inform Decision-Making

The recent expansion of critical quantitative work into deeper epistemological and theoretical considerations is not, in fact, new in the social sciences. The earliest use of quantitative research to document racial inequality beyond the numbers was that of W. E. B. Du Bois in his monumental study *The Philadelphia Negro* in 1899.[8] In this study, Du Bois embedded many statistical analyses of the Black community of Philadelphia in historical and theoretical discussions of education, housing, employment, crime, labor, and health, among others. Rather than letting the numbers speak for themselves and fall prey to the deficit logic used to blame Black community members for the racism surrounding their lives, Du Bois sought to explain the interconnections between culture, structure, and how policies can reinforce racial inequality in the everyday lives of community members.[9] Such a reorientation to statistical analyses of racial inequality to combat a fast-growing eugenic era that merged shallow analyses with policy prescriptions to fix the "race problem" in the nation laid a foundation for QuantCrit.

Early forms of QuantCrit in education used statistical analyses to document the student pipelines from primary school through graduate education and included detailed discussions of the structural impediments to educational pursuits for students of color. These analyses and discussions often ran counter to mainstream stories of why racial inequality existed in schools and colleges.[10] An important feature of this work is critical race theory and intersectionality as frameworks to reorient seemingly straightforward numbers and put them in a sociohistorical context to describe the complex processes that led to these statistical outcomes.[11] Both critical race theory and intersectionality frameworks are important for informing quantitative analyses. For example, a narrow but pluralistic interpretation of diversity looks at identity as a benign set of categories. In this view, identity is something people inhabit or take on rather than an attribute that shifts with context and is anchored in the culture and structure of organizations specifically and society more generally.[12] Both frameworks are increasingly applied in studies of schools and colleges, but most of this research is qualitative, leaving quantitative approaches underdeveloped regarding how they could be better utilized for pursuing racial equity.[13] Despite the increasing use of these two frameworks, higher education scholars Jessica Harris and Lori Patton's analysis of intersectionality in higher education research provide an important point that simply increasing the use of critical frameworks for analyses does not guarantee that they will be used appropriately.[14]

If we are to accept that racial inequality is shaped by our universities and that quantification can influence how we understand the opportunity structure, depending on our monitoring of different metrics for diversity, equity, and inclusion, then we must shift our analytical approaches. Our statistical analyses and interpretations should examine how inequality can variously result from universities' policies and processes. The emergent area of QuantCrit provides more nuanced perspectives because of its theoretical depth in framing quantitative analyses.[15] This approach can reorient how scholars, policy makers, and administrators use these quantitative methods in diversity and inclusion efforts.[16]

QuantCrit provides more information on the everyday experiences seldom captured in traditional quantitative work and pinpoints the patterns of inequality informing people's daily lives.[17] This work challenges the belief that more advanced statistical techniques can overcome theoretical and interpretative flaws. The idea is not to dismiss advanced quantitative approaches used in higher education or other sectors of society, but to charge the people using these analyses to consider the complexity of college campuses, for example, not just their equations. This work complements Wendy Espeland and Michael Sauder's examination of how quantification can shift the value of numbers in decision-making and people's preference for the simplification of complex social realities.[18]

Five working tenets inform QuantCrit scholarship. They challenge the role and value that quantification has gained not simply in higher education but also in society, and they can shape how decisions are made.[19] First, quantitative analyses are limited in their ability to capture the depth, complexity, and fluidity of systems of power and their connections. Second, quantitative methods and their products are not value-neutral; they can promote deficit perspectives of marginalized communities (i.e., the view that inequalities are the result of individual or group faults or limited capabilities). Third, categories used in quantitative analyses must be challenged and not taken for granted. Fourth, quantitative approaches must be coupled with qualitative research to take into account the experiences and perspectives of marginalized communities. Finally, quantitative approaches are an important component of social justice and transformation efforts, but they are not inherently valuable; they become valuable for different groups in varying ways in an unequal society.[20]

QuantCrit reminds us that statistical analysis is only one tool for documenting racial inequality as both an outcome and a lived experience.[21] As David Gillborn, Paul Warmington, and Sean Demack succinctly note, "numbers do not speak for themselves," but researchers do interpret numbers and must do so carefully to avoid implying that statistical significance eclipses the sociohistorical and political meanings of their findings.[22] With this primer of how QuantCrit can apply to diversity and inclusion in higher education, we must first consider the categories often used to analyze diversity in higher education. To do so, we will examine how different classification systems of the same campus can present different conclusions about student representation and diversity.

Race, Categories, and Diversity Obfuscation

Every day, higher education uses racial and ethnic categories without even questioning them. Whether they are calculating graduation rates, studying enrollment numbers, or exploring the diversity of faculty search pools, university personnel use these categories with different goals in mind. But these categories are not benign bins to place people in. They were created through literal centuries of sociopolitical battles over resources and opportunities. Thus, from a QuantCrit perspective, we should examine how recent changes in these categories may influence our understanding of diversity and inclusion in higher education. Aided by quantification, the racial categories used in higher education inform the core functions of universities as racialized organizations. Further, these racial and ethnic categories provide the foundation for diversity numbers.

A classification system can be helpful for organizing information and for quantified analyses, an integral part of decision-making.[23] But quantification begins to falter when it assigns meanings of race to the people who are grouped under these classification systems.[24] The creation of racial categories is a long-standing racial project that connects organizations and extends their underlying ideas and rules about race and inequality. Identified by Michael Omi and Howard Winant as a racial project, racial categories in higher education were not necessarily created by universities but were incorporated from the US Census. The categories follow a general process in which they and their associated meanings are created, modified, and destroyed over time.[25] For example, who is considered white has changed over time through census definitions, laws and policies, Supreme Court cases, and the social interactions in communities across the nation.

The quantification informing the construction of the census's racial categories and their often-required use for data collection in higher education reinforce the supposed objectivity and legitimacy of racial categories. Thus, these categories became important in people's understanding of diversity and racial disparities.[26] With the continual use of diversity measured and analyzed according to racial categories, universities still racialize people and explain away persistent racial inequality in higher education.[27] For example, in reviewing how the racial diversity of students is both constructed and presented by universities, Karly Ford and Ashley Patterson have found different omissions, aggregations, and additions of ethnic and racial categories. These practices can shift both the "cosmetic diversity" presented by university websites and realistic interpretations of student representation and what diversity looks like on campuses.[28]

QuantCrit requires us to further consider what racial categories mean for diversity and inclusion in higher education, and how relying on these categories, their measurements, and related analyses can lead researchers, administrators, and policy makers to reductionism.[29] Moreover, as Kerry Ann Rockquemore, David Brunsma, and Daniel Delgado eloquently describe, we must not confuse processes of racial identity, or how people identify with different groups, with processes of racial identification and categorization, which are aligned with more quantitative approaches to racial inequality. The quantification-related processes impose meanings of race on people and limit the approaches that higher education might consider for improving diversity and inclusion.[30] The push for accountability in society, and higher education in particular, has made quantification even more important in conversations about race and inequality. The challenges go beyond college access to how colleges can serve as vehicles for social mobility among marginalized groups.[31] The sociopolitical and legal push for strict scrutiny of race-conscious admissions policies is one pressure on higher education. Under such scrutiny, institutions feel pressure to transform racial categories into the purportedly best way to operationalize race and analyze racial inequality on college campuses.[32] Yet, QuantCrit reminds us that we cannot naturalize these categories under pressures to use convenient quantitative forms of data for bureaucratic purposes. These categories in no way represent people's complex life circumstances that we must understand in the pursuit of diversity and inclusion.[33]

Reconsidering Racial Categories in Federal Education Data

A wide range of racial categories do not neatly align with how people identify racially and ethnically in the United States.[34] The most popular group of categories used in American society is derived from the US Census, and these categories are part of the required data reporting by colleges and universities to the Department of Education if they wish to receive federal financial support such as financial aid for students. Before 1997, people could only identify with one racial or ethnic category. However, the Office of Management and Budget issued a directive that allowed people to select more than one race and ethnicity.[35] This new directive caused many headaches for researchers attempting to analyze changes in student demographics in higher education, for example, in studies related to diversity and inclusion. The directive also required the main warehouse of higher education data, the Integrated Postsecondary Education Data System (IPEDS), to change its reporting procedures for race and ethnicity data. Although the US Census rolled out the new multiple-box approach to race and ethnicity in the decennial census year of 2000, IPEDS did not allow for fuller reporting under the Office of Management and Budget directive until the 2008–2009 academic year.

If we consider student demographics prior to these changes, universities were only required to report students if they fit under one category: Hispanic, White, Black, Asian/Pacific Islander, Native American or Alaska Native, Race/Ethnicity Unknown, or Nonresident Alien. After these reporting changes, IPEDS included both new and old definitions for reporting data about racial and ethnic categories that researchers and administrators can use in analyses to align these changes. The 2008–2009 data collection year also included a new category, "Two or More Races," if a student selected more than one racial or ethnic group if a university's form allowed for such multiple choices. Reflecting the changes allowing for multiple group identification, IPEDS shifted to the "new" classification system that included the following groups: American Indian or Alaska Native, Asian, Black or African American, Hispanic or Latinx, Native Hawaiian or Other Pacific Islander, White, Two or More Races, Race/Ethnicity Unknown, and Nonresident Alien. Table 2.1 summarizes the IPEDS racial and ethnic categories before and after 2008 and highlights the grouping differences.

The reporting of racial and ethnic data is not as straightforward as going with whatever a student marked on a form, unfortunately. Complications include the type of forms used to collect this information and situations in which a student's identity differs on two university forms or when there is other possibly conflicting information about a student.[36] Quantification requires new systems of condensing and analyzing data.[37] Thus, IPEDS reporting standards have some wrinkles: students are not necessarily reported the way they may have identified themselves on forms. In general, people are not presented with options beyond the listed categories, and IPEDS dissuades university staff or administrators from offering any option or combination of options that allows the student to identify as "Unknown," to refuse or decline to respond, to check "None of the Above" on a form, or to identify simply as "Other" or "Nonresident Alien." People are supposed to choose from categories in the racial classification system that aligns closely with the US Census, but their choices are not fully acknowledged by the census approach to racial and ethnic groups. Table 2.2 illustrates how universities are instructed to report people's racial and ethnic identities using the IPEDS classification system.

As table 2.2 shows, the current IPEDS reporting instructions require the use of old organizational logic for reporting self-identified race and ethnicity.

TABLE 2.1 *Current racial and ethnic categories in the Integrated Postsecondary Education Data System (IPEDS)*

PRE-2008	POST-2008
AMERICAN INDIAN OR ALASKA NATIVE[a]	
A person having origins in any of the original peoples of North America and who maintains cultural identification through tribal affiliation or community recognition.	A person having origins in any of the original peoples of North and South America (including Central America) who maintains cultural identification through tribal affiliation or community attachment.
ASIAN[a]	
Existed in combination with another category.	A person having origins in any of the original peoples of the Far East, Southeast Asia, or the Indian Subcontinent, including, for example, Cambodia, China, India, Japan, Korea, Malaysia, Pakistan, the Philippine Islands, Thailand, and Vietnam.
NATIVE HAWAIIAN OR OTHER PACIFIC ISLANDER[a]	
Existed in combination with another category.	A person having origins in any of the original peoples of Hawaii, Guam, Samoa, or other Pacific Islands.
ASIAN/PACIFIC ISLANDER[a]	
A person having origins in any of the original peoples of the Far East, Southeast Asia, the Indian Subcontinent, and Pacific Islands. This includes people from China, Japan, Korea, the Philippine Islands, American Samoa, India, and Vietnam.	No longer exists.
BLACK OR AFRICAN AMERICAN[a]	
A person having origins in any of the black racial groups of Africa (except those of Hispanic origin).	A person having origins in any of the black racial groups of Africa.
HISPANIC OR LATINO[b]	
A person of Mexican, Puerto Rican, Cuban, Central or South American or other Spanish culture or origin, regardless of race.	A person of Cuban, Mexican, Puerto Rican, South or Central American, or other Spanish culture or origin, regardless of race.

PRE-2008	POST-2008
WHITE[a]	
A person having origins in any of the original peoples of Europe, North Africa, or the Middle East (except those of Hispanic origin).	A person having origins in any of the original peoples of Europe, the Middle East, or North Africa.
TWO OR MORE RACES	
Did not exist.	Category used by institutions to report persons who selected more than one race.
RACE/ETHNICITY UNKNOWN	
This category is used ONLY if the student did not select a racial/ethnic designation, AND the postsecondary institution finds it impossible to place the student in one of the aforementioned racial/ethnic categories during established enrollment procedures or in any post-enrollment identification or verification process.	Same definition as previously used.
NONRESIDENT ALIEN	
A person who is not a citizen or national of the United States and who is in this country on a visa or temporary basis and does not have the right to remain indefinitely.	Same definition as previous used.

Note: The above table was created from information on National Center for Education Statistics practices for IPEDS reporting available online (http://nces.ed.gov/ipeds). The following clarification of nonresident alien categories accompanies IPEDS reporting instructions: "Nonresident aliens are included here, rather than in any of the five racial/ethnic categories described below. Resident aliens and other eligible (for financial aid purposes) noncitizens who are not citizens or nationals of the United States and who have been admitted as legal immigrants for the purpose of obtaining permanent resident alien status (and who hold either an alien registration card (Form I-551 or I-151), a Temporary Resident Card (Form I-688), or an Arrival-Departure Record (Form I-94) with a notation that conveys legal immigrant status such as Section 207 Refugee, Section 208 Asylee, Conditional Entrant Parolee or Cuban-Haitian) are to be reported in the appropriate racial/ethnic categories along with United States citizens."

[a]Category was originally reserved for people not identifying as Hispanic.

[b]Latino was added to the IPEDS racial and ethnic categories in the new classifications system.

TABLE 2.2 *Reporting instructions for race and ethnicity categories in IPEDS*

INDIVIDUAL SELF-REPORT	ASSOCIATED IPEDS CATEGORY
Hispanic only, or Hispanic and any race category	Hispanic
Not Hispanic; American Indian or Alaska Native only	American Indian or Alaska Native
Not Hispanic; Asian only	Asian
Not Hispanic; Black or African American only	Black or African American
Not Hispanic; Native Hawaiian or Other Pacific Islander only	Native Hawaiian or Other Pacific Islander
Not Hispanic; White only	White
Not Hispanic; more than one race category	Two or more races
OTHER REPORTING CATEGORIES	
Refuses to respond to both questions	Unknown race and ethnicity
Responds "No" to the Hispanic question, but does not respond to the race question	Unknown race and ethnicity
Responds to the race question, but does not respond to the Hispanic question	Report race as outlined above, as if individual self-identified as non-Hispanic
Is a nonresident alien according to the visa and citizenship information on record at the institution	Nonresident alien

Source: Adapted from information provided by the National Center for Education Statistics, the manager of IPEDS, available online (http://nces.ed.gov/ipeds).

This requirement not only constrains the exploration of demographic realities across the nation but also ultimately restricts how people's identities are used to acknowledge possible campus issues related to their specific groups. For example, because of the structure of IPEDS data, we cannot examine trends such as graduation rates for students who identify as Black or white Latinx, despite noted differences in their experiences in higher education and society.[38] The changes in racial and ethnic categories also shift what the demographics of higher education look like because of the modification of definitions, the creation or elimination of categories, and changes in organizational reporting instructions.[39] Again, far from being color-blind or race-neutral organizations, universities rely on race and ethnicity as part of their everyday processes and policies both internally and externally, such as in fulfilling US Department of Education requirements.[40] IPEDS is not alone in providing a window into the shifting approaches to documenting racial and ethnic categories and using the categories for analyses. Higher education scholars Nichole Garcia and Oscar Mayorga elaborate on similar shifts in the often-used Freshman Survey of the Cooperative Institutional Research Program at the University of California, Los Angeles (UCLA) Higher Education Research Institute since the survey's founding in the 1960s.[41]

Despite IPEDS's requirement that universities report racial demographics using its racial classification system, many institutions are now expanding the number of categories that students readily identify with to provide additional information on the racial and ethnic diversity on their campuses. This broadening of categories can have many benefits for campuses aiming to improve decision-making to support student success. Educational researchers Samantha Viano and Dominique Baker also describe ways to expand the data used to inform both the construction of racial and ethnic categories for institutional analyses and the interpretations of identities and related inequalities on campus.[42] In light of changes to the federal reporting instructions for race and ethnicity, a new classification system was developed by the University of California (UC) system both to align with federal reporting standards and to address the need to focus on specific communities represented on UC campuses.[43] Use of the federal categories can hide diversity *within* student groups, and the UC approach allows for further examination of different student group experiences rather than relying on the federal categories. For example, the UC approach contains a category for Black and African American students that includes multiple groups such as African Americans, African and Caribbean students who also identify as Black, and other students who identify as Black or African American, or both, in some form.

As another example, the UC system allows Asian students to identify with sixteen ethnicities, including an "Other Asian" category, which is separate from categories identifying people with both Pacific Islander ethnicities and

Middle Eastern and North African ethnicities. The UC approach is quite uncommon in higher education data collection and has developed as other racial classification approaches for data come under additional scrutiny for homogenizing diverse groups.[44] For example, the ambiguity and shifting usage of Middle Eastern and North African as a racial and ethnic category by the census can complicate how student diversity and representation is constructed by universities that rely on this classification approach, while the UC approach provides one avenue of including a broader set of categories for these students to identify with and use in analyses.[45] Further, the UC approach offers additional ways to examine multiracial and multiethnic student enrollments.

UC's approach to racial and ethnic data is an improvement for examining diversity on college campuses partly because it allows researchers, administrators, and policy makers to further uncover disparities among students from different racial and ethnic backgrounds. Fitting in with a more QuantCrit approach, the UC system can also support a deeper examination of barriers to degree completion, such as a student's transferring, low-socioeconomic background, lack of US citizenship, and gender. Although not perfect, the UC approach to race and ethnicity data enables us to use quantitative tools to obtain more information and create more detailed descriptions of group experiences in higher education.[46] The conversation about diversity within groups, particularly panethnic groups such as Asian Americans, provides data-informed arguments against stereotypes about who succeeds or does not and why, to better inform higher education policies and initiatives.[47] These approaches to quantitative data can help debunk the homogenizing effects of stereotypes such as the model-minority myth and deficit perspectives targeting Black, Latinx, and other groups on campus.[48] Additionally, QuantCrit requires a more dynamic examination of racial and ethnic experiences and disparities in higher education. Sociologist Yasmiyn Irizarry provides one example of a multidimensional approach to race and ethnicity that incorporates immigration history and that can expand the work the UC system has already begun.[49]

Snapshot of Diversity Obfuscation

As I have noted, the different racial and ethnic classification systems used in higher education analyses can shift how administrators and policy makers view diversity and inequality. Let's briefly examine how UC's approach for one campus can provide a more nuanced understanding of student representation, even when we rely on the broader racial and ethnic categories. But these broader categories can also lead to confusion about who is being discussed, the consistency of classification and categorization, and how varied the campus data can be when compared with the federal data available in IPEDS. Each of these issues can exacerbate the impact of policies that use such data to inform decisions.

Table 2.3 compares UC and IPEDS data on undergraduate demographics for the University of California, Berkeley, in the fall of 2018. The categories are based on UC's data-collection approach and provide broad category totals (i.e., total across all possible subcategories for each grouping) overlapped with the IPEDS categories to show how the two approaches agree (or don't) for the totals of each category. The UC approach provides disaggregated (i.e., a wider group of racial and ethnic categories) and aggregated (i.e., collapsing related racial and ethnic categories into a smaller number of groups) data on student representation. The first column shows disaggregated data for US students by race and ethnicity. The second column presents the full racial and ethnic diversity of students on campus and includes non-US students in the totals. Both these columns use duplicated, or multiple-response, data for students. That is, these columns take into account that students could check more than one box for their racial and ethnical identity. The third column provides aggregated, unduplicated data (i.e., classifies students using a one-box approach) for student demographics more in line with the federally mandated reporting systems. The fourth column provides IPEDS data for Berkeley's campus. The remaining columns calculate the differences between each racial classification system, comparing the percentage differences for each group between (1) the disaggregated US-only calculations and the disaggregated data for all students, regardless of citizenship status from the UC system; (2) the disaggregated US-only calculations and the aggregated data from the UC system; (3) the disaggregated US-only calculations and IPEDS data; (4) the disaggregated calculations that include international students and IPEDS data; and (5) the aggregated UC system data and IPEDS data.

TABLE 2.3 *Comparison of student representation for University of California–Berkeley using UC system and IPEDS data sets*

STUDENT GROUP	UC SYSTEM				% CHANGE		% CHANGE FROM IPEDS		
	DISAGG US	DISAGG ALL	AGG	IPEDS	US-ALL	US-AGG	UC-US	UC-ALL	UC-AGG
American Indian/Alaska Native	0.86% (257)	0.76% (258)	0.44% (136)	0.09% (28)	0.10	0.42	0.77	0.67	0.35
Black/African American	3.49% (1,039)	3.32% (1,120)	3.37% (1,039)	1.85% (570)	0.17	0.12	1.64	1.47	1.52
Asian	41.91% (12,473)	46.16% (15,586)	39.29% (12,123)	35.10% (10,830)	-4.24	2.62	6.81	11.06	4.19
Hispanic/Latinx	15.76% (4,691)	14.92% (5,038)	14.70% (4,534)	15.24% (4,701)	0.84	1.07	0.53	-0.32	-0.54
Native Hawaiian/Pacific Islander	0.60% (178)	0.54% (184)	0.00% (0)	0.12% (37)	0.05	0.60	0.48	0.42	-0.12
Southwest Asian/North African	5.22% (1,553)	4.98% (1,680)	0.00% (0)	0.00% (0)	0.24	5.22	5.22	4.98	0.00
White	32.15% (9,568)	29.32% (9,901)	24.81% (7,656)	24.87% (7,672)	2.83	7.34	7.29	4.46	-0.05
Multiracial/ethnic	0.00% (0)	0.00% (0)	0.00% (0)	5.77% (1,779)	0.00	0.00	-5.77	-5.77	-5.77
Race/ethnicity unknown	0.00% (0)	0.00% (0)	4.42% (1,364)	4.00% (1,235)	0.00	-4.42	-4.00	-4.00	0.42
International	0.00% (0)	0.00% (0)	12.97% (4,001)	12.97% (4,001)	0.00	-12.97	-12.97	-12.97	0.00
Total students	29,759	33,767	30,853	30,853					

Figure 2.1 shows how the data can look different for the same campus, depending on the classification system used. As the table and figure show, the organizational logic solidified into policy for constructing and counting the racial and ethnic diversity among students varies and raises important questions not only about how data is used on one campus but also about how data available in national datasets such as IPEDS is used across several campuses. For example, if we focus on students classified as Asian, the US-only disaggregated data for the UC system reports nearly 42 percent of students identifying with the group. This percentage increases when international students are included in the data, and Asian students represent slightly more than 46 percent of students on campus. However, when students are aggregated to smaller groups and a one-box approach is applied for the UC system data, Asian students represent less than 40 percent of all students. This differs from IPEDS data that reports 35 percent of Berkeley students on campus that semester were identified as Asian.

The preceding example suggests how the four classification approaches that aggregate, disaggregate, include, or exclude international students, and identify students with only one racial or ethnic group or multiple groups for the UC system and IPEDs data, can shift the representation of student groups on campus. These differences illustrate how three core processes of quantification (the formulation of categories, the classification of people into those categories, and the enumeration of the people in a category) can influence the fourth core process (valuation) and operate as a form of racialization at the organizational level of higher education.[50] The classification approach used to present information on student representation can influence how administrators and researchers understand not only the disparities in outcomes and marginalization on campus but also who is affected and what resources may

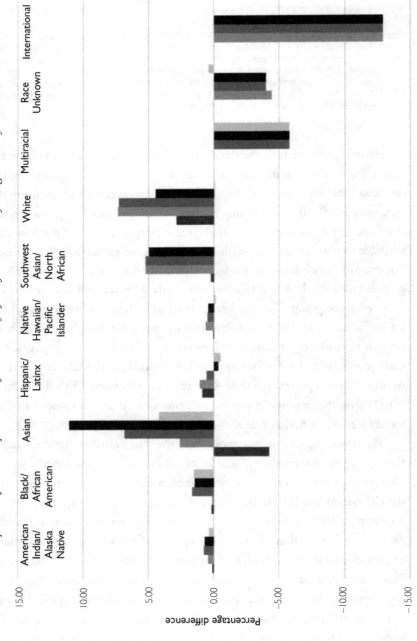

FIGURE 2.1 *Comparison of student representation for University of California–Berkeley using the UC system and IPEDS data sets*

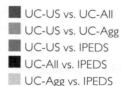

■ UC-US vs. UC-All
■ UC-US vs. UC-Agg
■ UC-US vs. IPEDS
■ UC-All vs. IPEDS
░ UC-Agg vs. IPEDS

Abbreviations: **IPEDS** = data presented in Integrated Postsecondary Education Data System form; **UC** = University of California; **UC-Agg** = the aggregated UC data and IPEDS data.; **UC-All** = the disaggregated calculations that include international students and IPEDS data; **UC-US** = difference between disaggregated data for US-only student and IPEDS data; **US-Agg** = difference between disaggregated data for US-only student and aggregated data from UC; **US-All** = difference between disaggregated data for US-only student and disaggregated data for all students.

be needed to provide a more equitable and inclusive experience for students. If we do not understand how these classification systems can change the composition of a racial group, then we cannot fully grasp how a suggested resource or support system may continue to undercut the academic achievement of students within that specific group.

The UC system's policies recognize that race and ethnicity are not solely a US social reality but exist globally. Thus, for example, the disaggregated approach allows researchers and administrators to identify how considering international students changes measures of student representation and could mask or overemphasize disparities in student experiences and academic achievement. These UC system's two disaggregated approaches also allow for the consideration of students identifying with more than one racial or ethnic group. These classification approaches differ from UC's aggregated form of student racial and ethnic diversity (the third column), which closely aligns with reported IPEDS data for the same campus (fourth column). International students are removed and treated as a separate racial-ethnic category and situates students' citizenship status as an overarching status that outweighs how race, ethnicity, and citizenship intertwine.[51]

A similar approach to using separate multiracial/ethnic and race and ethnicity unknown categories changes the perceived representation of student groups on campus according to which classification system is used to examine racial and ethnic diversity. These calculations show how some groups' representation is affected more by some racial classifications. Returning to the previous example, Asian student representation appears undercounted with the disaggregated US-only approach compared with the disaggregated system that includes international students into racial and ethnic categories, but then varies across which form of aggregated data is used for the campus. Nor is white student representation immune to these changes that are based on the classification system and data set used.

Suffice it to say that to see improvements in data collection, categorization, and classification with a critical eye, we must also evaluate the processes of quantification and how they fit the operations of colleges as racialized organizations that distribute resources and opportunities. We must examine quantification as a racialization process that moves from student identity to identification, categorization, classification, enumeration, valuation, and, finally, solidification into the underlying ideas and rules forming schemata, policies, and processes at an organizational level. Categories and their use are not benign university operations but have real consequences for students. We must not take these categories lightly if we are truly committed to promoting more equitable and inclusive higher education.

A Cautionary Note on Older Categories

A persistent yet subtle concern exists in data collection related to racial and ethnic categories. Researchers, administrators, and policy makers should be wary of a problematic practice in quantitative racial analyses in higher education and elsewhere: the use of eugenic categories and related explanations of inequality. Perhaps the most commonly used relic of the early twentieth-century eugenic era is the word *Caucasian* in reference to white people. *Caucasian* is used even in some of the more progressive approaches to documenting people's racial and ethnic identities; the term is used in UC's classification scheme. The history of this category's formation in support of the myth of white supremacy is perpetuated by the term's knowing or unknowing referral to a racial or ethnic group.[52] Relatedly, there are not "more scientific" categories to use, because race is socially constructed through human relations and holds real meaning for people's lived everyday experiences. Although recent scientific innovations in genetics and genomics suggest that racial or ethnic groups can be identified in the human genome, these findings only reinforce the pernicious myth that race is a biogenetic fact and not, as interdisciplinary research has documented for generations, a social one. Thus, we need to exert more care when considering the history and development of racial and ethnic categories in relation to people's racial and ethnic self-identification. We must scrutinize how this information is presented and, as discussed later, how it is analyzed and interpreted. In the meantime, *white* is the best available term in reference to student, faculty, and staff demographics.

Similarly, the category Nonresident Alien imposes a derogatory label on non-US students on college campuses and is used in federal immigration rhetoric. While the term *alien* is thought to refer to the person as a non-US student, the category and assumptions behind it also suggest these individuals are foreign to humanity. No person is an alien to humanity, and people from outside the United States who come to our universities to work and study should be treated better, even in statistical conversations. Additionally, the lumping of all students and faculty from outside of the United States into the Nonresident Alien IPEDS category constrains our analyses of how, for example, non-US students experience race and racism in higher education, and what differences exist for students who may identify differently racially and ethnically but come from the same nation. Again, QuantCrit requires us to be more responsive to the long sociohistorical trajectory of racial categories, their meanings, and current usage to transform data collection and analyses as well as better equip higher education leaders with information and perspectives to support these students, faculty, and staff on campus.

At an institutional level, universities should consider exploring how their data-collection efforts can reinforce harmful views of why racial inequalities exist on their campuses. As an initial step, universities could facilitate campus-wide studies to show that race and ethnicity are not neatly affixed to the categories used for data collection but relate to student, faculty, and staff experiences and processes of identity. This approach could assist with an understanding of how universities can work with students who are fighting for recognition of their experiences. Such studies could become part of the institutional processes and policies rather than the old, worn organizational standards for data collection, analysis, and interpretation; old approaches like these reinforce boundaries that hinder the development of more equitable and inclusive campuses.[53]

Because the organizational schema for racial classification requires universities to participate in a racialization process using federal guidelines for reporting such information, quantification legitimizes these categories and their associated diversity numbers as necessary for decision-making.[54] As Benjamin Baez reminds us, starting research and analyses without questioning the idea of difference and the categories that influence our view of difference and that simultaneously serve as the basis for comparisons of people's experiences in higher education can perpetuate the marginalization and oppression we are seeking to address.[55] This unquestioning view of racial and ethnic categories is the first step of how a university's organizational life can use quantification to falsely reconstruct itself as a color-blind, race-neutral organization all while contributing to racial stratification and inequality on campus.

As described in the introduction, an easy pitfall with the use of racial and ethnic categories is the belief that these categories adequately summarize individuals' identities, thoughts, and actions, absent sociohistorical and organizational contexts.[56] While social science research can produce important knowledge about inequality in higher education, thereby shaping public discourse about race-related issues, we must keep in mind that these differences and inequalities gain meaning through organizations' metrics and uses of this information.[57] Through the frequent use of this knowledge of difference, an organization's reliance on it becomes normalized, as do the underlying beliefs of those in an organization about racial inequality and why it exists. The underlying ideas of an organization coupled with individuals' beliefs can lead to deficit thinking that attributes the origin of the disparities to the students rather than to the processes, resources, and policies of a university that can perpetuate disadvantages.[58] The most frequently used data examines the "compositional diversity," or the representation of students from different racial and ethnic backgrounds, on campus in an increasingly diverse learning environment.[59] However, as we will see, the representation of different groups on our campuses reflects the opportunity structure of higher education influenced by organizational policies and processes.

Always Under the Microscope: Campus Diversity and Its Changes

A persistent theme in discussions about diversity in higher education is the changing demographics, particularly of students, on campus. Perhaps one of the most frequent observations in the last thirty years is that college campuses are becoming more racially and ethnically diverse. American higher education witnessed continued growth well into the recovery period after the Great Recession of 2008, climbing from 13.5 million enrolled students to slightly over

21 million in 2011. However, college enrollment recently plateaued before the COVID-19 pandemic as people once seeking additional education and training are landing jobs in the postrecession economy. Enrollment dropped by nearly 1 million students over roughly the past decade to level off at around 20 million total postsecondary students in 2019.[60]

During this same thirty-year period, college-going rates increased for students of all racial and ethnic backgrounds as the average percentage of high school students pursuing some form of postsecondary education increased from approximately 60 percent in 1990 to nearly 70 percent in 2019.[61] Despite increases across the board, these college-going rates differ by racial and ethnic student group. In 2019, white students' college-going rate after high school mirrors the overall rate, while Black students have an approximately 10 percent lower college-going rate; Latinx students are nearly on par with white students.[62] Asian American students, on the other hand, far outpace other student groups, with a current college-going rate of nearly 85 percent. These differences in who makes it to college classrooms are obviously a result of broader issues beyond student drive and desires; these issues include the inequitable system of K–12 education and inequitable admissions processes that students must navigate.[63]

Who enrolls in college also reflects the immigration system of the United States, which privileges some communities over others while targeting some groups by overpolicing, and is insidiously used to make narrow cultural arguments about racial or ethnic groups.[64] Additionally, students vary in how soon after high school graduation they enroll in postsecondary education, and longer delays correspond to lower rates of college completion. As the American Council on Education's in-depth report *Race and Ethnicity in Higher Education* documents, despite a slowly increasing rate of students enrolling in college immediately after graduating high school since the mid-1990s, these rates differ by race and ethnicity. Nearly 87 percent of Asian American students enrolled in college in 2016 immediately after high school graduation, followed by Latinx and white students, with slightly more than 70 percent enrolling after high school, and Black students, with the lowest immediate enrollment rate of approximately 57 percent.[65]

From 1990 to 2017, higher education witnessed many changes in racial and ethnic representation. Among US students, white enrollment fell from approximately 80 percent of all postsecondary students to nearly 57 percent across all sectors of higher education (including two- and four-year degree-granting institutions). Black student representation increased from 9 percent to slightly over 13 percent, Latinx representation increased from just under 6 percent to nearly 19 percent, Asian Americans from 4 to 6 percent, and Native American representation remained steady at just under 1 percent of all post-secondary students during this nearly thirty-year period.[66] International students increased from slightly under 3 percent of all postsecondary students in 1990 to approximately 5 percent in 2017. Not all of these changes are reflected in every undergraduate degree program. Many students of color, for example, are underrepresented in bachelor's degree programs and overrepresented in associate degree programs relative to their higher education population size.[67]

Undergraduate enrollments by race and gender present a more complex picture. Approximately 57 percent of college students are women, but the gender composition of different student groups can influence the identification of resources that may be needed to support them. Among international students, for example, men and women are evenly split in representation. Women constitute 62 percent of all US Black students, 60 percent of multiracial students, and 58 percent of Native Hawaiian and Pacific Islander students in undergraduate degree programs across the country.[68] However, these enrollment breakdowns also miss nonbinary students, who are only recently gaining more attention as researchers document institutions' related policies on gender and binary students' experiences on college campuses.[69]

Disaggregating undergraduate enrollments by socioeconomic status and age adds even more complexity to the issue of underrepresentation on college campuses. Differences in socioeconomic status and age in addition to race and ethnicity can shift what administrators identify as solutions to address student needs. For example, less than half of all Native American, Black, and Native Hawaiian and Pacific Islander undergraduate students are younger than twenty-three, while nearly two-thirds to three-quarters of Native American and Black students come from homes in the bottom two income quartiles, and half of Native Hawaiian and Pacific Islander students come from similar socioeconomic backgrounds.[70] As seen in these brief examples, there is more diversity to the diversity on our college campuses than is often reflected in analyses. Administrators and policy makers should carefully consider which students they are discussing when evaluating initiatives or policy changes, because of the great variation in who is represented on college campuses beyond the purported cut-and-dried racial and ethnic enrollment numbers.

Racial Segregation Across Higher Education

Segregation in higher education manifests itself across the different types of institutions. Representation at public institutions can differ from that at private ones. Even at public universities and colleges, opportunities and resources are unequally available. Thus, student representation differs across higher education. Despite the general increase in college-going rates among all students, there are differences in where students land for their college education and in the degrees they pursue. Research often examines how changes in student demographics reflect diversity, not segregation. But we must view diversity and segregation as related in higher education. Increasing diversity must not be considered the same as decreasing segregation, however; nor should it be equated with inclusive policies in higher education.

Overall, white students are more likely to be found at public and private four-year institutions, while other student groups have more variation in the colleges they attend. This difference is particularly notable in both racial-gender and socioeconomic breakdowns of where college students pursue their degrees. For example, Black women enroll more in for-profit institutions than Black men do, whereas public two-year colleges are disproportionately educating Native American students.[71] These enrollment statistics reflect the predatory practices of many for-profit institutions. They seek Black students and other students of color, who often come from lower socioeconomic positions. The institutions enroll these students to collect federal student aid with little intent of supporting students once they are enrolled or providing a viable pathway to social mobility and career opportunities.[72] The higher percentage of Native American students attending two-year institutions probably reflects the easier access to two-year institutions, including tribal colleges near many reservations. This structural impediment to attendance at a more distant four-year college results from early settler colonialism that purposely undercut Native American communities.[73] The complex issue of where and why students of different races and ethnicities pursue their college degrees is further complicated by the students' gender and socioeconomic backgrounds.

But we must also examine how admissions processes can encourage segregation across higher education.

Although there are slight variations in how researchers classify the selectivity of universities' admissions processes, we find that segregation is solidified as selectivity increases. Segregation and selectivity go hand in hand as processes of exclusion. Thus, college admissions selectivity should be framed as a mechanism of segregation in higher education, not a meritocratic process (as discussed in chapter 1). College rankings reward universities for being more exclusionary, and quantification aids in justifying such institutional rewards. Thus, these higher education policies and processes further reinforce how colleges and universities can operate as racialized organizations that differentially distribute resources and opportunities, influencing life chances along racial and ethnic lines.[74] When this reality is layered onto the unequal resources found across higher education whereby the most selective institutions hold the most opportunities for their students, these policies of segregation have a greater impact than many may realize.[75] It is difficult to achieve the proverbial American dream when structural obstacles impede your progress at each stage of education and then when institutions explain away these issues as individual deficits.

Slightly over half of all college students attend moderately selective four-year institutions (i.e., institutions in the middle two quartiles of admissions rates and admissions test scores as defined by the National Center for Education Statistics). However, the segregation of opportunities and resources disproportionately hurts Black, Latinx, and Native Hawaiian and Pacific Islander students, as they are underrepresented at the most selective colleges and universities. Conversely, these same student groups, in addition to Native American students, are pursuing their degrees at underresourced open-admissions institutions.[76] Socioeconomic-based segregation through college selectivity can have varying effects on students' higher education experiences and outcomes. While more Asian American students, regardless of socioeconomic background, were enrolled in very selective institutions (i.e., institutions admitting less than one-third of applicants), Latinx students were more likely pursuing degrees in open-admissions institutions.[77]

Other research also points to the segregation of public flagship universities that are often the standard-bearers of public higher education opportunities.

Research analyst Mark Huelsman found that, despite the increasing high school graduation and college-going rates of Black students, these students only represent approximately 5 percent of all students at public flagship institutions and that Black student enrollment is often declining at these institutions. These disparities in student representation are manifest most distinctly in Southern states with a long history of explicit and official exclusionary policies, both in higher education and in the community.[78] Additional research by Georgetown University's Center on Education and the Workforce further elaborates on why these disparities in public higher education matter as Black and Latinx students graduate at rates similar to those of their white peers from selective institutions, when they are admitted. Further, not only does access to well-resourced institutions such as public flagship universities correspond with higher degree attainment, but these institutions can also provide additional financial aid that can reduce student loan debt that disproportionately affects Black graduates and other graduates of color.[79]

One final way to pinpoint segregation in higher education is by looking within institutions to identify a practice often noted in the public K–12 system: racialized tracking. Through this structural aspect of school curricula, students are sorted by their purported ability and potential. For example, many high schools offer students different levels of English classes, including AP, honors, regular, and remedial classes. A wealth of research provides evidence that the popular tracking system in US education promotes whiteness and condemns blackness and brownness and is layered with socioeconomic inequality that rewards students from higher socioeconomic backgrounds.[80]

In higher education, a corollary of tracking reinforces educational inequality that accumulated throughout students' precollege lives and that limits access to certain majors. If students have limited advanced mathematics and science courses in high school, for example, they may find it more difficult to prepare for and pursue science, technology, engineering, and mathematics (STEM) degrees in college. Across higher education, we find underrepresentation in different fields. The American Council on Education focused on STEM degree programs, which have been increasingly deemed the most valuable and needed degrees in society, to provide a snapshot of this segregation in a recent report. The council found that a majority of students pursuing STEM degrees attend public four-year institutions, but that racial, ethnic, and gender disparities persist regardless of which institution's data is examined. Asian American students pursue STEM degrees at higher rates than those for the overall student body, but Asian American men have higher representation in these degree programs than do Asian American women. Native American students are dramatically underrepresented in STEM fields. Only 17 percent of Native American men and 8 percent of Native American women pursue such degrees at public institutions, and the underrepresentation is so low in private institutions that it cannot accurately be statistically identified in these fields.[81]

If we focus on education degrees, we can identify from this same data how the paucity of teachers of color in US schools is perpetuated by limited opportunities to pursue these degrees, particularly for men of color. This data does not discount the role of teacher bias that can contribute to the segregation found in higher education. But the segregation of opportunities and resources is a systemic problem in higher education, a patterned outcome of organizational policies and practices that hinder the education of some student groups while promoting the education of others. The differences in completion rates by race, ethnicity, gender, degree level, and field of study reinforce the structural reality of higher education segregation that students must navigate.[82] This unequal terrain can shape not only who is in the classroom to learn, but also who will one day be at the front of the room teaching and heading the offices on campus.

Diversity and Segregation Among Graduate Students

The tracking that begins in the K–12 system carries forward. It affects not only whether a student makes it to college but also, as noted, what degrees the individual pursues. These segregated opportunities in higher education have obvious impacts on the career endeavors of students and shape the pipeline of future faculty and staff on university campuses. The patterns of underrepresentation and segregation found at the undergraduate level are manifest at the graduate level as well. Approximately half of all college graduates in 2007 enrolled in a graduate degree program by 2012, with women having a slightly higher enrollment rate than men did. This slightly larger number for women echoes findings at the undergraduate level. Differences exist by race and gender in graduate enrollments as well. Nearly 64 percent of Black women pursue graduate degrees, compared with 45 percent of Black men. While Latinx men and women as well as multiracial men and women have comparable graduate enrollment rates, more white and Asian American women pursue graduate degrees than do men in the same racial groups.[83]

Graduate enrollments show little fluctuation with socioeconomic background. Students from the lowest income quartiles have slightly lower enrollment rates, but some groups, such as Black students, have a reverse effect: lower socioeconomic students pursue graduate degrees more frequently than do students with higher socioeconomic status, and multiracial students have a bimodal socioeconomic representation in graduate degree programs.[84] Private institutions appear to be educating more graduate students of color than public institutions do. However, for-profit institutions have an alarmingly high percentage of students of color enrolled in graduate degree programs, despite these schools' questionable academic credibility.[85]

Zooming in on doctoral students, the budding faculty of tomorrow, we can identify another layer of segregation that hinders the career ambitions of students. The for-profit sector is educating half of all Black doctoral students in the United States—a strikingly higher percentage than that for any other racial or ethnic doctoral student group.[86] For a brief comparison, only 16 percent of white doctoral students pursue degrees at for-profit institutions. Asian American and Latinx students are more likely to pursue doctoral degrees at private institutions, while international students are more likely to go the public institution route. Turning to doctoral degrees fields, 31 percent of students pursued a STEM degree, but 60 percent of international students were STEM doctoral students, followed by 28 percent of Asian American students, 25 percent of white students, 22 percent of multiracial students, 18 percent of Latinx students, and slightly less than 14 percent of Black students. Native Hawaiian, Pacific Islander, and Native American students had such low representation in STEM doctoral degree programs that their percentage of representation could not be accurately calculated. In doctoral degree programs in education, 30 percent of students are Black, followed by nearly 23 percent white, slightly less than 19 percent multiracial, 18 percent Latinx, and slightly more than 7 percent Asian American.[87] We also find differences in student persistence across graduate school programs. Like the undergraduate completion differences, these graduate school differences reinforce the racial and ethnic inequality of higher education.[88] Thus, similar patterns of racial and ethnic representation and segregated majors continue into graduate school and can have an obvious impact on the faculty and staff ranks now and in the future.

Faculty and Staff Representation Across Higher Education

Among all higher education faculty, regardless of institution where they are employed, nearly 73 percent are white. Asian Americans represent 9 percent of all faculty on college campuses, Black faculty almost 6 percent, Latinx faculty approximately 5 percent, international faculty 3 percent, and the remaining faculty groups less than 1 percent.[89] Higher education has undergone a dramatic change in the type of faculty employed, with a surge in contingent faculty, many of who are employed under per-class contracts while the percentage of tenured or tenure-track faculty continues to decline. The majority of faculty members at every rank are white, though representation slightly decreases as one moves down the seniority ranks. While Asian American faculty representation has somewhat increased in tenured and tenure-track ranks, Black, Latinx, Native Hawaiian, Pacific Islander, and Native American faculty have higher representation among contingent faculty positions.[90]

Faculty and staff diversity provides a concerning picture in higher education. Faculty of color are more frequently relegated to the least-secure positions and are often employed in for-profit and two-year institutions that have the least amount of resources in higher education.[91] A similar underrepresentation of people of color is prevalent for administrators and staff on campus. White people represent a majority of university leaders such as college presidents, while the representation of presidents and chancellors of color somewhat varies by the type of institution.[92] Again, white people represent an overwhelming majority of administrators and staff across higher education, regardless of what area of employment is considered. They represented fully 75 percent (chief student affairs administrators) to 92 percent (chief facilities officers) of all those employed as administrators in higher education.[93] The overwhelming majority of those employed in professional staff positions in higher education are also white.

Staff members of color are most highly represented in safety offices and other educational offices, representing about one-third of all employees. However, overall, they represent only a tiny percentage of all professional positions in higher education.[94] The least diverse offices were those facilitating fundraising, advancement, and alumni affairs. The people with the most decision-making power, that is, university leaders, mostly continue to be the only group able to have such opportunities in the past: white people. Campus leaders are not perfect, but as I make clear throughout this book, if we continue to grant power to the same types of people who have had it in the past, we will accomplish little in diversity and inclusiveness in higher education. Most likely, the organizational policies, processes, and interests will continue to reflect those of the group in power.[95]

Other staff positions such as office, clerical, technical, service, manufacturing, and service roles have more racial and ethnic diversity, although white people are still a majority of these employees. Service and maintenance positions, often the lowest-paid and least-secure jobs on college campuses, constitute the most diverse sector of staff employment, with slightly more than 40 percent being staff of color, while approximately a quarter of the largest category of staff members, office and clerical staff, were people of color.[96] A related analysis I conducted with colleagues Sarah Ovink and Rachelle Brunn-Bevel using data from the National Center for Education Statistics reveals how segregation in higher education employment is even deeper if you consider gender.[97] This analysis did not break down employment by full-time or part-time status, but given the trends previously mentioned and in other studies, college employees of color are more likely to be found in the most tenuous employment situations such as part-time positions that are often low-paying and not eligible for benefits. We would expect gender differences to carry over to these positions as well.

So far, we have raised many issues for researchers, administrators, and policy makers to grapple with. Researchers and college leaders must continue to examine how some student groups are underrepresented on campus and face difficult pathways to their college degrees and why faculty members with particular backgrounds funnel through the institution as if it were a revolving door. Whether the focus is on recruitment and access, persistence and retention, or anything in between for understanding the racial and ethnic diversity on college campuses, the quantification of diversity and inclusion obviously matters in higher education. An overarching point is that the quantified data on these features of campus life should not be viewed as natural, fixed, and infallible.

As I described earlier in the comparison of the UC system's approach to race and ethnicity data with the federal government's IPEDS database, these categories, who they represent, and how they are created and used in analyses change frequently. Moreover, we must not necessarily aim to gather more accurate data about race and ethnicity in the traditional sense. Improving our data collection to understand student experiences on campus, for example, requires us to examine how students' racial and ethnic background can inform their navigation of an inequitable experience.

But we cannot assume that a student identifying with a particular group will do so forever or that identifying with a group reduces the person's life to the disparities that other group members experience.[98] This more nuanced approach is difficult for many researchers, especially those relying on quantitative data. They struggle with this approach when conducting their analyses and interpreting results about how and why race and ethnicity matter in varying ways for conversations about diversity, equity, and inclusion in higher education. As I note later, this complexity can be embraced in quantitative methods but should be cautiously explored, given the many assumptions informing our analyses.

Advanced Analyses to Inform Decision-Making

The preceding examples employing descriptive analyses of how segregation can proliferate across college campuses by considering where students study, where faculty teach and in what capacity, and which staff positions employ different racial and ethnic groups on campus provide useful information on diversity and inclusion. Yet, a criticism of early QuantCrit is its reliance on descriptive analyses and its limited use of more advanced methods.[99] Though not exhaustive, this section describes some of the recent studies using a QuantCrit approach for analyzing inequality. Campus leaders and policy makers might consider these studies useful for improving their exploration of diversity, equity, and inclusion in higher education. The information in this section may be most useful for researchers and institutional analysts, who produce reports to inform decision-making. Nevertheless, education leaders and policy makers also need to understand how some analytic approaches might fail to provide the most informative perspective on various issues. Thus, even if you are not involved in the analyses yourself, you will want to understand their limitations.

Inserting dichotomous or binary variables for each group is a common way to integrate race and ethnicity into advanced statistical analysis.[100] This approach allows for simple comparisons between people identified with different racial and ethnic groups. However, scholars question this approach for different reasons, including faulty interpretations that may result from analyses instead of constructing separate group-specific models that can better examine intracategorical intersectionality quantitatively.[101] Irizarry's multidimensional approach to race in quantitative analyses demonstrates how race, ethnicity, and immigration history intersect, invalidating our assumption that people can be neatly organized into distinct categories.[102] Other research provides examples of how multiple data sets can help compare differences in degree completion with differences in citizenship status, which is often constructed as an overarching status in data sets such as IPEDS and does not allow researchers, administrators, and policy makers to disaggregate how this attribute may relate to structural barriers in higher education.[103] To obtain more accurate, fine-tuned results from quantitative research, analysts should use a QuantCrit lens to carefully scrutinize the assumptions in their research. Lisa Bowleg provides a cautionary note about how to interpret the assumptions in both quantitative and qualitative studies utilizing an intersectional lens. She suggests that preliminary additive approaches (e.g., race + gender + socioeconomic status) can sometimes provide useful information about how people experience different forms of discrimination. Bowleg also warns that quantitative analyses may hide people's experiences of discrimination or amplify them if studies exclude important contextual information on people's complex identities.[104]

Echoing these cautionary tales of how intersectionality is framed as a testable hypothesis in advanced analyses, Ange-Marie Hancock describes the pitfalls of not exploring other modeling approaches that include intersectionality in their assumptions, modeling strategies, and interpretations. She explains that modeling intersectionality not only can improve our understanding of inequalities but also can be applied in legal arguments and policy-making.[105] Educational researcher Lauren Schudde echoes many of Hancock's points and suggests the possibility of examining heterogeneous effects to explore intersectionality with quantitative data, but again, she cautions researchers to not eschew theory for more advanced methods; they must work together.[106] The limitations of common quantitative approaches should be openly discussed with campus leaders and higher education policy makers to help them make sound decisions about the opportunities and resources students have access to and the institutional efforts to promote racial equity.

What does student success look like when we are comparing group experiences in degree programs? This is not a straightforward question if we consider which groups are succeeding more than others in higher education today and how this information can inform our data analysis and what decisions may be made, in light of our analyses. For example, in quantitative studies about student success, it is not apparent which racial group best serves as the benchmark. Work by sociologist Nancy López and colleagues illustrates how advanced quantitative studies can use readily available information to challenge the default assumption of who is successful in education. They use an intersectional approach to create groups of students facing varying degrees of marginalization in higher education and situate white middle-class women as the reference group, given their higher academic success (as measured by enrollment and graduation rates) compared with other groups.[107] These researchers also describe innovative ways of framing statistics, such as the interclass correlation, to tap into a deeper, intersectional approach to higher education data.

However, inequality manifests itself differently in specific fields of study, and an understanding of this variability can help researchers shape their assumptions of how quantitative models should be constructed and interpreted. Instead of simply viewing some students as achieving and others as not, we can shift who we understand to be academically successful on campus. Doing so can change campus leaders' perspectives of which programs may support student achievement and could be expanded to better support other student groups on campus. The changes address policies and programs rather than measuring gaps between students and viewing their achievement as unrelated to the resources and opportunities provided by an institution.

One concern about intersectional quantitative research is the small number of people in some groups. As noted earlier, there were sometimes too few Native American students, for example, in a sample for a study to produce statistically meaningful results. With this so-called small-N problem, researchers have fewer cases than they need to conduct more advanced statistical analyses. A QuantCrit approach reminds us that we should ask why there are so few members of certain groups in the first place, rather than viewing the small sample size as an analytical problem. That is, it's not about a small N; it's about a small group of students, faculty, or staff whose experiences we are trying to understand in our analyses. This adjusted view of the data can also help us ask how the sampling for supposedly nationally representative data sets can skew our interpretations about group experiences, trajectories, and needs. Central to these questions are discussions of college recruitment and access, student persistence and retention in college, and institutional transformation. Questions like these do not rely on victim blaming and deficit perspectives. We also need to raise our institutions' accountability of persistently low representation of different student, faculty, and staff groups because these patterns are a major detriment to the racial equity efforts of a campus. The institution should be held more responsible for doing little to support these small groups of students.

Garcia and Mayorga showcase how this reorientation to data and sampling raises important questions for secondary data analyses, such as where Latinx students are located within the higher education system and why the sampling for national surveys may misrepresent these students' experiences. They suggest more purposeful sampling and an awareness of how the sampling frame can affect results. Similarly, Schudde explores how large-scale data from the National Center for Education Statistics and other federal- and state-managed data sets may be tentatively used to look at smaller populations of students. [108] One simple way to assemble more cases to conduct advanced statistical analyses is to pool data, if possible, across years. Researchers can also include a variable for each survey year to begin obtaining tentative answers for smaller groups on campus. As noted, campuses trying to use quantitative data to examine different group issues but facing persistent limited data for a student group with low representation on campus must first tackle a fundamental question. They must ask why they have such low representation of these students on campus in the first place, not how to analyze them statistically. This observation echoes the groundbreaking work by Alejandro Covarrubias, who documents how the educational system can undercut the academic and career pursuits of Chicana/o students; the research encourages further examination of why a limited number of students may reach certain levels of education or pursue different academic majors.[109] Again, raising institutional accountability requires researchers to explore new approaches and communicate clearly the limitations of the more common quantitative analyses for decision-making. Otherwise, they will find themselves perpetuating some of the central racial equity issues they seek to change through their work.

Other studies offer useful examples of how to better contextualize quantitative analyses through the incorporation of organizational and community factors.[110] Sociologist Alyasah A. Sewell looks at the "racism-race reification process" to examine racial health disparities that could readily apply to analyses of higher education data.[111] Sewell uses an intricate model that includes different factors at the community, organizational, and individual level to explain health disparities among Black community members. This method complements scholar Jenna Sablan's instructive discussion of how measurement theory and scale development can be useful to explore the existence of students' different concepts and experiences, such as the cultural wealth of students attending Asian American and Native American Pacific Islander–serving institutions.[112] Additionally, multigroup structural equation models (which compare how a similar model connecting different variables and processes may more or less accurately reflect the experiences and outcomes of some student groups compared with others) can help universities understand how some campus features can operate as barriers to academic success for certain student groups while possibly supporting the academic pursuits of other students. All these approaches can better inform campus decision-making, give policy makers much-needed information about student experiences, and help leaders develop more effective policy interventions in higher education. Although these different considerations for advanced statistical analyses utilizing a QuantCrit approach are helpful, researchers and policy makers must remember not to rely solely on quantitative research. The use of mixed methods in research can add depth and context to the data and can shed light on persistent patterns and their causes.

The Importance of People's Voices

The experiences and issues facing marginalized groups are not readily accessible through strictly quantitative approaches, and these issues add another layer of complexity to our work to create more equitable and inclusive college campuses.[113] QuantCrit provides examples of how incorporating mixed-methods approaches may be done for single institutions or across multiple institutions aiming to tackle similar issues. Covarrubias and colleagues' research provides a useful model of how this mixed-methods approach can assist our efforts. In examining Latinx pathways toward college degrees, the researchers infuse their analyses with *testimonios* that center the data on people's knowledge, experience, and agency rather than projecting interpretations out of sync with the people at the center of the analyses.[114] A key tenet of QuantCrit work is to "listen to the voices, not just the numbers," and to further incorporate the voices of marginalized communities to better contextualize quantitative analyses.[115] In the rest of this section, I provide a few useful examples of how mixed-methods research that further incorporates qualitative approaches can assist campus leaders and policy makers in their decisions. Through these approaches, they can think deeper about racial inequality on college campuses and can limit their reliance solely on quantitative metrics of diversity, equity, and inclusion.

A wide range of work couples quantitative and qualitative research to better explain the hows and whys of persistent racial inequality in higher education. This research provides a glimpse into why researchers, administrators, and policy makers should make greater efforts to listen to the voices behind the diversity numbers. Julie Park's recent overview of research that debunks many of the myths about race in higher education describes another useful approach to coupling different forms of research rather than relying on one form for decision-making.[116] For example, Park tackles the common belief that students of color, particularly Black students, self-segregate on college campuses. Using a mountain of quantitative research, she shows that the disparate social interactions across racial and ethnic lines do not hinge on one group's isolating themselves from other groups, as the myth purports. Instead, she describes how all college students tend to lessen their interactions across racial and ethnic lines and that this practice is more common for white students than it is for students of color.[117]

Park incorporates some of her earlier research examining the difficulties of students who were part of a religious organization as they tried to cultivate cross-race interactions, break down stereotypes, and push forward more racially progressive activities and views in light of the California ban on affirmative action.[118] The students' struggles that Park describes not only are touching, but also reveal the obstacles to creating more equitable campus communities when policies change or different racial tensions arise on campus. The quantitative research may say that students need to interact with one another to reduce their reliance on stereotypical views of different groups or that promoting intergroup dialogue programs for whole campuses are necessary. Yet, the depth of these numbers ends in fully explaining how universities should do the work to cultivate such a reality through programming, initiatives, or different policies in orientation programs, curricular offerings, and faculty trainings. Natasha Warikoo's research is also insightful on this point. She recounts how two universities pursuing similar goals with similar programs end up with different outcomes among students.[119]

Even if we focus on how universities recruit and retain students of color in STEM fields to combat racial and ethnic disparities, a purely quantitative study might indicate that offering more financial aid to students of color will increase their enrollment in STEM disciplines. However, qualitative analyses reveal that factors such as competitive pressures and stereotype threat situations, whereby students of color must actively work to avoid conforming to stereotypes of group's capabilities, in these disciplines quickly debunk the assumption that offering more financial aid to students of color during recruitment will help overcome the discriminatory issues in these programs.[120] Therefore, the success of recruitment offices in reaching equity and inclusion goals may be diminished when universities fail to listen to students about their experiences and instead rely on limited surveys that do not tap into these experiences in the end. To support students of color from recruitment to graduation, universities must consider multiple research methods to eliminate deleterious assumptions about what may be driving racial inequality on campus.

Similar benefits from these approaches can be applied to the issues of diversity and inclusion of faculty and staff on college campuses. Although a wealth of data is available on college students, much less data exists on the inequalities facing faculty and staff in higher education. While UCLA's Higher Education Research Institute collects data nationally on faculty, and Harvard's Collaboration on Academic Careers in Higher Education (COACHE) provides a more in-depth look at faculty experiences for institutions that participate in the survey, we have little wide-ranging data on this issue. Many institutions conduct their own studies of faculty life, and this research can be useful for identifying problems and developing solutions. However, many of these surveys are limited to campus climate surveys that are designed for more general examination of issues across multiple constituents, such as students and staff. This general focus restricts how much information can be collected to identify issues of marginalization and discrimination.

We have much more qualitative data than quantitative data on faculty life, and the data that we do have can assist us with equity and inclusion efforts. But higher education desperately needs to play catch-up with quantitative data to obtain more holistic information on how to support faculty across the nation.[121] These efforts must include contingent faculty members, who are continually growing in presence and responsibility for educating students in higher education. The limited quantitative data available on faculty prevents leaders from fully recognizing that faculty of color, particularly women, are more likely to be placed in the least supported faculty roles on campus and that their scholarly pursuits are devalued and dismissed.[122]

While few people would explicitly argue that qualitative and mixed-methods research is less valuable in policy and program decision-making, the privileging of quantitative work in these conversations, as evidenced in broader society as well, shows otherwise.[123] Again, the two types of research must be combined to limit misinterpretations of larger structural patterns found in quantitative data and to understand how thicker descriptions of processes and experiences detailed in qualitative research can support more effective programs and policies to undercut unequal campus opportunities. Without additional dynamic research approaches that provide more a contextual understanding of the numbers driving different decisions, higher education is likely to repeat many of the same mistakes of the past and perpetuate inequalities on campus instead of finding remedies to them.

Although more mixed-methods approaches are being utilized today, the evolving contours of research on diversity and inclusion in higher education also challenge a recurring question related to this work: at what point is a university "too white?" The next section considers this question.

What Makes a University "Too White"?

In this chapter, I focus mostly on the demographic aspect of this question. Clearly, having fewer students on campus who identify as white does not necessarily lessen the whiteness of the university.[124] But representation absolutely matters, and it would be foolish to argue that it doesn't for students' academic and social growth during their college years.[125] There are two important critiques of this commonly asked question. First, asking if a university is "too white" relies on binary thinking that QuantCrit analyses directly challenge. We know that diversity and inclusion are continua of representation and experience and are not neatly fixed to either-or approaches. Similarly, as noted previously, there is no singular "Black college student experience" or "Latinx college student experience." Such labels would homogenize the diversity within groups and limit our examination of the complexity of people's lives—an examination that can promote better solutions to the systemic inequalities on our campuses. As Baez elegantly describes, the homogenizing of groups relies on the essentialism of experiences.[126]

Second, the question of whether a campus is "too white" relies on a reductionist definition of diversity and inclusion in higher education and how they should be examined.[127] This question relates to a point in chapter 1 about college access and admissions. The reliance on a narrow concept and operationalization of critical mass in attempts to pinpoint how much student diversity is needed to cultivate its educational and social benefits oversimplifies why diversity and inclusion matter to higher education.[128] The emphasis of critical mass reduces diversity to a singular number. Doing so ignores the broader contexts of college campuses and the need for mixed-methods research and qualitative inquiries into the dynamics of student, faculty, and staff experiences. A reductive critical-mass approach is therefore detrimental to institutional efforts to fight the inequality they reproduce each day.[129] This ongoing tension with aiming for the unquantifiable also suggests how the power of, and assumptions behind, quantification continue to grip universities and possibly counter their efforts at institutional transformation.[130]

Assuming that colleges and universities are racialized organizations, then what makes an institution "too white" is more than compositional diversity among students or faculty; institutional whiteness is emblematic of an organization's policies, processes, and underlying ideas and unwritten rules for how it operates each day.[131] Whiteness, then, is also related to the cultural realities that reinforce the structural inequalities that students, faculty, and staff must navigate.[132] To determine if an institution is "too white," we therefore need further analyses of the campus culture that reinforces unequal organizational policies and processes. Luckily, a long-standing and important area of research focuses on this aspect of colleges and universities. Research on the campus's climate and more specifically, for our discussion, its racial climate, emphasizes the importance of diversity and inclusion in higher education and society by identifying the mechanisms that create these benefits.[133]

Conclusion

Despite its promise, a large part of campus climate research relies on the supposedly reliable quantitative approaches that can reinforce pernicious views about diversity and inclusion. As Baez discussed as far back as 2004, the social science approaches to this area of research are important in many ways, including supporting universities' cases for why race-conscious admission policies matter in the promotion of the educational benefits of diversity in higher education. These same social science approaches and their corresponding policies, however, are still susceptible to the pitfalls of reductionism and essentialism.[134]

With that said, we now move from examining how quantification can shift our understanding of the composition of our college campuses to delving into the research that argues why diversity and inclusion matter. As we will discuss in the next chapter, the quantitative-only examination of campus racial climate can limit arguments for diversity and inclusion in higher education and reify many issues that can undercut efforts to cultivate equitable and inclusive campuses.

CHAPTER 3

The Other Climate Science

Researching Race and the Campus Climate

CREATING ORGANIZATIONAL CHANGE is difficult, to say the least. Research can help universities document what they need to change to achieve their goals. Put simply, the main goal for universities is to help students learn and prepare for work and life once they graduate. As noted earlier, research supporting the educational benefits of diversity generally argues that better representation of students from different racial and ethnic backgrounds and with different experiences and perspectives can enhance the learning opportunities of college students in various ways.[1] To what extent a critical mass of students from different backgrounds is needed depends on many circumstances at the university, and cannot be boiled down to a handful of numbers for administrators to aim for regarding student representation. The answer is a more dynamic perspective than simply diversifying the student and faculty bodies.[2] Although most administrators and other higher education professionals recognize the educational benefits of diversity, a paradox emerges about how to promote it on college campuses.

In light of a wave of student protests of racism and inequality on their campuses at the University of Missouri in the fall of 2015 and the recently rekindled demonstrations after the murders of George Floyd and Breonna

Taylor as the world faced a pandemic, college campuses needed to do some soul-searching. One could argue that administrators had to acknowledge that despite their embrace of the educational benefits of diversity, perhaps their campuses were not making as much progress toward equity and inclusion as they once thought. However, administrators were quick to suggest that it was not as bad as students were asserting. In a survey of university presidents during this period, they were likely to rate campus race relations as good or positive, a perplexing assessment as students issued a wide range of demands and staged sit-ins for institutional change on the very same campuses.[3] How could university leaders not fully connect the research they supported—the other climate science, if you will—with the everyday realities of marginalization on their own campuses? What aspects of campus climate research resonated with them for programmatic and organizational change on their campuses?

One possible answer is that the trajectory of campus climate research in the past thirty years has shifted, allowing administrators to disconnect how the data applies to their own campuses. These leaders might then ignore systemic inequality and attribute the problem to individuals. If we are seeking organizational changes for college campuses to improve students' lives as well as those of faculty and staff, we must take into account our research methods and their application. Campus climate research seems to have evolved in that it now mostly recommends individual and small group changes. These conclusions from the research allow university leaders to perhaps ignore systemic problems and the need to adapt the research to affect organizational change in higher education.

This chapter tackles these potential challenges by examining the evolution of campus climate research since the early 1990s. Using a unique analysis of published empirical scholarship examining race-related campus climates from 1992 to 2019, I summarize what this other climate science focuses on to examine the main obstacles to equity and inclusion efforts in higher education. This chapter also explores how policy suggestions garnered from this research may present additional obstacles to efforts to increase racial equality on college campuses, because the suggestions focus on individuals and small groups and are disconnected from organizational-level processes. An integral component to this discussion is how to avoid misinterpreting the data, processes, and outcomes from this highly important research area. Such misinterpretation can lead one to view campus climate as the result of individual action rather than the result of the larger system. This chapter provides readers with insights on how to better conduct and apply this research area for organizational changes that have impacts on students, faculty, and staff.

Before studying race-related campus climate research in detail, we should have a foundation of how this research area developed. I briefly review the trends in the literature on campus climate research as they pertain to racial and gender inequality. I also discuss levels of analyses (e.g., individual versus organizational). Next, I describe the popular framework used for campus climate research. This framework incorporates the many decades of research into a holistic model of how diversity, equity, and inclusion can influence student academic and social outcomes, among many other facets of college campuses that surround students. The campus climate framework provides important insight into what has been published over nearly three decades of research. Following the discussion of how campus climate research has evolved, we consider what these findings mean. We examine the use of this research in implementing organizational change in higher education in general and different college campuses in particular.

An Introduction to Campus Climate Research

A large literature exists on campus climates in higher education, and the terminology has expanded since the 1980s, when the term *campus climate* was incorporated into everyday conversations among higher education professionals. Identifying some of the key terms and their connections with each other is helpful for a deeper examination of the evolution of the literature. This initial analysis suggests the approaches needed for institutional change at colleges and universities to promote diversity, equity, and inclusion. Furthermore, a broad, "30,000-foot view" can reveal the literature's potentially unhelpful focus on changing the actions of individuals and small groups to address racial inequality on campuses nationwide.

General Climate Trajectories

The term *campus climate* has existed in the scholarly literature since the 1960s as researchers and administrators turned their attention to the many issues facing their campuses with desegregation. However, the study of campus climates did not markedly increase until the publication of Roberta Hall and Bernice Sandler's pivotal report on women faculty on college campuses in 1984 and a follow-up 1986 report, which expanded the focus to women in administrative and graduate student positions.[4] From the mid-1980s into the early 1990s, the study of campus climates continued to grow, and after the publication of Sylvia Hurtado's study of the campus racial climate in 1992, it increased exponentially.

Although the popularity of campus climate research began with the study of gender inequality and marginalization, after Hurtado's key study and others in the 1990s, campus climate research began to skew toward racial and ethnic inequality and marginalization. These changes, also marked by more complex theoretical frameworks for examining campus climates, were attributable to Hurtado and the burgeoning research area in the 1990s. The growing research trend continued after the affirmative action cases against the University of Michigan in 2003. At that time, the university used social science research to support its position that cultivating diversity through college admissions policies is one part of university efforts to provide students with added educational benefits while pursuing their degrees. As described earlier, this argument is better known as the educational benefits of diversity.[5] Therefore, I focus specifically on the studies examining race and campus climates that have grown more central to the conversations about the educational benefits of diversity.

To begin examining the diverging trajectories of campus climate research focused on race and gender, I compared the frequency of certain phrases in books using Google Ngram, a tool to identify words and phrases across all American English-language books digitized for the Google Books project. With this tool, I could plot how often the term *campus climate* is linked to the words *race*, *racism*, *sexism*, and *gender* (figure 3.1).[6] From 1980 to 2008, *campus climate* was most frequently associated with *race* throughout this nearly thirty-year period, although writings about campus climate and gender increased during the 1980s and 1990s before decreasing after the turn of the twenty-first century.[7] Additionally, in line with Victor Ray's and other scholars' argument that organizations, including colleges and universities, are seldom understood as parts of systems of power and inequality, statements about campus climate and racism and sexism are much less frequent in the available publications in the Google Books project.[8]

FIGURE 3.1 *Frequency of the phrases* campus climate, race, *and* gender, *1980–2008*

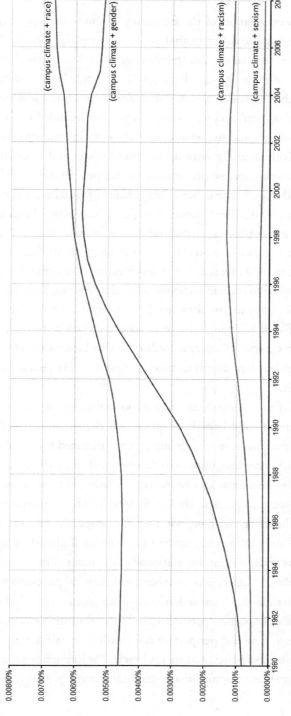

(campus climate + race)

(campus climate + gender)

(campus climate + racism)

(campus climate + sexism)

Source: Created from Google Books Ngram Viewer (http://books.google.com/ngrams), using a database of books written in English, published in the United States, and included in the Google Book project.

Further examination of the frequency of the term *campus climate* and other terms related to different analyses in higher education could help identify how organizational policies and processes bear on campus climate and the experiences of different groups. Figure 3.2 is a Google Ngram plotting *campus climate* and the words *individual, culture* and *cultural*, and *structural. Institutional, organizational*, and *discrimination* are also included in this figure. If, as argued, colleges and universities operate as racialized organizations that connect individuals and groups to systems of power and inequality through organizational policies and processes, then campus climates may be the integral feature that pulls these many components of racialized organizations of higher education together.[9] However, as figure 3.2 shows, this is not the case indicated in printed books. Reflecting the highly individualized approach to inequality in the United States, the most frequent discussion of campus climates relates to individuals and, to a lesser extent, to cultural features, which are closely linked to individual behaviors and attributes. The phrases that are the least linked to campus climate relate to organizations, institutions, and structures of society. Though discrimination is the least utilized phrase today connected to campus climate, according to this broad view of this research area, it is not clear how discrimination is constructed in relation to any of the other features.

These brief analyses underscore an important aspect of campus climate research and theory, and I further explore it in the remainder of this chapter. We need to examine campus climate as a multifaceted feature that can situate people within organizations to understand their experiences and outcomes. These organizations must also be placed in relation to their histories, politics, and broader societal contexts. The two figures show how infrequently researchers connect these features to provide a holistic perspective of campus climate as an integral feature influencing campus inequalities. Rather than review all the developments of defining and operationalizing campus climate as they relate to racial inequality, I focus on a comprehensive theoretical perspective that has developed through in-depth research of college campuses over the last thirty years. While this is an important perspective in higher education research, as will be examined later, how this perspective is quantified can shift what researchers, administrators, and policy makers understand as important takeaway points about how and why campus climates matter for diversity, equity, and inclusion.

FIGURE 3.2 *Frequency of the phrase* campus climate *and other phrases linked to different levels of analysis, 1980–2008*

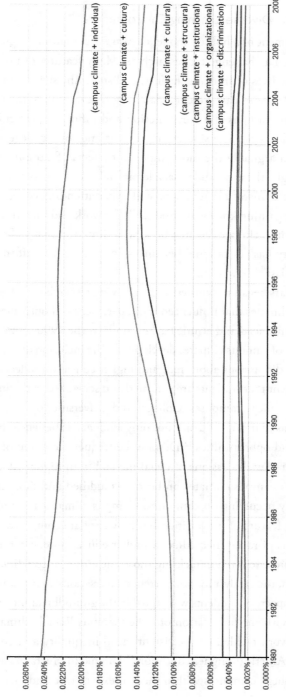

(campus climate + individual)

(campus climate + culture)

(campus climate + cultural)

(campus climate + structural)
(campus climate + institutional)
(campus climate + organizational)
(campus climate + discrimination)

Source: Created from Google Books Ngram Viewer (http//books.google.com/ngrams), using a database of books written in English, published in the United States, and included in the Google Book project.

A Model for Diverse Learning Environments

The development of a holistic model of campus climates in higher education has long been a challenge for researchers. Many features of universities can influence the lives of students, faculty, and staff. The sheer magnitude of all these considerations can present a daunting task of pulling them together to focus on how campus climates function and influence particular elements of higher education. Considering the importance of a college education in society, then arguably the most important effects of campus climates are, unsurprisingly, those of student academic and social outcomes. This view of why campus climates matter aligns with what attending college is supposed to be about: gaining knowledge and skills for work and life. Thus, it's easy to see how campus climate research became an important part of the argument that diversity has educational benefits—an argument in affirmative action cases of the last thirty years.[10]

As scholars began to synthesize the growing research on different features of campus climates that influenced the experiences and outcomes of students from different racial and ethnic backgrounds in the 1990s, an emerging understanding of campus climates developed.[11] The inclusion of campus climate in everyday discussions about race and higher education reflects people's acknowledgment that students are educated and socialized in distinct racialized contexts on college campuses. Colleges and universities operate as racialized organizations that can influence not only students' experiences but also their resources and opportunities.[12] Despite the frequent mention of campus climate in everyday discussions of racial inequality in higher education, what constitutes a campus climate can become muddled and disconnected from what is truly occurring on campuses. Campus climates are spoken of as an overarching feature of universities, but how they are composed and distilled into patterns of racial inequality in higher education can sometimes elude those who are interested in tackling those patterns of inequality.

As noted, the catalyst for our current conversations about campus climates and their impacts on students was arguably the groundbreaking work of Sylvia Hurtado. With the publication of "The Campus Racial Climate" in 1992, Hurtado's work tackled the persistent racial inequality and conflict facing students in American higher education.[13] Unique to Hurtado's approach was situating college campuses within the contexts of race and racism in society to enhance the research area known as *college impact studies.* This area, which focuses on how the different features of an institution influence students' academic and social experiences and outcomes, developed over several decades of research.[14] At the time, Hurtado provided one of the most comprehensive analyses of the institutional contexts for racial tension on college campuses to further explain how campus climates shape student learning and social outcomes. Hurtado studied a cohort of students from 1985 to 1989 to examine how this heightened tension on campus, similar to more recent racial tensions on college campuses, influenced the experiences and attitudes of white, Black, and Chicano students at 116 colleges and universities. Ultimately, Hurtado described campuses where students' perceptions of racial tension were linked to institutional features and how student-centered a campus was; she highlighted the multifaceted connections of campus climate with student experiences and outcomes. She also described how perceptions of the campus climate differed for students from different racial and ethnic groups and for students attending different types of institutions (public, private, research, liberal arts, more competitive, etc.).[15] From the early 1990s to today, Hurtado has developed a more complex model documenting the importance of campus climates for organizational processes and student outcomes.

Particularly since the turn of the new century, higher education has witnessed the development of a more formal guiding framework for campus climate research and policy. The Multi-contextual Model for Diverse Learning Environments (MMDLE) assesses how institutional and societal features influence students' experiences and outcomes while they pursue their college degrees.[16] Key to the development of the MMDLE was a literature review and theoretical synthesis led by Hurtado; this synthesis created the foundations for the campus climate framework.[17] This first iteration of the model posited that external circumstances related to the history, government, and policies of universities can influence the campus racial climate. Within an institution, four interrelated dimensions were identified: (1) a historical legacy of inclusion or exclusion; (2) structural diversity; (3) the psychological climate; and (4) a behavioral dimension. From the theoretical synthesis of the literature and coalescing their findings into this early campus climate model, Hurtado and colleagues explained how each aspect of the campus climate could influence student experiences and learning. The researchers explored how campus leaders and state policy makers could promote more diverse climates for higher education through financial aid policies, intergroup dialogues, and institutional strategic planning, among other key areas.[18]

In 2005, nearly five years after the original model was proposed by Hurtado and her colleagues, Jeffrey Milem, Mitchell Chang, and anthony antonio proposed an updated version of the original campus climate model; they included a specific organizational dimension.[19] This dimension included how diversity can benefit groups on campus, and it examined everyday university functioning such as tenure policies, budgets, general education curricula, admissions and hiring practices, and other related features. The importance of further incorporating an organizational focus for campus climate research sparked by these efforts is also notable because, as Hurtado and colleagues explain, "these are often the institutional mechanisms that reproduce inequality and shape diversity dynamics on campus."[20] With the addition of an organizational dimension and its structural features, Milem, Chang, and antonio relabeled the previous structural diversity dimension as "compositional diversity" to speak more clearly about student, faculty, and staff representation on campus. Additionally, Milem, Chang, and antonio consistently described each area of the campus climate as a dimension to better organize the theoretical framework and describe its features. This label solidified the terminology and its application to the campus climate framework developed earlier by Hurtado and colleagues.[21]

In the most recent iteration of the MMDLE, Hurtado and colleagues sought to overcome previous models' limitations concerning (1) the connection between diversity and cross-race social interactions on educational outcomes, (2) how diversity-related aspects shape curricular and cocurricular areas of campus life, and (3) ways for faculty and staff to promote diversity, equity, and inclusion in higher education generally and in student educational outcomes in particular.[22] The current iteration of the model also more fully incorporates an organizational lens to examine campus climates and the interconnections of each component.[23] These corrections, done to ensure that the MMDLE considers the impact of campus climates on students, reflect not only a theoretical need, but also a sociopolitical need in a recurring era of anti-affirmative-action lawsuits.

The incorporation of an organizational lens to examine campus climates acknowledges that a predominant approach previously focused extensively on psychological and behavioral components of campus life. This focus in early campus climate research probably also reflects the heavy social psychological foundations of the field of higher education.[24] Organizational approaches to campus climates can also limit the consideration of societal contexts and "fail to specify the dynamics between actors within the institutions."[25] Reflecting on limitations of previous models, Hurtado and colleagues refined the MMDLE (1) to better understand the importance of intersectional positions of people and how these positions influence the navigation of unequal college campuses and (2) to develop a more contextual understanding of how campus climates can shape, for example, student learning outcomes.[26] Hurtado and colleagues' revised model identifies higher education institutions as part of a racialized society that facilitates inequality; the model highlights the organizational processes and policies that can influence student experiences and outcomes. Additionally, it allows researchers to stay attuned to the complex identities and positions that people hold to navigate campus inequalities.

Dimensions and Processes of Campus Climates

The MMDLE has five dimensions and multiple features. Consistent with its racialized nature, the university is presented as a multilevel organization where race and racism are interwoven into policies, practices, experiences, and outcomes.[27] Each dimension of the model is necessary for identifying how a university policy or a state policy can, for example, influence student representation. These interconnected pieces allow for a more thorough understanding and examination of how race is an integral part of everyday life in American higher education. All the dimensions in a university can shape curricular and cocurricular contexts such that the campus climate is not relegated to simply a welcoming or hostile atmosphere among individuals on campus. Instead, the climate shapes many processes and outcomes related to teaching, learning, research, and everyday social interactions, all of which can have lasting impacts on individuals, groups, and institutions themselves.

The first part of the MMDLE discusses the external circumstances that can influence how universities pursue diversity and inclusion. The *external forces* includes the connections between universities and their communities, whether a community be the immediate surrounding area or a broader community such as land-grant universities with missions to serve a state's residents through different programs and support services. This aspect of the university-community connections is sometimes referred to as *town-gown relations*, reflecting universities' outreach efforts, or lack thereof, in the community. Sometimes, the relationship is strained as universities expand in communities and assume that the area will automatically benefit from the expansion without fully considering the needs of community members.[28] Outreach programs through different projects include real estate deals and management, internships, volunteering opportunities, and high school programs for local children, among many other possibilities. More broadly, external forces reflects sociohistorical influences on institutions and people who work and study in relation to these institutions. Additionally, changes in policies such as affirmative action, student eligibility for different forms of financial aid, and university accreditation can influence students' access to resources and their degree progress, faculty teaching requirements, and institutional financial sustainability in many ways.[29]

The *organizational dimension* is the first institutional-level layer for the MMDLE. One modification to the organizational dimension of the model I propose relates to where institutional history is incorporated. Whereas Hurtado and colleagues posit a specific historical dimension of campus climates separate from the organizational dimension, I integrate the historical component into the organizational dimension. An institution's history reflects the policies and practices that cannot be removed from the conversation of how universities operate as racialized organizations over time. If we are to understand how race is embedded in policies and practices today, we must understand how it was part of them yesterday as well. Most closely aligned with situating universities as racialized organizations, the organizational dimension examines many features of a campus. Hurtado and colleagues list them as the "structures and processes that embed group-based privilege and oppression or confer resources that often go unquestioned, such as tenure processes, decisions on recruitment and hiring, budget allocations, curriculum, and other institutional practices and policies."[30] These features can suggest the true institutional commitment to diversity, equity, and inclusion beyond symbolic actions because resources, policies, and infrastructure are built to support the features. In addition to the historical legacies of inclusion and exclusion, which I further discuss later, several other features are integral to the organizational dimension of campus climates.[31]

- *The institution's policies and plans for organizational transformation:* This feature includes advisory groups (e.g., diversity task forces), diversity strategic plans, diversity-related research activities, employee training, recruitment, and other related activities.
- *Academic support initiatives aimed to cultivate diversity and inclusion:* Examples of these initiatives are mentoring, advising, tutoring, and other related support services.
- *Curricular efforts:* Such initiatives include diversity requirements in the general education curriculum; certificate programs; and the creation or expansion of academic programs, departments, or concentrations (e.g., ethnic studies departments).
- *Diversity-related cocurricular initiatives:* Examples are rituals and celebrations, workshops, and intergroup dialogues on campus.
- *Safe-space initiatives aimed to support underrepresented students:* These efforts can include residential hall initiatives, specific student identity and cultural centers, and ethnic student organizations.
- *Interdisciplinary programs connecting multiple campus units:* Initiatives like these can facilitate diversity-related student learning and social growth. For example, there are study-abroad opportunities, living-learning communities, service learning, high school-to-college programs, structured cohort programs, and undergraduate research.

As noted earlier, another critical feature of the organizational dimension is a university's historical legacies of inclusion and exclusion. These multiple legacies are intertwined with a university's cultural traditions, policies, and everyday norms of social interaction.[32] An institution may support Black students, for example, but does it necessarily include all Black students or possibly just certain groups? The historical trajectory of a university tells the story of how racial inequalities and other inequalities they intersect with (e.g., gender, class, sexuality, and disability) developed over time. And although inequities are difficult to assess in research using, for example, quantitative methods, mixed-methods approaches can pinpoint how inequality historically became entrenched in university policy. For example, Gina Garcia shows how history is an important feature of the organizational dimension for universities identified as Hispanic-serving institutions (HSIs).[33] Although these institutions are noted for their missions and demographics that align with being an HSI, their policies, practices, and cultural leanings do not always mean they fully support Latinx students on those campuses. Without the historical feature in the organizational dimension, universities can repeat their marginalizing and oppressive practices from the past, using the justification of ignorance, simply because these universities never thought diversity and inclusion were important in the first place.[34]

The second dimension of the campus climate is the *compositional dimension* (once referred to as the structural dimension). Frequently discussed in conversations about diversity-related outcomes, the compositional dimension focuses on the numerical representation of students, faculty, staff, and administrators from diverse social identities and positions.[35] Representation on campus has been linked to many student outcomes as part of the educational benefits of diversity. This perspective proposes that some level of critical mass of underrepresented students, or some amount of student diversity in general, increases social interactions and reduces prejudice and stereotyping.[36] Campus representation is also notable for its relationship to identity development and students' sense of belonging and for combatting stereotype threat situations that could undercut student learning and academic achievement.[37] As discussed earlier, numeric representation is only one feature of campus climate and not the be-all and end-all that universities should aim for in their efforts. Aiming for a critical mass of students, for example, misses why diversity, equity, and inclusion are important for academic and social outcomes; it misses the dynamism of diversity.[38]

The third dimension of campuses climates is the *behavioral dimension*, which, according to Hurtado and colleagues, "refers to the context, frequency, and quality of interactions on campus between social identity groups and their members."[39] Central to this dimension are the formal and informal interactions of everyday life on and around campuses. Formal interactions are part of classroom and cocurricular settings related to educational practices, while informal interactions happen outside of campus-designed activities.[40] These interactions include microaggressions through social interaction, experiences with direct discrimination, and the often-examined intergroup interactions.[41] These behavioral features also extend to pedagogical practices of instructors to create more equitable and inclusive classroom spaces or possibly to perpetuate a hostile learning environment. For example, student affairs practices may alienate and marginalize underrepresented students or cultivate a welcoming community that fosters a great sense of belonging on campus. And more recently, researchers are focusing on how the educational and social benefits of a diverse campus relate to campus activism for racial and social justice, such as signaling civic engagement. In general, research on the behavioral dimension of campus climate aims to promote more equitable and inclusive social interactions that can improve student learning and understanding of societal contexts and inequality.[42] Researchers have consistently found that both formal and informal interactions are important to increasing equity and inclusion on college campuses.[43]

The fourth dimension of the MMDLE is the *psychological dimension* that "involves individuals' perceptions of the environment, views of intergroup relations, and perceptions of discrimination or racial conflict within the institutional context."[44] Research has generally found that students of color perceive the campus climate differently from how their white peers view it, and these perceptions often describe an unwelcoming and hostile place. However, more recent research has further incorporated discussions about social identities and their development within the college contexts as a way of distinguishing the psychological dimension from the behavioral. This research, which examines the affirmation and validation of social identities that often intersect, can influence not only how students or faculty may view themselves in relation to race, gender, class, sexuality, disability, and other identities, but also how they view themselves in relation to their studies and their work.[45] These connections about self and campus life are important in countless ways, including how someone may lack a sense of belonging to an institution and their peers or colleagues.[46] By examining how students navigate larger social pressures related to their connections with their academics such as stereotype threats, we can expand our conversations about the importance of campus climate for an individual's well-being.[47] Further, we can look at students' understanding of unequal opportunities and resources undergirding persistent social inequalities to identify how students' beliefs can influence what they get out of diversity-related curricular or cocurricular initiatives.[48]

The fifth dimension I propose for the MMDLE modifies the behavioral and psychological dimensions slightly. Perceptions of the campus climate have long been a focus of researchers who are monitoring possible campus tensions. These perceptions effectively operate as a bridge that merges the behavioral and psychological dimensions of the campus climate to some degree. The model describes the different ways the dimensions can overlap to create the contours of campus climates and influence student learning. As Hurtado and colleagues' note, perceptions of campus climates can straddle both the behavioral and psychological dimensions and better fit one or the other, depending on the measurement of these perceptions.[49] For example, if a survey of undergraduate students asks how welcoming they felt the campus climate was for them, this wording leans more toward the psychological dimension of campus climates. However, if the question asks students how often they witnessed unwelcoming behaviors on campus, their institutions' commitment to diversity, or their institution's framing of possible hate speech as a free-speech issue, then the wording leans more toward the behavioral dimension of campus climates. These bridging perceptions always have one foot in each dimension, and the question becomes to what extent these perceptions are gauging more of one dimension or the other. Given the inconsistency with what perceptions of the campus climate are tapping into across an abundance of research in the area, this bridging-perceptions dimension can add depth to researchers' exploration of the behavioral and psychological dimensions.

The use of the MMDLE to identify what impact campus climates have on students and, subsequently, faculty and staff, is important in many respects, but so is the need to understand the evolution of this research area that contributes to higher education decision-making. Arguably the most common measures of campus climates and their impacts are quantitative. The popularity of quantification reflects the increased pressure on higher education to document student success.[50] This pressure can influence research on campus climate as a whole. Some previous research about campus climate was limited to quantitative studies of student outcomes or was focused on the campus climate assessment process.[51] Yet, the possible centrality of quantitative approaches for campus climate research is still unclear. This limited research could also privilege which findings are utilized in complex decision-making on college campuses, in higher education policy circles, and, as the continual attacks on race-conscious admissions policies attests, even in the courtroom. Further, by examining how campus climate research has evolved, we can begin to pinpoint how universities operate as racialized organizations. Through the methodologies they use to study race and inequality, universities often wind up individualizing systemic inequality and ultimately influencing future research trajectories, policy-making, and institutional decision-making in ways that undercut the goal of creating more equitable, inclusive, and just learning environments.

Evolution of the Research

Much has been written on race and campus climates over the years. The amount of information and the great number of perspectives in the literature could be difficult to sift through. To focus on the policy suggestions and organizational approaches that may be derived from the voluminous literature on race and campus climates, I examined empirical articles published from 1992 to 2019 in thirteen journals popular among higher education researchers. The start date marks the publication of Hurtado's groundbreaking analysis of the campus racial climate. An initial search of these journals identified 977 possible articles for inclusion to study how research on race and campus climates evolved over nearly thirty years. After screening for relevance, I retained 558 articles. The goal was to analyze how research related to race and campus climates has evolved and what role, if any, quantification has played in these changes that could influence what higher education does to promote equity and inclusion. Then, I used Hurtado and colleagues' MMDLE and related research as the framework to code the articles' methodologies and results discussions to examine how researchers' perspectives on campus climates have changed over time.[52] The appendix contains additional information on my methodological approach.

Changing Research Methods

Before we can examine whether quantitative research has shifted what we know about campus climates in higher education, we first must identify whether quantification has increased over the years. Figure 3.3 and table 3.1 provide an overview of the number and percentage of empirical articles using quantitative, qualitative, or mixed methods. The total number of articles that examined some aspect of campus climates in relation to racial inequality dramatically increased since Hurtado's 1992 article. In 1992–1995, only nine empirical articles

FIGURE 3.3 *Methodological approaches to studying race and campus climates, 1992–2019*

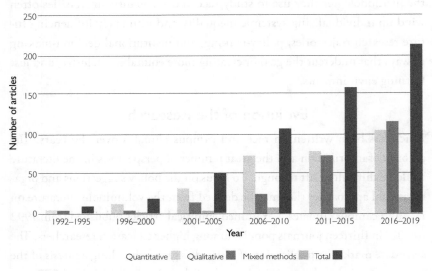

examined race and the campus climate, but the number roughly doubled over each five-year period for the next fifteen years to 106 articles in 2006–2010. In the final group of years examined for this analysis (2016–2019), 213 empirical articles on campus climate and race were published.

The rapid increase of campus climate research was arguably the result of quantification in the 1990s into the early 2000s. Approximately two-thirds of all empirical articles on race and campus climate were quantitative until 2010. However, quantitative research has somewhat plateaued in its representation among campus climate articles the last ten years. Qualitative research, on the other hand, has become a more integral part of campus climate conversations since 2010. In the last years included in the analysis (2016–2019), slightly more than half of all the articles were based on qualitative research. Generally speaking, quantitative studies of race and campus climate represented approximately half of all published studies across this nearly thirty-year period, with the greater part of their contribution occurring before 2011.

Lacking Definitions of Campus Climates

With the expansion of campus climate research, we would expect that this research would eventually develop a standard definition of a campus climate.

TABLE 3.1 *Methodologies and inclusion of explicit definitions of campus climates among empirical articles examining race and campus climates, 1992–2019*

	NUMBER OF ARTICLES (% OF TOTAL)		
YEAR	QUANTITATIVE METHODS	QUALITATIVE METHODS	MIXED METHODS
1992–1995	5 (55.6%)	4 (44.4%)	0 (0.0%)
1996–2000	13 (65.0%)	4 (20.0%)	3 (15.0%)
2001–2005	32 (62.7%)	14 (27.5%)	5 (9.8%)
2006–2010	73 (68.9%)	25 (23.6%)	8 (7.5%)
2011–2015	78 (49.1%)	73 (45.9%)	8 (5.0%)
2016–2019	76 (35.7%)	116 (54.5%)	21 (9.9%)
Total	277 (49.6%)	236 (42.3%)	45 (8.1%)
Number of articles that included definition of campus climate (percent of total)	87 (31.4%)[a]	35 (14.8%)[a]	11 (24.4%)

[a]Means comparison (*t*-test) revealed quantitative and qualitative studies of race and campus climates significantly differed between their incorporation of an explicit campus climate definition (*p* < .05).

Having a clear and straightforward definition could benefit not only the research but also university administrators in their efforts to promote equity and inclusion on campus. One pitfall in efforts to quantify campus climate is the difficulty in defining it. As with most quantitative research, researchers trying to define a phenomenon rely on the measures they have access to. As a result, researchers define campus climate only by what they can actually measure in their studies. Therefore, we may miss the breadth and depth of these features of our universities by relying on quantitative studies and their definitions.

The 558 research articles included my analyses reveal a somewhat concerning trend. As table 3.1 shows, less than a quarter of all empirical articles examining race and campus climates included an explicit definition or framework of campus climate. Quantitative studies had the highest percentage of articles that included an explicit definition (31.4 percent). Despite their relatively small number, mixed-methods studies had the next-highest percentage of articles with definitions of campus climate (24.4 percent). Qualitative studies had the smallest percentage of articles with definitions (14.8 percent). Supplementary analyses not presented here show that the number of articles that included explicit definitions has not increased during the period studied. Since 2000, less than a quarter of articles (22.5 percent) discussing race and campus climates included an explicit definition or framework of campus climate. Also, the methodological differences generally hold for the percentage of studies that include such discussions, regardless of years examined. Among all studies that included an explicit definition or framework, fully 52.6 percent (70 out of 133 studies) utilized an iteration of Hurtado and colleagues' model of campus climates to guide their research.[53] Without a clearer description of what they are examining, researchers can struggle to connect their research with related dimensions of campus climates. That is, without an explicit definition, the idea of campus climate is a nebulous feature that allows racial inequality to persist at universities under the guise of good-faith efforts.

Campus Climate Dimensions

One challenge with the examination of campus climates is how this research area may limit proposals for organizational change. The concern is actually twofold: quantification can narrow the research to individual-level aspects of campus climates, and policy makers may struggle to fully connect the research results with real changes needed at the organizational level. Quantification can promote additional narrowing by focusing only on the data that can be neatly quantified, such as survey data.[54] Although quantification is advantageous for studying certain aspects of campus climates such as how taking an ethnic studies course can benefit student learning, quantitative approaches may not easily apply to assessing other aspects of campus climates. That said, what methodological differences do we find in researchers' examinations of campus climates at colleges and universities?

To compare what parts of campus climates researchers focused on in their studies, I used Hurtado and colleagues' MMDLE, along with a few other connected readings, to identify the dimensions, features, and processes that were included in the methods and results sections of the 558 empirical articles in the sample.[55] Because authors could mention different aspects of campus climates throughout their articles—a practice that could skew interpretations of the main focus of the research—I only focused on what was studied and the results in the articles. Table 3.2 compares quantitative, qualitative, and mixed-methods approaches to the study of campus climates by the dimensions of the MMDLE and the corresponding features of each dimension. I identified whether an article included each feature under the dimensions, and I calculated the total number of features for each dimension an article included in its methodology and results sections. The table shows the average number of dimension features included in each type of campus climate study and the proportion of articles that included each campus climate feature under each dimension. Finally, I compared the dimensions and their features between each methodological form to show the significant differences between the three types of studies.

The first component examined in the MMDLE is the external forces. This component focuses on the policies and sociohistorical circumstances that can influence how universities approach diversity, equity, and inclusion and how people experience these aspects of campus life each day. This group of features was the least studied in terms of the average number of possible features researchers could have included in their studies of race and campus climates across the nearly thirty years of empirical articles examined here. Of a possible total of five features of this component, the authors of each methodological approach averaged less than one feature included in their studies. The broader sociohistorical context followed by community relations (i.e., "town-gown relations") were the two most included items of the external dimension of campus climate. Some variation existed among the three methodological approaches, as quantitative studies included fewer external dimension features than did the qualitative and mixed-methods studies.

The first dimension, the organizational dimension of campus climates, was the most incorporated one on average across all the journal articles. This dimension was included the most often by mixed-methods studies, followed by qualitative and quantitative studies. In general, researchers incorporated some aspect of the historical inclusion or exclusion of universities the most. Next, researchers similarly included academic support initiatives, curricular and cocurricular learning initiatives, and safe-space initiatives such as retention services, ethnic studies courses, diversity requirements in the general education curriculum, intergroup dialogues and workshops, and specific student

TABLE 3.2 *Campus climate dimensions and their features included in quantitative, qualitative, or mixed-methods studies, 1992–2019*

CLIMATE DIMENSION AND FEATURE	ALL (N = 558)	QUANTI-TATIVE (N = 277)	QUALI-TATIVE (N = 236)	MIXED METHODS (N = 45)	MEANS TESTS
External forces (0–5 features)	0.52	0.33	0.70	0.73	a, b
Sociohistorical contexts	20%	9%	30%	27%	a, b
Access (affirmative action)	8%	5%	11%	9%	a
Access (financial)	6%	4%	8%	7%	
Attainment policies	2%	3%	1%	7%	c
Community relations	16%	12%	20%	24%	a, b
Organizational (0–7 features)	1.70	1.49	1.84	2.24	a, b
Historical inclusion/exclusion	43%	38%	46%	62%	b
Institutional policies	14%	3%	23%	29%	a, b
Academic support initiatives	25%	22%	25%	38%	b
Cocurricular initiatives	21%	22%	17%	27%	
Curricular initiatives	27%	25%	29%	31%	
Safe-spaces initiatives	30%	25%	37%	31%	a
Interdisciplinary learning initiatives	10%	14%	6%	7%	a
Compositional (0–3 features)	0.67	0.55	0.77	0.91	a, b
Student diversity	53%	43%	62%	67%	a, b
Faculty diversity	12%	9%	14%	18%	
Staff/administration diversity	2%	3%	1%	7%	c
Psychological (0–6 features)	1.45	0.88	2.06	1.78	a, b
Social identities	53%	34%	72%	69%	a, b
Sense of belonging	35%	21%	49%	49%	a, b

CLIMATE DIMENSION AND FEATURE	ALL (N = 558)	QUANTI-TATIVE (N = 277)	QUALI-TATIVE (N = 236)	MIXED METHODS (N = 45)	MEANS TESTS
Validation	15%	3%	31%	11%	a, c
Stereotype threat	4%	1%	8%	9%	a, b
Implicit/unconscious biases	7%	1%	14%	7%	a
Racial attitudes or prejudice	30%	27%	32%	33%	
Bridging perceptions	55%	43%	67%	62%	a, b
Behavioral (0–6 features)	1.06	0.78	1.36	1.20	a
Microaggressions	20%	6%	34%	31%	a, b
Discrimination	18%	12%	25%	22%	a
Intergroup contact/ relations	39%	43%	33%	38%	a
Pedagogical practices	13%	11%	16%	16%	
Student affairs practices	6%	1%	11%	7%	a
Activism	10%	5%	17%	7%	a

Note: The average number of features under each campus climate dimension is presented along with the percentage of each study that incorporated a feature under each dimension. "Bridging perceptions" is a single item and is thus represented as a percentage of studies that included it.

[a]Significant difference between quantitative and qualitative studies after Bonferroni correction ($p < .05$).

[b]Significant difference between quantitative and mixed-methods studies after Bonferroni correction ($p < .05$).

[c]Significant difference between qualitative and mixed-methods studies after Bonferroni correction ($p < .05$).

organizations such as ethnic student organizations. Although there are slight variations across the methodological approaches, all the articles focus on the organizational dimension to a similar extent. One interesting difference is the qualitative and mixed-methods articles' increased examination of diversity-related institutional policies and practices, such as diversity training; strategic planning; and programs to diversify faculty, academic support programs, and curricular learning initiatives.

The second dimension of campus climates, the compositional diversity of faculty, staff, and students, was also one of the least included dimensions by researchers. Again, the qualitative and mixed-methods studies incorporated some aspect of this dimension more often than the quantitative studies did.

All three methodological approaches overwhelmingly focused on diversity among student populations. Faculty representation was the second-most examined item under the compositional dimension, again, with qualitative and mixed-methods studies including these items more often than quantitative studies included them. As these observations show, we urgently need further examination of staff representation as part of the compositional dimension of campus climates. Less than 10 percent of any study included some analysis or discussion of this feature of campuses.

The model's third dimension, the psychological one, was the second-most examined area of campus climates among the articles included in the current study. People's social identities, their sense of belonging, and racial attitudes or prejudice were the most examined features of this dimension. Qualitative and mixed-methods studies focused on each of these items, particularly social identities, sense of belonging, and stereotype threat, more often than quantitative studies did. Each methodological approach to campus climate similarly focused on racial attitudes or prejudice.

The bridging dimension, which focuses on student, faculty, or staff perceptions of campus climate (a hostile climate, a welcoming one, institutional commitment to diversity, the use of policy to frame hate speech as free speech, etc.) was included by more than half of all studies examined in the analysis. As was the case for other dimensions, qualitative and mixed-methods studies include campus climate perceptions more than quantitative studies did.

Finally, the behavioral dimension was the third-most incorporated aspect of campus climates studied by researchers. The increasing focus on micro-aggressions in higher education is notable in two ways. First, it is the most incorporated feature of the behavioral dimension. And second, like the other dimensions, the behavioral dimension was incorporated more often in the qualitative and mixed-methods studies than it was in the quantitative ones. Additionally, given the importance of the MMDLE's relationship to the educational benefits of diversity perspective, the second-most examined feature of this dimension was intergroup contact or relations on college campuses.[56] The other features, such as discrimination and activism, were not examined nearly as frequently. Notably, for nearly all behavioral dimension features, quantitative and qualitative studies differed in the frequency with which they incorporated these features, and differed from mixed-methods research regarding the examination of microaggressions as well.

Across all these dimensions and features, the psychological and organizational dimensions of campus climates are evidently the most studied across all the methodological approaches. However, the methodological approaches to race and campus climates have one apparent difference. Quantitative studies of race-related aspects of campus climates often significantly differed from qualitative studies in the features and dimensions they included, although mixed-methods studies also differed from quantitative studies in many respects. How has the choice of which features of campus climates are examined in research changed over time? Moreover, how has the way people have studied these features—the methodology—changed over nearly thirty years of research?

The Methodological Divide

Research articles on campus climate illustrate a methodological divide between quantitative and qualitative approaches. As discussed in the preceding section, qualitative and quantitative researchers differ in their examination of campus climate dimensions. This methodological divide, a historical feature of research and higher education in general, has important implications for administrators and policy makers attempting to put this research into practice and to make campuses more equitable and inclusive. Therefore, we must explore whether this divide is widening, shrinking, or staying the same over time. As we saw in figure 3.3, the number of quantitative articles on race and the campus climate have somewhat plateaued in the last ten years, while publication of qualitative research has skyrocketed. These differences may suggest a widening divide in which dimensions are examined in published research.

Figure 3.4 compares the dimensions of campus climates examined by quantitative and qualitative approaches from 1992 to 2019. For each group of years, I calculated the difference between the average number of features included in the quantitative studies and the average number in the qualitative studies. A score of zero indicates that quantitative and qualitative research on race and campus climates focused on a dimension equally during that period. Positive scores indicate that quantitative studies focused more on one

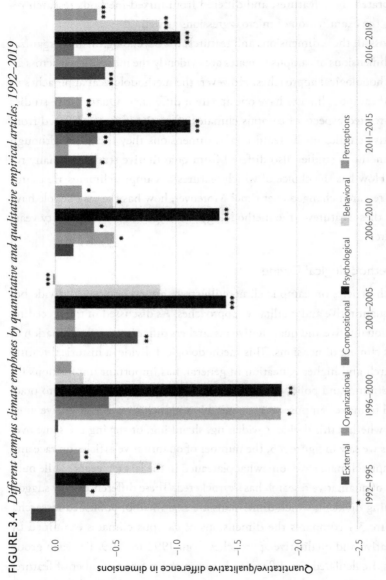

FIGURE 3.4 *Different campus climate emphases by quantitative and qualitative empirical articles, 1992–2019*

Note: Data points below zero suggest that qualitative research focused more on the dimension than quantitative research did. Data points above zero suggest the opposite: that there was more quantitative research on the dimension than there was qualitative. Asterisks mark significant means differences (t-tests) between quantitative and qualitative studies for each period (*p < .05; **p < .01; ***p < .001).

dimension than did qualitative studies, while negative scores indicate the opposite, that qualitative studies focused more on a certain dimension.

The quantitative and qualitative methodological approaches to research on race and campus climates appear to be converging. In the 1990s, qualitative research, not quantitative, was more likely to consider organizational and psychological dimensions. Quantitative research on campus climates in the 1990s also focused slightly more on the external forces that can influence these climates. However, since 2000, quantitative and qualitative research has included similar numbers of items for each dimension, with slightly more items included in qualitative studies. The one exception is the psychological dimension. Qualitative research includes many more features of this dimension on average than does quantitative research. These differences are meaningful, despite being small.

Since 1995, the additional qualitative focus on the psychological dimension significantly differs from quantitative studies of the same dimension (shown by asterisks for each appropriate bar in the figure). From 2011 to 2015, the qualitative focus on the external and compositional diversity dimensions of campus climates significantly differs from quantitative studies, while in the last grouping of years (2016–2019) qualitative studies significantly differ from quantitative studies for incorporating measures of external forces, organizational, and behavioral dimensions. Since 2005, the quantitative and qualitative approaches also significantly differ for bridging perceptions. These are important differences, but how do they shape administrators' and policy makers' decisions when these leaders are attempting to create more systemic change on college campuses? We still must learn how campus climate researchers connect the external forces and other dimensions to the organizational dimension to help cultivate systemic change in higher education.

How Research Can Miss Organizational Issues

To examine the possible connections (or lack thereof) between the organizational, psychological, behavioral, and bridging dimensions of campus climates, I used a two-pronged analytic approach. First, I studied which factors relate to the changes in incorporating organizational dimension features into race-related campus climate research. Second, I created difference scores between the organizational, psychological, and behavioral dimensions to see if incorporating more of either psychological or behavioral dimensions in a study comes at the expense of the organizational dimension. These analyses can demonstrate how campus climate research may suggest initiatives that do not necessarily correspond to organizational changes.

Table 3.3 shows three regression analyses of the factors that shape the incorporation of more organizational features in race-related campus climate research. The first model includes external forces and the other campus climate dimensions: compositional, psychological, behavioral, and bridging perceptions. Studies that included more external, compositional, and behavioral dimension features also included more organizational dimension features. Studies with a stronger focus on the psychological dimension had fewer organizational features. Studies that included an explicit definition of campus climates had more organizational dimension features included than did studies without such definitions. Also, studies that were qualitative or mixed methods compared to quantitative contained more organizational dimension features. Thus, some initial methodological differences contribute to the likelihood that a study focused more on the organizational dimension of campus climates.

The incorporation of organizational dimension features in studies and the changes associated with including more psychological and behavioral dimensions may be accentuated by how each dimension connects with the bridging perceptions of campus climates. Thus, two analyses included interaction terms between the psychological and behavioral dimensions with bridging perceptions of campus climates. The second model included the interaction term between the bridging perceptions and psychological dimensions. Again, more features related to the compositional and behavioral dimensions of campus climates corresponded to more of an organizational focus in studies as well. Conversely, articles focusing more on the psychological dimension and those examining perceptions of campus climates corresponded with fewer organizational dimension features. Interestingly, the interaction term between the psychological dimension and bridging perceptions of campus climates is positive, meaning articles that focused more on the psychological dimension and examined campus climate perceptions had more of an organizational dimension focus.

The third model of the analyses included the interaction term between the behavioral dimension and bridging perceptions of campus climates.

TABLE 3.3 *Multivariate analyses of change in organizational dimension usage in race-related campus climate research, 1992–2019*

VARIABLE	MODEL 1		MODEL 2		MODEL 3	
	>ß	SE	ß	SE	ß	SE
Dimension						
External	.08†	.07	.05	.07	.09*	.07
Compositional	.16***	.08	.16***	.08	.17***	.08
Psychological	−.09†	.05	−.28***	.08	−.08	.05
Behavioral	.18***	.06	.16***	.06	.33***	.11
Bridging perceptions	−.00	.12	−.16*	.17	.09	.16
Bridging of dimensions						
Perceptions × psychological	—	—	.31*	.10	—	—
Perceptions × behavioral	—	—	—	—	−.24*	.14
Other article information						
Campus climate defined	.12**	.14	.12**	.13	.13**	.14
Student data	−.06	.13	−.06	.13	−.06	.13
Qualitative	.09†	.14	.10*	.14	.09†	.14
Mixed methods	.11*	.22	.11*	.22	.11*	.22
Year published	−.04	.01	−.04	.01	−.05	.01
F	8.10		8.50		7.91	
R^2	.11***		.13***		.12***	
N	558		558		558	

Note: SE = standard error. ß = beta value, represents standardized coefficients.

†$p < .1$

*$p < .05$

**$p < .01$

***$p < .001$

Although similar positive findings for the compositional and behavioral dimensions were found in the model, neither the psychological dimension nor the bridging perceptions were significant. However, the interaction term did significantly relate to how much the studies focused on the organizational dimension. Studies that incorporated more behavioral dimension features and examined perceptions of the campus climate had fewer organizational dimension features in the end.

These findings, though intriguing, leave open the possibility that research examining one dimension may not necessarily incorporate another dimension. To better understand how these three dimensions (behavioral, psychological, and organizational) and the bridging perceptions connect with one another, we need relational measures. One way to identify the relationship between researchers' use of organizational, psychological, and behavioral dimensions features of campus climates is to create a difference score between the dimensions. I created two difference scores, one between the organizational and psychological dimensions, and another between the organizational and behavioral dimensions. For the first difference score, I subtracted the number of psychological dimension features from the total number of organizational dimension features for each article. A positive score suggests that an article incorporated more organizational features in the study, while a negative score suggests the opposite—that an article included more psychological features. I used a similar process for the second difference score, subtracting the number of behavioral dimension features from the total number of organizational dimension features for each article.

Table 3.4 presents multivariate analyses examining the changes in the relationships between the organizational, psychological, and behavioral dimensions of campus climates. Two models examined changes in the difference scores between the organizational and psychological dimensions, and the remaining two models identified changes in the difference scores between the organizational and behavioral dimensions. Similar to the above models, interaction terms between the bridging perceptions and the psychological and behavioral dimensions were included in the analyses.

In the multivariate analyses of organizational-psychological difference scores, the first model found that a greater focus on the external forces and compositional dimension corresponded with a greater focus on the organizational

TABLE 3.4 *Multivariate regression analyses assessing changes in relationship between organizational dimension with psychological and behavioral dimensions in race-related campus climate research, 1992–2019*

VARIABLE	ORGANIZATIONAL-PSYCHOLOGICAL DIFFERENCE				ORGANIZATIONAL-BEHAVIORAL DIFFERENCE			
	MODEL 1		MODEL 2		MODEL 1		MODEL 2	
	ß	SE	ß	SE	ß	SE	ß	SE
Dimension								
External forces	.14**	.09	.17***	.09	.05	.08	.04	.08
Compositional	.10*	.11	.10*	.11	.14**	.10	.14**	.10
Psychological	—	—	—	—	−.20***	.06	−.29***	.10
Behavioral	−.02	.08	.20*	.14	—	—	—	—
Bridging perceptions	−.10*	.16	.03	.22	−.11*	.14	−.18**	.20
Bridging of dimensions								
Perceptions × psychological	—	—	—	—	—	—	.15	.11
Perceptions × behavioral	—	—	−.32**	.17	—	—	—	—
Other article information								
Campus climate defined	.16***	.18	.18***	.18	.06	.15	.06	.15
Student data	−.17***	.16	−.16***	.16	−.04	.14	−.04	.14
Qualitative	−.24***	.18	−.23***	.17	.01	.16	.02	.16
Mixed methods	−.07	.29	−.06	.28	.08†	.25	.08†	.25
Year published	−.10*	.02	−.11*	.01	−.03	.01	−.03	.01
F	11.13		11.23		6.37		5.98	
R²	.14***		.16***		.08***		.08***	
N	558		558		558		558	

Note: SE = standard error; ß = beta value, represents standardized coefficients.

†p < .1   *p < .05   **p < .01   ***p < .001

dimension than on the psychological dimension in race-related campus climate research. A focus on perceptions of the campus climate related to less focus on the organizational dimension in this research area. The second model includes the interaction term between campus climate perceptions and the behavioral dimension. Similar findings existed for the connections between the external forces and compositional dimension and inclusion of the organizational dimension features in race-related campus climate. However, campus climate perceptions was not significant. Studies with more behavioral dimension features also had more organizational dimension features and fewer psychological dimension features. The interaction term was also significant, but negative, meaning that studies examining both campus climate perceptions and more behavioral features had fewer organizational dimension features and more psychological dimension ones. In both analyses, this shift away from the organizational dimension toward the psychological dimension has gradually occurred across the period studied.

In the multivariate analyses of organizational-behavioral difference scores, the first model found that, similar to earlier analyses, studies with more of a focus on the compositional dimension had a stronger focus on the organizational dimension than on the behavioral dimension of campus climates. Studies that incorporated more of a psychological focus had less of an organizational focus than on the behavioral dimension. Relatedly, studies that examined campus climate perceptions also had less of an organizational focus. The second model included the interaction term between bridging perceptions of campus climates and the psychological dimension. This analysis had similar findings to those of the previous model. However, the interaction term was not significant, meaning that studies that further incorporated campus climate perceptions and the psychological dimension did not shift the relationship between organizational and behavioral dimensions in race-related campus climate research. These findings did not differ over time. Moreover, the findings suggest that the relationship between bridging perceptions and the behavioral dimension can obscure the connection between social interactions and psychological processes and organizational circumstances, particularly policies and programs.

Taken together, these results suggest that the shift in race-related campus climate research toward the psychological dimension is slow and not fully discounting organizational dimensions. Though not wholly concerning, this gradual shift means that initiatives and policies may not catalyze organizational change as much as anticipated, because of what is becoming a predominant feature of this research area: individual-level processes with less organizational connections.[57]

Improving the Research

A central aim of *Behind the Diversity Numbers* is to explore why quantifying diversity, equity, and inclusion in higher education can be both a strength and a liability in university efforts. Despite the usefulness of quantification studies, previous scholarship also notes the limitations of these tools for decision-making and policy-making. Quantification studies are particularly ill equipped to document how race is incorporated into policy conversations and to explain racial inequality and its relationship to other social inequalities found on campuses and in higher education policies.[58] As discussed earlier, quantification aligns with the unwritten ideas and rules of organizational schemata in certain ways that discount the importance of race in admissions reviews while emphasizing specific academic characteristics of students. Yet, an examination of the research literature on campus climate suggests that efforts to address racial inequality on campuses through policies and programs need to further incorporate organizational features of campus life. Thus, an important limitation of this research area is not relegated to quantitative approaches but encompasses the field as a whole. Without additional organizational connections in our research, we will struggle to establish long-term, achievable goals whose progress we can monitor. In the following sections, I summarize the main findings of the analyses and make four recommendations for how universities and policy makers can begin addressing the organizational disconnects.

Both-And: The Need for Numbers and Voices, Together

Somewhat countering the perspective that numbers generally, and quantitative methods specifically, are taking hold of research in recent years, the use of quantitative approaches to study race and campus climates has plateaued since the early 2000s.[59] Instead, qualitative approaches have dramatically increased since around 2010. Additionally, mixed-methods studies have increased as well, though much less sharply. The broadening of methodical approaches to examining the different features of campus climates is a welcoming trend, particularly in light of the many criticisms of quantitative methods.[60] Each form of methodology has its own strengths and can inform decisions and policies affecting campus life. For this reason, we must pursue more mixed-methods research to uncover the complex features of campus climates and how they manifest themselves on different levels and shape people's lives in higher education. Campus leaders and policy makers alike should avoid data mining and relying on quantitative data for decision-making and policy proposals. Otherwise, they run the risk of glossing over the nuances of racial and other social inequalities on campus and overlooking how a policy or program change may exacerbate these inequalities instead of reducing them.

The added benefit of pursuing more mixed-methods research is the combined strengths of quantitative and qualitative approaches. For example, of the 558 journal articles that I examined, the quantitative studies frequently included explicit definitions and frameworks of campus climates. Approximately a third of the quantitative studies used such definitions and frameworks, while less than 15 percent of the qualitative studies did so. Without describing clearly what is being examined and its components, analyses of racial inequality on college campuses can miss how the inequality also reflects organizational processes and policies. We have to clearly and consistently name and identify how campus climates are integral to the extent that a university can reproduce racial inequality in everyday life, on multiple levels of operation, and for different community constituents on and off campus.[61] We must also hold each other accountable in the identification of campus climate features in research, policy, and practice. Otherwise, we could succumb to what sociologist James Thomas describes as "condensation." When we condense an issue, we describe certain campus features as simply part of a ubiquitous diversity or campus climate reality, but these features are overlooked in our discussions of, or approaches to, addressing specific issues.[62] Without combining both qualitative and quantitative methodologies under a more coherent approach for campus climate research, we run the risk of misinterpreting the meanings of diversity, equity, and inclusion for policy and program changes and ignoring how an individual's experience relates to an organizational deficiency.

A final benefit of mixed-methods research is the amount and depth of what can be studied. Remarkably, qualitative studies incorporated more items related to each dimension of campus climate than did quantitative studies. This pattern held consistently across the nearly thirty years of research in this area. The pattern also confirms the limitation of the quantification of social phenomena; quantification relies on specific, measurable data that fits the methodological framework for analysis.[63] However, when the narrowness of quantitative methods is compensated for through qualitative approaches to the same campus climate features, researchers can draw more connections to the organizational dimension. Qualitative studies better incorporated organizational features than did quantitative studies, but mixed-methods studies added features that the other methodological approaches did not consider. For example, mixed-methods research can better examine the connection between some behavioral features of campus climate and organizational policy. As a result, the research helps pinpoint the changes needed to improve individuals' experiences and outcomes and to reach organizational goals.

The Dangers of Individualizing Racial Inequality

A troubling finding is that race-related campus climate research, particularly quantitative analyses, saw a slight erosion of the organizational dimension over the years. However, this reduction applies to all campus climate research, not just the quantitative type. The danger with the decreased attention to the organizational dimension of campus climate lies in how the closely connected psychological and behavioral dimensions, along with the bridging perceptions of campus climate, are perceived. When organizational factors are largely ignored, these other dimensions assume more prominence than perhaps they should. The research thus often fails to connect individual outcomes with organizational inequality, and these disconnects are intensified by perceptions of campus climates and institutional commitments to diversity, equity, and inclusion. Researchers and campus leaders must recognize that the data collected on individuals reflects the influence of university policies and practices. This common association of inequality with individuals and not with the organizational reality of college campuses exemplifies how universities operate as racialized organizations; the organization is framed as race-neutral despite much evidence to the contrary.[64]

Why has research on race and campus climate incorporated more psychological and behavioral dimension considerations at the cost of the organizational dimension? One possible explanation is that an increasing amount of research does not clearly connect the psychological and bridging dimensions with the campus climate that informs people's understanding of their positions on an unequal campus. By focusing mostly on the psychological dimension, researchers may not fully consider how a person's social identities, sense of belonging, and validation, for example, relate to the social structure and culture of the organization. As will be further discussed, if the research ignores the microclimates people must navigate on campus, their documented individual-level experiences and outcomes will have little bearing on organizational evaluation of what needs to change to promoted diversity, equity, and inclusion.

On a related note, researchers' categorization of people's perceptions of campus climates as a behavioral feature links these perceptions mainly with social interactions and ignores the broader campus issues. The multivariate models further bolster this individualizing of the campus climate into social interactions and their influence on psychological processes, also devoid of any campus context. This approach is a quintessential feature of racialized organizations: they frame inequality as an intergroup or ideological feature, not as an organizational reality.[65] With this framing, initiatives to address racial inequality center on what's wrong with people (implicit biases, cultural insensitivities, etc.) more than on the organization that people must navigate. A constant focus on group behavior and individual outcomes may be important for learning goals, but research is not further elaborating how such outcomes correspond to organizational goals, policies, and processes. A similar disconnect is found by sociologist Natasha Warikoo in her study of elite college students' views of race and inequality. Warikoo shows how the much-lauded intergroup dialogue approach can entrench the view that individual behavior and perceptions take precedence in combatting racial inequality when the organizational contributions to the problem are ignored. Under these circumstances, students fail to understand how racial inequality is about systemic inequity rather than solely about individual intent and capabilities.[66]

The work of Garcia and Thomas further describes the dangers of these organizational disconnects for perpetuating racial inequality, especially under the guise of serious efforts at diversity, equity, and inclusion. Garcia's critical work on HSIs shows how the changing demographics and the federal requirements for designation leave room for both ideological divides about what makes an institution an HSI and what this answer means for supporting Latinx students.[67] According to Garcia, the norms of higher education reflect and value whiteness by curtailing the transformation of academic, cocurricular, and overall organizational practices that would provide more equitable and inclusive learning environments, even when a majority of students on campus are people of color.[68]

While Garcia's work discusses the obstacles facing organizational transformation for federally designated HSIs, Thomas's work centers on an organizational reality facing many institutions described as historically white institutions. He documents how the increasingly elaborate "diversity regimes" of larger universities present conflicting, decentralized approaches to diversity, equity, and inclusion and can obscure and increase racial inequalities on campus.[69] Both Garcia and Thomas critique universities for transforming diversity into an issue of individual performances with diluted meanings and actions that never fulfill universities' commitments for organizational change. Researchers and campus leaders must carefully reconnect the organizational dimension of campus climates in their discussions of inequality on campus. If they fail to do so, they will continue to miss why marginalization is not a feeling but an experience reflecting inequality on an organizational level.

The Microclimates of Campuses

The third recommendation builds on the recommendations in the preceding two sections. It elaborates on how organizational policies and processes work at multiple levels, which can increase racial inequality and complicate people's navigation of racialized campuses. As noted earlier in this chapter, campus climates are often discussed in broad terms as an overarching feature of a university. Hurtado and colleagues' MMDLE for campus climate research provides an important step to inform decision-making and organizational change. Although the model is useful in many ways, recent exploration of climates within climates, or *microclimates*, allows researchers and college administrators to think about how the campus climate can be distilled into multiple intersecting environments that people must deal with. Originally developed by Martha Ackelsberg and colleagues focusing on faculty experiences, the concept of microclimates refers to "a small, relatively self-contained environment within which a faculty member operates."[70] Although originally focused on faculty members, this concept can be easily extended to students' and staff members' navigation of different structures of campus life, including departments, committees, and cocurricular initiatives.

A few examples can provide helpful information about the need to expand campus climate research to understand how racial inequality can proliferate throughout an organization despite what may be found at a university level of analysis. Garcia takes an in-depth look at how faculty, student affairs practitioners, and administrators understand the construction of a university as an HSI through their institutional locations in different departments, offices, and programs.[71] Representation of different student, faculty, and staff groups can fluctuate by departments and offices such that a campus may seem diverse and inclusive as a whole, but examining microclimates can reveal pockets of underrepresentation and marginalization through policies, processes, and leadership practices. Kimberly Griffin also discusses how pursuing more diversity, equity, and inclusion in STEM fields requires understanding the fields' cultural differences that operate as barriers for the degree and career pursuits of students of color, particularly women.[72] By assessing the unique contexts and ways the campus climate manifests itself within these departments and programs, campus leaders can work closely with faculty and staff to develop different initiatives and support programs to promote more collaborative and engaging learning environments for students.

Finally, Annemarie Vaccaro's study of LGBTQ student, faculty, and staff experiences provides further support for documenting the microclimates within the broader campus climate.[73] Vaccaro's research describes the extent that people's social identities intersect with their social locations on campus (i.e., undergraduate or graduate student, staff member, faculty, administrator, etc.) and the campus organizations they are connected to and how these connections shape their perceptions, experiences, and pursuits. Therefore, more detailed study of these microclimates within the larger campus climate could better inform campus decision-making by highlighting the interconnections of different campus units and the needs of student groups. By showing that inequity and marginalization may exist for students, faculty, and staff, the documentation of microclimates can also help policy makers target certain academic and support programs.

Recognizing Important External Forces

While most of this chapter focuses on how research on campus climates rarely incorporates the organizational dimension into studies, my analyses revealed another issue that could have additional far-reaching implications for higher education and society. Researchers' limited attention to the external forces of campus climates challenges administrators and policy makers to better examine how an outside policy or an external pressure from society can have implications for diversity, equity, and inclusion. Of course, higher education researchers do examine, for example, the impact of federal or state policies on universities' college admissions processes and policies or how certain college degrees may grant graduates access to better-paying jobs. However, research on other external forces would not only strengthen the connections made between specific federal or state policies and campus climates but also strengthen the theoretical contributions of the field by embracing aspects of the social psychological traditions the field has always relied on.

Race-related campus climate research has consistently been a feature in policy discussions and amicus curiae briefs since the *Regents of the University of California v. Allan Bakke* decision supporting the foundations of what became the argument for the educational benefits of diversity.[74] However, we need a better understanding of how the interaction of higher education and society is related to racial equity concerns, particularly along the lines of sociohistorical contexts, not just policies.[75] Policies that influence higher education are a reflection of societal circumstances, and without including more of these elements in campus climate studies, our understanding of why policy debates matter for racial equity on campus will be incomplete.

The development of affirmative action bans, an issue closely related to campus climate research, illustrates why including more sociohistorical background in research can help with higher education's policy-making. These bans occur at state levels and notably reduce the racial and ethnic diversity of the student body.[76] One particularly informative study was conducted by educational scholar Dominique Baker. The study examined whether the perceived racial threat of the move to diversify student bodies at public flagship universities was an underlying reason for many states' affirmative action bans passed from 1995 to 2012. As the proportion of white students on campuses declined, the likelihood that a state would propose and pass a statewide affirmative action ban increased because of the perceived scarcity of highly valued educational resources.[77] Baker also connected these bans across larger, multistate areas to show why this context matters. Taken together, this research provides an important example of how the study of more external forces could refine not only our understanding of how external sociohistorical and policy changes are related to one another but also what impacts they have on campus racial equity efforts.

The limited inclusion of external forces in campus climate research also suggests an underlying problem with higher education in general. Because the institution of higher education is only loosely connected to the ongoing debate about race and racism off campus, any changes to promote diversity, equity, and inclusion on campus will be more difficult. A small but growing segment of campus climate research focuses on immigration. Immigrant students, and undocumented students, including those under the Deferred Action for Childhood Arrivals policy, face many challenges. Students contend with questions like how to access higher education opportunities, pay for college, balance the challenges of work and family life, and navigate campuses, given their identities and positions. This research on immigration is an important example of how universities could help these students by recognizing the sociohistorical effects of policies on multiple aspects of higher education. This awareness could also encourage faculty and staff to support these students as they pursue their college degrees in uncertain and fearful times.

As Hurtado and colleagues aptly describe, the importance of university and community connections must not be lost on how our campuses support equity efforts.[78] The colloquial term *town-and-gown relations* does not fully confer how the connections between our institutions and their communities can shape student learning and experiences. Additionally, by reasserting the importance of societal structure and culture for campus climate research, researchers can strengthen their theoretical connections to important social psychological approaches such as the social structure and personality framework.[79] At the same time, by providing more concrete evidence of how universities and their communities are interconnected, the researchers can help promote diversity, equity, and inclusion on many levels and for many community members on and off campus.

Finally, we need additional research that clearly demonstrates the connections between campus climates and societal changes; such research would benefit campus leadership and policy-making for racial equity. Unfortunately, the recent waves of student protests against racial injustice on campus and in broader society have been met with disjointed perspectives by campus administrators. They perceive the campus racial climate as rather harmonious despite agreeing that racism in the rest of society is rearing its ugly head.[80] Such framing of campuses as better than, and possibly separate from, broader society when it comes to racism and racial inequalities is quite common. Higher education scholar Eddie Cole conducted an in-depth examination of how campus leaders explain away or possibly amplify campus racism and the connection of their institutions to white supremacy; his observations should make everyone cautious about how they relate to racial injustice.[81] By situating racism in higher education and society as an aberration, a phenomenon outside everyday organizational processes and policies, campus leaders and their approaches will increase racial inequality on campus and throughout their institutions rather than effectivity addressing it. Such perspectives will also continue to focus organizational transformation approaches on individual and group changes that are fairly loose in structure and action.[82] These perspectives among campus leaders also inform policy-making. And when a university's response to racial inequality is limited to individual-level efforts, with little attention to the broader connection between higher education and society, university policies could increase inequality on campus.

Conclusion

To say that race-related campus climate research has been and continues to be important is an understatement. This research area, a fixture of higher education research in general, informs decisions on campuses and in the courtrooms. Yet, we need to refine how this research is conducted and how it affects university efforts to promote diversity, equity, and inclusion. My analyses of the campus climate literature published over nearly thirty years highlights many strengths of the work but also areas of concern. Although the quantification of diversity, equity, and inclusion are central themes in this book, the campus climate literature shows an overall move away from incorporating data and discussions about the organizational dimension of campus climates. As discussed in the previous chapters, however, data are critical for good decision-making on campus as well as for policy-making that can improve higher education, make an impact on society, and, hopefully, promote racial equity and inclusion. The use of bottom-line numbers for these decisions and proposals without the contextual information and voices of those affected means these decisions will seldom hit their mark. And if they do, it may not stick for long. From admissions to changes in student, faculty, and staff representation on college campuses and to the obstacles they face in their educational and career pursuits, numbers matter in many ways. However, we need to rethink why these numbers and research in this area matter and why diversity, equity, and inclusion are important for higher education as universities face mounting pressure to address racial injustice on campus and by their institutions in society. We now turn to what is needed for universities to envision racial equity and justice as a future public good rather than relying on the narrowness cultivated behind the diversity numbers currently used in higher education.

CHAPTER 4

What Universities Can Do About Racial Equity

MY PARTNER AND I were on our way back from an extended trip on the East Coast at the beginning of March 2020, first for a conference in Philadelphia and second to see family in Virginia on the edges of the suburbs of Washington, D.C. Like many flights, our flight was delayed thirty minutes, but then a staff member from the airline announced that we were waiting on another plane because of a mechanical issue the airline discovered when checking the plane before boarding was set to take place. Good for us that the preflight check had spotted a problem, but bad for us as well because we had to wait nearly two hours before we could board our flight. While waiting, I looked at the television hanging from the ceiling and frowned as news scrolled about Seattle and New York City facing the spread of the novel coronavirus, COVID-19. My partner had a similar concerned look on her face. We were in for a long, arduous experience. It was something you could sense at that moment; things were about to change. A few days later, my colleagues and I received word from a department administrative assistant that campus leaders were planning to close the university and that we should grab what we thought we needed from our offices for a few weeks, perhaps a month. The next day, the university was ordered closed at the end of the week, and the state followed suit not too long afterward as cases surged.

Nearly three months into the stay-at-home orders, I milled around a small apartment trying to write, think, and simply do something besides dwell on the continuing rise of cases and deaths attributed to COVID-19 and the seeming desire in the United States to do everything but address the public health crisis. As my colleagues and I talked with one another across the nation, we agreed that trying to get back into some of our projects felt pointless. Children were home all the time now, and some people either took in other family members or temporarily moved to take care of ailing family members as health-care facilities and practitioners became strapped because of the virus. Assistance with university tasks fell onto many faculty members' plates as a new type of service requested during a pandemic. Among other tasks, I worked on rapid grant proposals and helped create a survey of student needs for the summer to identify what resources and issues would need attention as the university planned for the fall semester. All the while, I was trying to keep as much communication with colleagues and students as I and they could manage.

In between the many new tasks and the deluge of emails about constant changes and uncertainty during the pandemic, I kept trying to work on this book. Yet, nearly each time I sat down to write, I would hit a roadblock and find myself thinking, "You're writing about how universities use quantitative measures for diversity, equity, and inclusion efforts and operate in a way that may undercut their own work. Why does that matter at a time like this? People are dying, and you are playing with numbers." I was simply at a loss. At this same time, many colleagues who worked on racial health disparities began publishing commentaries and calling attention to the dramatic impact the coronavirus had on marginalized communities across the nation. The numbers were important, but the question was how they fit into the emerging conversation about tackling the pandemic and racial health disparities simultaneously. Colleagues observed that the entrenched institutional discrimination of the health-care system, of which higher education has contributed to as well, was an underlying factor for the disparate impact of the coronavirus on Black, Latinx, and Indigenous communities across the United States.[1]

Then, on May 25, 2020, in Minneapolis, a man named George Floyd was killed by a police officer whose knee slowly choked the life out of him while onlookers yelled for the police to let him go. Next came to light the tragedy of Breonna Taylor, who had died from police gunfire in March as she lay sleeping in her apartment. A no-knock warrant was used to break into the apartment to arrest a drug dealer who was already in custody. The incident was part of a larger gentrification scheme to clear a segment of a predominately Black neighborhood for possible redevelopment. Taylor's boyfriend heard people breaking down the door, and because the police did not identify themselves, he fired at the intruders. They fired back, killing Taylor. George Floyd, Breonna Taylor, and Ahmaud Arbery, who was attacked and shot dead as he went for a jog in Georgia, became household names because of the circumstances that led to their deaths. Protests were immediate and widespread beyond Minneapolis.

Why this book matters beyond the research and theoretical discussions came back to light at this moment. W. E. B. Du Bois, reflecting on the lynching of a Black man in rural Georgia, wrote, "One could not be a cool, calm, and detached scientist while Negroes were lynched, murdered and starved."[2] Fast-forward more than fifty years since Du Bois's writings, and we find ourselves in another wave of resurgent racial justice movements across the nation. As colleague and fellow sociologist Rashawn Ray wrote in the midst of these movements and the uncertainty of the pandemic: "Some of us do not have the luxury to sit in the Ivory Tower and do 'pure research.' And, our research is no less important for being community- and policy-relevant. Rather, I would argue that this research is more significant . . . Being disconnected from local communities outside of the symbolic and physical barriers of the Ivory Tower that detach universities from the neighborhoods they are located in is a privilege that some of us do not have."[3]

In light of the monumental changes that the year 2020 brought to society, I reexamined the purposes of this book—helping eliminate racial inequality in higher education—and thought about the many pressures higher education was under. In light of the pandemic, universities were changing nearly everything, and both K–12 schools and higher education were under immense pressure to do so as the virus continued to spread throughout the summer. However, as my public health colleague William Lopez and I wrote, the constant changes of higher education in universities' many attempts to physically reopen campuses and facilitate coursework did not factor in the racial and socioeconomic inequality that students navigate every day on and off campus.[4] Without universities' consideration of this important context, these inequalities would only increase during the pandemic, regardless of how much planning was done. Higher education needed to change how it operates and the assumptions behind why it does so.

The coronavirus pandemic provides higher education with an opportunity to commit to, and invest in, the diversity, equity, and inclusion efforts necessary to support marginalized students, faculty, and staff. While many campus leaders, boards of trustees, and higher education policy makers suggest more austere practices of cutting and consolidating as the pandemic wears on, I argue the opposite. There is no better time to invest in higher education and make a significant push for equity and inclusion than the present. Now is not the time for the happy talk of diversity, but a time for action. We must now prove that a university's commitment to diversity, equity, and inclusion is more than statements, underfunded offices, and, simply put, window dressing to how the institution functions each day.[5] If colleges and universities are racialized organizations, and if many institutions' usual quantitative approaches do not fully support the stated goals and ideals of equity and inclusion, then we need to envision a better university. With that in mind, I explore a few areas that could help us promote racial equity in and by higher education in the future.

Embedding Racial Equity Further into Universities

In the introduction, I extended Victor Ray's theoretical perspective of the racialization of organizations to the similar ways universities operate.[6] I also explored how quantification can perpetuate harmful perspectives, processes, and policies for universities aiming to promote diversity, equity, and inclusion.[7] Clearly, organizations' operations, which reflect their underlying, unwritten ideas and rules for working toward their goals and policies and the ideology of those who work in the organization individually and collectively, can influence racial inequality. We must recognize that a true transformation of colleges and universities to promote diversity, equity, and inclusion and not reinforce racial inequalities requires that the institutions refrain from dumping into the laps of individuals the responsibility for organizational change. Universities, as racialized organizations, can create and maintain racial inequalities without individual malice and even with people's best intentions.[8] In this chapter, I suggest some ways that universities can begin fulfilling their stated diversity, equity, and inclusion goals.

Equity and Inclusion from Dynamic Diversity

As an initial step, institutions can revisit their use of the perceived educational benefits of diversity research and can reconsider why race matters for higher education and society. The continuing legal challenges to the use of race in holistic college admissions decisions spotlights the political battle for access to valuable resources and opportunities that highly selective and well-resourced universities provide for their students. However, as discussed in chapter 1, these ongoing battles have spurred universities to rely on research about the educational benefits of diversity in ways that are somewhat antithetical to their own arguments. Part of the problem is universities' reliance on mostly quantitative analyses of the importance of diversity, specifically racial and ethnic diversity, in the educational and social development of college students in an increasingly contentious environment that is requiring a narrower tailoring of race-related policies and accountability. This situation results in a delicate balance of efforts both to dequantify race in university policies and to quantify its importance despite legal restrictions of doing so.[9]

To promote racial equity and inclusion, universities could build on the foundational work of Sylvia Hurtado and colleagues, who elaborate on the complexity of campus climates; the connection of campus climate to student learning, as described in Liliana Garces and Uma Jayakumar's work on dynamic diversity; and Julie Park's discussion of the fluidity of racial diversity and the benefits of diversity for student learning.[10] To reiterate Garces and Jayakumar's central point, we must reject the narrow description of critical mass—a description that says a quantifiable proportion of students from certain racial and ethnic groups produces the educational benefits of diversity. This limited view is ineffective both in universities' future arguments about why racial diversity matters and in how researchers explore the connection between racial diversity and student learning. Although we need to rely on existing research, we also must invest more in research of different forms to effectively target organizational processes and policies that reinforce rather than reduce racial inequality on college campuses.

Researchers must identify how a university's promotion of diversity, equity, and inclusion benefits student learning; they need to focus on the important details of the campus climate, the university's historical trajectory, and other institutional-specific contexts. Without clearly describing how the dynamics of diversity are manifest on an individual campus, researchers will struggle to identify how a university should pursue organizational change to promote equity and inclusion. In this case, generalization beyond a campus is not important, because campus leaders need to avoid applying generic talking points about why racial diversity, equity, and inclusion matter. They must instead talk specifically about the benefits their students, faculty, and staff receive from the university's own efforts. This approach puts more pressure on the leaders to be accountable. It will quickly pull back the curtain on hollow statements of support—the so-called happy diversity talk—without substantive action.[11]

From the examinations of individual universities, we can develop a better understanding of how an institution's particular circumstances matter for creating organizational change in higher education. Although I have noted a large literature that suggest how these changes could be made in higher education, campus leaders and higher education policy makers need to follow specific, not universal, approaches. Because generalized approaches to diversity, equity, and inclusion take the mere talking points of diversity as the full body of information, they reduce a university's capacity for change and its ability to support marginalized students. Sarah Ahmed, Gina Garcia, and James Thomas all note that these general, and frequently essentialized and hollowed-out, perspectives on diversity work become a cover for serious accountability, hiding behind image management as individuals and institutions try to present themselves as "good diversity workers."[12] Researchers nevertheless need to identify commonalities within the broader patterns for similar institutions across a multitude of data to pinpoint what efforts work in specific organizational situations so that we may gain greater traction on the road to racial equity and inclusion in higher education. This approach can also facilitate collaboration among similar institutions. They can share information and other resources to increase the equity and inclusion on their own campuses, given their similar circumstances and potential obstacles to these efforts. Further, this collaborative work could be informative for state higher education agencies and university policy makers looking for more specifics to improve higher education's contribution to communities through equity and inclusion data and dialogue.

While I was finishing this book, the US Department of Justice issued a statement to Yale University about the university's use of race in college admissions reviews.[13] In part, the statement threatened to sue the university if it did not stop considering race, because, the department argued, an analysis of the data about the admissions review found discrimination against white and Asian American students. These arguments against Yale's admissions policies and practices, however, further underscore this book's assertion that the reliance on strict quantification of diversity can be detrimental to equity and inclusion efforts in higher education, even for critics of affirmative action, in which capacity the federal office was operating in this case. The Justice Department's framing of diversity as a measurable component of college admissions contradicts the recommendation that universities treat racial equity and inclusion as a complex and contextual reality of higher education rather than a metric attached to people.

The Justice Department compared Yale's holistic admissions review process, which considers race for all applicants, with the University of Texas at Austin's review process, which only considers race for a secondary pool of applicants after using a percentage plan (see chapter 1).[14] This comparison falsely equates the policies, applicant pools, actual review processes, and contexts of how Supreme Court rulings apply to each institution. Interestingly, the Justice Department argued that "Yale's diversity goals are not sufficiently measurable. Our investigation indicates that Yale's diversity goals appear to be vague, elusory, and amorphous. Yale's use of race appears to be standardless, and Yale does virtually nothing to cabin, limit, or define its use of race during the Yale College admissions process."[15] The catch, however, is by following a dequantification approach to diversity to make it less measurable and expanding what counts as diversity in holistic review, as required under Supreme Court rulings, Yale is blamed for not making diversity more of a fixed, quantitative metric. The Department of Justice's threat to Yale is in line with the faulty belief that diversity as a critical mass means universities must seek a certain proportion of racial and ethnic diversity through college admissions to promote an educational benefits of diversity.[16]

Of course, higher education will continue to face scrutiny for considering race at all in any organizational policy and process, not only in college admissions. Such scrutiny reveals how important race is to the functions of universities as racialized organizations and why college admissions is such a battleground for debates about racial inequality.[17] These lawsuits and critiques also clearly show that institutions cannot rely only on the quantification of diversity, equity, and inclusion to argue why these components are important for student learning. To put it bluntly, neither quantifying nor dequantifying diversity will save you. What will help instead are arguments that are more specific and grounded in careful theoretical frameworks and well-designed research programs, to guide strategic planning in the promotion of the educational benefits of diversity and to reduce the marginalization of some people on campus. Universities cannot separate their arguments for diversity as an educational benefit from their efforts to reduce marginalization and racism on their campuses. Doing so would further entrench diversity, equity, and inclusion efforts as mainly a benefit for white students without creating a more equitable and racism-free environment for students of color. If diversity does matter, then ending racism on campus must be an integral part of those efforts. Universities must expand how they understand racial inequality to exist on their campus as both outcomes and, more importantly, experiences that need to be addressed simultaneously.

Improving Institutional Equity Research

Promoting racial equity and inclusion requires organizational change in institutional efforts at equity research. Institutional research offices, a vital part of evaluating and monitoring diversity, equity, and inclusion, can shape university policy. These offices are often charged with a wide range of data collection, analysis, and reporting responsibilities, which include collecting data on student, faculty, and staff representation and calculating the space of an institution's facilities. These research offices are also responsible for reporting data to the US Department of Education, particularly for its Integrated Postsecondary Education Data System (IPEDS). An important step in improving diversity, equity, and inclusion on campus is to evaluate how we collect data about these aspects of campus life.

As noted in chapter 2, reconsidering the racial and ethnic categories, how they are collected, and how they are interpreted can help campus leaders understand who is on campus and what their experiences are. Universities should work with their institutional research offices to explore different approaches to collect racial and ethnic data that may provide further information about the people working and studying on campus. Similar to the University of California approach that evaluated how the aggregate racial and ethnic categories limited campus leaders' understanding of equity and inclusion issues, many other campuses are also facing similar constraints because of their data-collection approaches. Institutional research offices are important for helping universities identify better data-collection approaches to improve decision-making and policy-making. Rather than going it alone, the offices could work with the central diversity, equity, and inclusion office on campus to explore how data collection and reporting could be improved without perpetuating narrow views of campus groups.

Researchers need to explore an expanded set of racial and ethnic categories carefully and should work with faculty who are experts on issues of race and ethnicity in these efforts. Additionally, universities should conduct focus groups with students, faculty, and staff about their views of different groups, how they are identified, and how this data is used for institutional efforts to uncover any underlying issues that may be hidden by the diversity numbers, however they are constructed. Given that race is socially constructed and fluid in everyday life, qualitative research can provide additional information to help institutional research offices and campus leaders understand that the racial and ethnic categories are messy and will continue to be so. This perspective requires deeper thinking about what this data reveals about a campus before decisions are made and initiatives and policies are created.

Although an expanded set of racial and ethnic categories for data purposes is important in many ways, we should not treat these categories as static, homogenizing markers of who people are or what they experience.[18] For example, once data about a category is collected, campus leaders and researchers must avoid describing the "Black student experience" on their campuses. Black students, among many other marginalized student groups, are not a monolith with singular experiences and needs. Expanding how people identify themselves in studies evaluating and monitoring diversity, equity, and inclusion also requires campus leaders and researchers to change how they interpret this data, that is, to change how they interpret people and their experiences. As higher education scholar Shaun R. Harper has noted in speeches and conversations for many years now, we must remember that "*N* equals people." Stated another way, the numbers we collect and use for research and decision-making are about people's lives. As the groundbreaking work of Du Bois reminds us, racial inequality is not simply an outcome; it's an experience as well.[19] Quantitative data is useful for patterns, and institutional research offices are important for collecting and reporting on these patterns. We need to extend more care in both the collecting and the reporting of racial and ethnic-related data to avoid spreading faulty perspectives about why racial inequalities persist on a campus and to propose solutions that may decrease, rather than increase, such inequalities.

Expanding the capacity of these research offices with staff members charged with focusing on diversity, equity, and inclusion on campus can promote not only additional data collection and reporting but also more care and attention to the nuances of racial inequality and its connections to other social inequalities at universities. Institutional research offices, again, are often given many responsibilities, but too often, mixed-methods research to better inform decision-making and policy-making is not one of them. To support better decisions and policy-making on their campuses, these offices need to integrate qualitative research to investigate the impact of policies beyond quantified metrics. Rather than assume and simply calculate the benefits of a new financial aid policy, for example, we should ask people what happened when it was implemented. The work of higher education scholars Sara Goldrick-Rab and Robert Kelchen describes these ineffective approaches. Campus leaders and higher education policy makers try to create policies that meet someone's calculated financial need, but the policies wind up leaving the student still struggling financially.[20] To learn how and why these policies are ineffective, leaders must discover the other needs that are left unmet for students and that quantitative methods cannot elucidate.

Another approach to increasing the institutional research efforts to promote diversity, equity, and inclusion is to expand the research capacities of central diversity offices and their staff. Central diversity offices, led by a chief diversity officer for the university, are responsible for many aspects of the policies, cocurricular opportunities, and assessment for diversity work. However, these offices seldom have a researcher on staff. Although staff members may hold advanced degrees and have research experience, a full-time researcher could assist with diversity efforts. By analyzing institutional data, conducting interviews and focus groups, examining documents, and doing other research tasks this staff member could explore how the institution could become more equitable and inclusive. This in-house researcher could work closely with the different units around campus to identify potential issues and strengths. By continuing these activities throughout the year, the researcher would overcome the limitation of campus-wide climate analyses conducted only every few years.

Equity researchers in the central diversity and institutional research offices could provide campus leaders with consistent, in-depth information about what is happening on campus. These staff could also coordinate with other units around campus to explore specific diversity-related questions such as how a new ethnic studies requirement is implemented in the general education curriculum, what students are gaining from these courses, and what pedagogical techniques could promote more learning in these course offerings. Additionally, when equity researchers are further incorporated into the university's organization, they could help coordinate the many projects, particularly surveys, that other units are interested in completing so that students, faculty, and staff do not experience "survey fatigue." This coordinating effort could lead to fewer, but more in-depth, projects that help multiple units at once without competing for campus community members' attention and time more than necessary. Thus, the equity researchers could facilitate a wide range of projects that could lead to more effective policies and programs to be implemented while also building in more student, staff, and faculty voice about their needs and experiences on campus.

One way this expansion of institutional equity research efforts can accrue multiple benefits is the opportunity to create buy-in from students through their participation in, and support of, these research endeavors. One avenue of increasing student participation is to ensure that researchers in both units have graduate assistants to work on the projects, write reports, and do other related tasks. Student participation would have two benefits. First, it would increase the experience of future campus leaders as they complete graduate work. Second, it would continuously expose the researchers to new theoretical and methodological perspectives that can enhance their research and increase the likelihood that it will lead universities closer to their equity and inclusion ideals. While many institutions have no graduate programs, undergraduate students bring enthusiasm, ideas, and skills that could support these research efforts as well. Capstone courses that explore specific topics in diversity, equity, and inclusion could be useful and could lead to more student buy-in because the students are part of the process of identifying solutions to ongoing equity and inclusion concerns on their campus.

A similar result is likely if researchers work closely with faculty and staff on issues related to their experiences on campus as well and not limit the focus to students only. This more collaborative and institutionalized, mixed-methods approach to evaluating and monitoring diversity, equity, and inclusion could provide more data than can be obtained from quantitative-only approaches and can consequently create more effective decisions and policies.[21]

Drawbacks of Some Literature on Higher Education Policy

A consistent theme throughout *Behind the Diversity Numbers* is the need for more analysis and explanation of how racial inequality and the processes creating the multiple forms of it in higher education cannot be measured and analyzed by quantitative metrics alone. A popular quantitative group of higher education books provide the hard-and-fast numbers that can guide decision-making and policy-making. A significant strength of these volumes on higher education policy is the large amounts of data they analyze and the clear, straightforward way the results are presented for readers to digest and use to think about important topics in higher education. Most analyses are limited to small groups of variables that help identify the impact of certain policies or experiences during college on a person's academic and social outcomes. This narrow scope is a marker of quantification: simplifying the complexity of the social world into the variables and outcomes that you need to know.[22] Yet, the world is complex, and so are the reasons we have racial inequality throughout higher education. Thus, we must embrace this complexity to demonstrate, for example, that a policy to improve financial aid to meet students' needs must do more than consider a finite amount of student information.

Embracing complexity also requires us to be comfortable with theoretical and methodological approaches that accommodate this complexity and suggest what is still missing from these analyses despite their strengths. Quant-Crit is of these helpful perspectives. One study cannot tell us everything we need to know about a topic, yet the popular, quantitatively focused books on higher education policy are presented as *the* definitive authority on these issues. This attitude is arguably the result of framing quantitative work as more objective, rigorous, and unwavering.[23]

If there were a low-hanging-fruit approach to expanding the discussions of these popular books in higher education literature, it would be to incorporate more qualitative research to add more context to the analyses provided in these books. I don't mean to suggest that after researchers conduct their quantitative modeling, they go out and collect interviews, conduct focus groups, or even complete a year-long ethnography for their projects. There exists a more straightforward approach to deepen these books' conversations and explain why they matter for students, faculty, and staff: simply incorporate more qualitative research to help explain the results you have. Little qualitative research is used in these popular books for theoretical framing or explaining results. They offer instead a truncated explanation that relies solely on the quantitative analyses presented in the book. There is little exploration of more complicated possible solutions suggested by the research for policy-making and decision-making.

As an example of one topic that highlights the glaring omission of, and, some would say, the dire need for, qualitative research is the pernicious discussion of the overmatching and undermatching of students, or the *mismatch hypothesis*.[24] The general argument of this research area is that some students are more prepared for completing a degree at a highly selective institution than other students are, and researchers mostly focus on how this difference perpetuates racial inequality. A student is considered a good match for an institution if their academic profile matches the average student who matriculates at the institution. Focusing on the performance of the student afterward provides a justification, if you will, for why administrators do not want mismatched students. If a student is mismatched, the hypothesis suggests they will either overperform or underperform during college. The general argument follows that an underprepared student admitted to college will have lower grades and a higher likelihood of dropping out than will peers who better match the institutional student profile.[25]

These discussions of the mismatch hypothesis, however, pay little attention to the structural and cultural aspects of colleges as racialized organizations that can influence whether students pursue a particular degree or how well they do in an academic program. Thus, the mismatch hypothesis is under-prepared itself to explain how a smart, hardworking student is considered undermatched. The hypothesis focuses only on individual academic outcomes and not the circumstances that often lead to such outcomes.[26] Furthermore, these arguments are supported by flimsy anecdotes that are ultimately de-bunked by the large qualitative literature that helps explain why we may find such results from quantitative analyses.[27] By incorporating more qualitative research, scholars can provide a more holistic discussion. They can note that their analyses are not the whole story and that other factors are at play. By using more qualitative research to contextualize these numbers, researchers can limit how much students are seen as the problems for racial inequality and can shift the focus to where change is needed most: on the institutions.

Many books on quantitative higher education policy are also limited in their consideration of how such policy suggestions will influence higher edu-cation as a whole. These books overwhelmingly focus both on highly selective institutions that are also the most well-resourced institutions in the nation and on gaining access to those institutions. Even when looking at public universi-ties, these analyses are restricted to exclusive flagship universities. As Barrett Taylor and Brendan Cantwell's examination of higher education institutions shows, the depth of social inequality means we should not focus exclusively on how policies will influence highly selective institutions and ignore their influence on the rest of higher education.[28] Most students will never attend these prestigious universities, and if we want to promote equity and inclusion in higher education, we should center our analyses on the institutions doing most of the work. We should be less concerned with colleges that select stu-dents who are academically successful and who can afford the high price tags once the students are admitted.

Reiterating a key point of chapter 1, the focus on these well-resourced and highly selective institutions as an example of racial inequality and the impact of policies such as considering race in college admissions highlights how or-ganizational processes and policies can solidify racial advantages in higher education. While books on quantitative higher education policy may speak to racial segregation and inequality in a general sense, they overlook how institutions reproduce such outcomes and experiences. Because these books consider this topic to be outside their scope, they ultimately limit the impact these analyses can have on equality and inclusiveness in higher education.

A last area of improvement for books on higher education policy is the need to broaden the scholarship consulted in discussions of racial inequality. Scholars of color are barely cited in these books. This near absence of scholars of color who have created theoretical perspectives, initiatives, and methodological approaches to identify paths to promote diversity, equity, and inclusion could easily be framed as an outright error, not simply a limitation, of this type of higher education literature. It is difficult to argue that you are concerned with racial equity and inclusion in policy discussions when you neglect to include those who experience marginalization and who would be the most affected by the policy suggestions in your analyses. This near omission of scholarship from researchers of color, particularly on discussions of racial equity and inclusion, is not relegated to the quantitative higher education literature; it is a feature of academia writ large and can undercut the contributions of research as well as the careers of researchers.[29] Therefore, we must consider how our work may exclude particular voices and perspectives that are vital to our discussions, in this case, racial equity in higher education, to ensure strong research and to practice equity and inclusion within the research process itself, a cornerstone of academia. Further, as I will discuss, notably absent from common quantitative analyses of higher education policy is how universities influence racial equity off campus in more than individual terms.

Universities as Arbiters of Racial Justice

Authors will often try to present a final chapter or section of their book as an agenda-setting discussion. As noted at the beginning of this chapter, I had an original vision for what this final chapter would include, but the pandemic and resurgent momentum of Black Lives Matter highlight a need for universities to develop their agendas in collaboration with marginalized communities. Too frequently, universities are described as beacons of light and knowledge and contributing a public good, but they also simultaneously hide more insidious actions that reproduce racial inequality in the communities surrounding them.[30] As higher education scholars Adrianna Kezar, Tony Chambers, and John Burkhardt note, universities have increased their focus on revenue generation and the individual benefits of higher education while somewhat reducing their visions of, and initiatives for, broader social benefits and policies.[31] Although the literature frequently discusses the social mobility of individual students who attend different institutions (notably highly selective universities), these discussions still situate higher education as mostly a private good for individuals and their families, but not for communities. We must also ask how arguments for higher education as a public good must critically examine higher education's continued exclusion of marginalized communities, despite the increased diversity on college campuses, and we must identify avenues for racial equity and justice in the future.

Amid the protests following the deaths of George Floyd, Breonna Taylor, and many others, colleges and universities faced new calls and demands for change to address racism of the past and present. Many of these calls built on generations of racial justice activism on campus as well as the wave of student activism after the deaths of Tamir Rice, Trayvon Martin, Sandra Bland, and Michael Brown, among many others. The rise of the Black Lives Matter movement also catalyzed student protests and demands, first at the University of Missouri and then across the nation.[32]

The demands to address racism happening on campuses and maintained by institutions of higher learning came in many forms and even created contentions points in certain disciplines. For example, members of sociology departments are reflecting on how their discipline has perpetuated racial violence against Black communities by promoting policing practices that profile and target marginalized communities. A poignant example of these reflections and calls for change includes the University of Minnesota's Department of Sociology, which educated some of the officers responsible for the murder of Floyd.[33]

Universities are facing the need to confront how pushing for increased student enrollment in high-demand fields such as criminology can contribute to on- and off-campus racial inequality and violence that they are complicit in. In the specific case of Minnesota's sociology program, graduates of the program later become police officers who surveil their former classmates. Looking at enrollment numbers, including increased diversity because of many of these degree programs, and tuition dollars, we must ask whether these high-demand programs contribute to the public good of higher education or are a detriment to the vision of racial equality. In a related matter, campus police forces have grown and can target marginalized communities that may include past, present, and future students.[34] We must ask, how do these programs and features of a university signal how it operates as a racialized organization by restricting opportunities, promoting negative campus climates, and influencing the diversity, equity, and inclusion measured in annual reports?

While working with and in communities, universities must consider how they influence racial inequality beyond educational opportunities. Not all the diversity-related numbers that must be monitored are education-specific. Universities can influence the segregation of their surrounding communities as well. An analysis I conducted with Jacob Rugh examined the evolution of residential segregation around universities since the 1980s.[35] Despite a slight reduction in racial segregation in the United States since the early 1990s, a unique picture exists for college towns. Racial segregation, in general, is lower around colleges and universities than in most other communities around the United States. However, the decline in segregation has somewhat plateaued for college towns since 2000. As higher education is becoming more racially diverse on campus, the communities around universities are not becoming more integrated.

Further, we found that more racial segregation off campus corresponded to less racial diversity among students in later years, a disturbing set of findings, to be sure. Therefore, if we want to measure a university's impact in the community, this quantitative data suggests a troubling relationship. Different directions of university growth, such as real estate, athletics-related business, and even positions on transportation issues, can all provide or cut off opportunities for community members.[36] These opportunities may benefit the university but not the community itself. What's more, when we talk to students about how they understand town-gown race relations, we learn that higher education's troubles have deepened. As higher education scholar Amalia Dache notes, the strong connection between college students and the surrounding community in light of movements against racial violence means that students are not simply demanding change on campus; they are demanding that their institutions be more accountable, equitable, and just in their relationships off campus as well.[37]

Universities must increase their interactions with communities, and students are often the best people to work with to increase racial equity on and off campuses. Students know, and have experiences with, both spaces. Student input is one way campus leaders can learn the context behind diversity numbers to better guide their interpretations, policies, and other decisions. These decisions have far-reaching ramifications, even if these consequences are not initially recognized by campus leaders and policy makers. However, the work of student activists, the rhetoric of institutional transformation, and anti-racist practices must not be co-opted and effectively watered down. [38] Doing so could undercut trust among students and communities; weaken needed organizational changes, including the many campus diversity initiatives promised after student demands; and ultimately increase racial inequality. Additionally, co-opting student-initiated efforts wrongly suggests that students are responsible for creating the change on campus and that campus leaders are absolved of responsibility and accountability for making their campuses more equitable.

Throughout history, and in recent waves of student antiracism activism in particular, students consistently pinpoint the depth of racism on and off campus for campus leaders to address. University leaders must understand that they have been given a roadmap for implementing racial equity and justice; they cannot ignore students and reduce student actions as those of "wayward youth."[39] In light of student demands, universities may want to show that they are increasing their diversity, equity, and inclusion efforts. For example, they could explain how they have increased the number of ethnic studies courses, have added such courses to curriculum requirements, have hired new faculty or staff of color, and have created new budgets for doing such work. Although these are all important areas to develop, analyze, and report on, such efforts can easily fall prey to the reductionist pitfalls described throughout this book. Universities must beware of simply showing the right numbers and performing "good diversity work" without doing much good with the work.

It would be disingenuous to say diversity, equity, and inclusion are easy tasks, among the many more that are needed of our universities, but they are not supposed to be easy. Because race is embedded in the very fabric of higher education, it complicates how campus leaders, faculty, staff, and students understand and navigate racial inequality in their everyday lives. Creating change this important requires difficult work now and for generations. If universities are to be arbiters of public goods, then they must also be arbiters of racial justice. There is no wavering on this front; we must be truly committed to diversity, equity, and inclusion but, more critically, committed to the necessary work of antiracism. On this path to organizational change, we must not view our progress in narrow, linear ways that quantification and common scholarly and popular perspectives support.[40] There will be fits and starts, and unfortunate regression, for colleges and universities on this path toward equity, inclusion, and justice. In today's renewed calls for antiracism, we must not solely focus on individual changes. We must, above all, pursue organizational and policy changes for lasting impacts. People come and go, but as witnessed with the long history of racial inequity and injustice behind the evolving diversity in higher education, racialized organizations can last forever.[41]

We must work diligently to create organizational and policy changes so that we can remake higher education to the ideals we hold true. Just as there was a failure on a massive scale to address the COVID-19 pandemic throughout 2020, there has also been a continued failure to hear and take up the racial justice demands that emerged in late spring of that year. Universities were again a battleground for societal changes, and like generations past, we have witnessed slow change on some campuses, significant progressive feats on others, and little change for still others, as the demands by students and community members for addressing racial injustice on and off campus fell into the institutional void. Quantification can be part of the solutions but also part of the barriers to these efforts. At the core of what needs to change is how our colleges and universities hold fast to race and racism but take little responsibility for racial inequality. Regardless of how we measure this inequality, allowing our institutions to continue absolving themselves while they crush and erase people's dreams will only have us faulting each other. We will perhaps wind up echoing arguments in the *Students for Fair Admissions, Inc. v. President and Fellows of Harvard College* case, asserting that we simply need to adjust our statistical models rather than change the larger organizations we hold dear. Until we are willing to challenge where, how, and why we work in higher education, we will continue to be surrounded by racial inequality and will remain ignorant about how we can change that reality now and in the future.

APPENDIX

Methodology for Examining Campus Climate Research

EXAMINING THE WIDE RANGE of campus climate research published over the decades can impose a monumental task for anyone, and a clear understanding of how this research area evolved requires a series of methodological decisions. This research area is pivotal to careers, court cases, leadership models, and campus initiatives, and most importantly, it shapes lives beyond formal education. Moreover, the research on campus racial climates is what propelled me to pursue graduate school and the work that has formed my career to this point. All of this is to say that an analysis of the campus climate literature is critical beyond the research endeavor itself. An analysis helps reveal how this research, an area that I have now been connected with for nearly twenty years, can move closer toward its ideals of making educational environments more diverse, equitable, and inclusive. Thus, the content analysis that formed the core of chapter 3 tries to document the details of an evolving research area central to equity efforts in higher education, even as the implications of these efforts changed over time.

Theoretical Frameworks as Coding Schemes

The research on race and campus climates in higher education is, simply put, vast. To clarify how I was to eventually code articles for what features of the campus climate they explored, I needed to establish a coding scheme focused on the core components of the research area in light of the many extensions of campus climate research that have developed over the years. This coding scheme was no straightforward task. Nor did it get easier after I decided what constituted the pertinent features of campus climates. A series of stops and re-starts, although frustrating at the time, were unavoidable as I continued with the analysis. I had to refine how I was examining race-related campus climate research in general and coding articles to document this area in particular.

To solidify my coding scheme, I sought a theoretical framework to guide the development of codes to explore campus climate research. The approach was similar to using critical race theory by Nolan Cabrera and María Ledesma as a guiding framework for their recent content analyses.[1] To base my cod-ing on the literature and to examine the evolution of race-related campus climate research, I turned to the Multi-contextual Model for Diverse Learn-ing Environments (MMDLE), led by Sylvia Hurtado and developed with her colleagues since the 1990s, as the guiding framework for a coding scheme.[2]

Utilizing this model serves two main purposes. First, the MMDLE has been developed through an ongoing synthesis of existing literature. The model aims to draw theoretical and empirical connections between how campus cli-mates operate as part of a diverse learning environment and how they can lead to various student academic and social outcomes. Therefore, using the MMDLE as the foundation for a coding scheme on campus climates means the scheme would be solidly connected to the literature. Second, if a central goal of campus climate research is to promote organizational change in higher educa-tion, the theoretical framework relied on for the coding scheme must contain specific features aligned with organizational policies and processes. The model includes an organizational dimension, which allows for different analyses to identify to what extent higher education researchers are including features of this dimension in their research. Results from analyses of the organizational dimension can also influence campus leaders' and policy makers' decisions on how to promote diversity, equity, and inclusion in higher education.[3]

The model specifies four dimensions of campus climates: organizational, compositional, behavioral, and psychological. It also specifies broader external forces to examine the sociohistorical, government, and policy contexts that can influence campus climates. Using Hurtado and colleagues' iterations of the MMDLE, I derived key features that fall under each of the four dimensions and external forces.[4] I then expanded the campus climate dimensions by identifying other important items from several analyses. I used Shaun Harper and Sylvia Hurtado's nine themes of campus climate research at that time point and Nicholas Bowman's themes of diversity experiences influencing student cognitive development. I also incorporated Nida Denson's curricular and cocurricular diversity experiences influencing racial bias among students. Finally, I used Hurtado and colleagues' analysis of campus climate assessments, particularly their seven identified components of such assessments and four related student outcomes.[5]

Given how the bridging capacity of people's perceptions of the campus climate connect the behavioral and psychological dimensions, I separated this item from the behavior or psychological dimension and established, as its own category, the *bridging dimension* of campus climates (see chapter 3 for more details).[6] This approach to base a coding scheme on the theoretical framework of the MMDLE and related research established the external forces, five internal dimensions, and twenty-eight campus climate features to use when I coded each journal article selected from the pertinent literature. As noted below, one item (activism) was prominent in recent research but had not been fully captured in the model; activism was included in the final list of twenty-eight campus climate features. Table A.1 provides an overview of each campus climate feature that was coded for by the MMDLE dimensions along with the "bridging dimension" that I separated from the behavioral and psychological dimensions (described further in chapter 3).

Data Sources

As noted in chapter 3, the direction of campus climate research arguably split in the early 1990s as researchers gave particular attention to race-related features of campuses and how these features affected student academic and social outcomes. Many of these studies, buoyed by ongoing litigation around

TABLE A. I *Campus climate dimensions and related features included for coding*

External forces	Psychological dimension
Sociohistorical contexts	Social identities
Access (affirmative action)	Sense of belonging
Access (financial)	Validation
Attainment policies	Stereotype threat
Community relations	Implicit/unconscious biases
	Racial attitudes/prejudice

Organizational dimension	Behavioral dimension
Historical inclusion/exclusion	Microaggressions
Institutional policies	Discrimination
Academic support initiatives	Intergroup contact/relations
Cocurricular initiatives	Pedagogical practices
Curricular initiatives	Student affairs practices
Safe-spaces initiatives	Activism
Interdisciplinary learning initiatives	

Compositional dimension	Bridging dimension
Student diversity	Perceptions of campus climate
Faculty diversity	
Staff/administration diversity	

race-conscious admissions policies, formed the core of campus climate research today. To examine this research area, I limited my collection of journal articles to those published from 1992 to 2019. The starting year marks the year that Hurtado published her groundbreaking article on the initial theory and empirical analyses of the campus racial climate.[7] As just mentioned, not long after this key article was published, campus climate research saw a split, with scholars focusing more on race than on gender; gender had been a central feature in campus climate literature in the 1980s, after the work of Roberta Hall and Bernice Sandler was published.[8] The endpoint of my analysis, 2019, marks the year this book was being written.

This nearly thirty-year period that I analyzed witnessed many changes in higher education and society as a whole, including multiple affirmative action cases; the election and reelection of the first Black US president, Barack Obama; the resurgence of racial justice movements such as Black Lives Matter; and, concurrently, the growth of white supremacists movements. These external features of society can shape what occurs on campuses. Universities do not exist in a vacuum, and the MMDLE specifically notes the importance of such external pressures as these on campus climates.[9]

Although theoretical contributions to campus climate research are important, I was most interested in exploring how researchers examine features of campus climates in their studies. If we hold data-informed decision-making as a strong marker for serious diversity, equity, and inclusion work in higher education, then focusing specifically on empirical articles can help us identify what areas of campus climates not only are studied, but also have proposed changes to guide campus leaders' efforts. If researchers study one campus climate feature more than they study another, then we would expect more implications around the studied feature. Empirical articles can give us a window in the justifications given for certain equity efforts on college campuses.

As mentioned previously, the campus climate literature is quite expansive. A quick search through Google Scholar for articles on race and campus climates returns nearly twenty thousand results. While these results are not solely empirical articles, this quick window into the research literature suggests the importance of narrowing the sampling approach to empirical articles in journals known for higher education research. In the current study, I chose thirteen peer-reviewed journals to collect empirical articles published from 1992 to 2019 and journals known for their prominence among higher education scholars. Seven of these journals were examined by Harper in his analysis of how scholars minimize racism in higher education, and the remaining six journals I added to capture as wide of swath of campus climate research as possible.[10] Here are the journals from which I collected articles:

American Educational Research Journal
American Journal of Education
Community College Journal of Research and Practice (formerly *Community Junior College Research Quarterly of Research and Practice*)
Community College Review
Educational Researcher
Equity & Excellence in Education
Journal of College Student Development
Journal of Diversity in Higher Education
Journal of Higher Education

Journal of Student Affairs Research and Practice (formerly *NASPA Journal*)
Research in Higher Education
Review of Higher Education
Sociology of Education

Literature searches were conducted in Google Scholar for each journal, which I have used successfully in previous studies, given its comprehensive collection of publications that are often omitted in other databases.[11] Additionally, unlike biomedical science publications, which can be searched with Medical Subject Headings numbers or structured keywords across journals, the higher education and social science literature does not allow for a similar search approach to identify all possible articles on campus climates. Thus, a broad string of search terms was used to capture the breadth of race-related campus climate studies: "campus climate" and "race" or "racial" or "diverse" or "diversity" or "ethnic" or "ethnicity" or "campus racial climate".

The preceding search allowed for an identical algorithm to be used across each journal. I could change the search approach slightly when relying on individual journals' website search engines. This search retrieved approximately 1,196 possible publications for inclusion in the current study. From this initial search, I screened the identified articles to ensure that only articles in the thirteen specified journals were included. Some of the initial results included journals that had similar names such as *British Journal of Sociology of Education* or *Research in the Sociology of Education* instead of *Sociology of Education*. This initial screening also eliminated articles that may have been reprinted in another issue of a journal. At this stage of data collection, I decided to keep articles that were published online but were not given a specific volume or issue number for a journal (i.e., forthcoming). These articles are just as accessible as are other published articles that assigned specific journal issues. I also verified that each article was published and available on journal websites. After this first round of screening, I was left with 977 articles. Table A.2 provides an overview of the number of articles kept and the percentage of the initial sample. Overall, 81.7 percent of articles were kept at this stage.

In the second stage of data collection, I screened the 977 articles for their relevance to race and campus climates. Because an article that only tangentially mentions "campus climates" or "race" or both would be captured in

TABLE A.2 *Search results and initial screening of journal articles on race-related campus climate, 1992–2019*

JOURNAL	SEARCH RESULTS	INITIAL SAMPLE	% RETAINED
American Educational Research Journal	26	25	96.2
American Journal of Education	7	7	100.0
Community College Journal of Research and Practice	72	70	97.2
Community College Review	33	27	81.8
Educational Researcher	11	8	72.7
Equity & Excellence in Education	47	43	91.5
Journal of College Student Development	243	208	85.6
Journal of Diversity in Higher Education	156	147	94.2
Journal of Higher Education	165	90	54.6
Journal of Student Affairs Research and Practice	168	143	85.1
Research in Higher Education	111	96	86.5
Review of Higher Education	145	107	73.8
Sociology of Education	12	6	50.0
Total	1,196	977	81.7

searches for possible articles, the screening helped reduce the number of articles included for further examination. In some cases, articles would discuss race only as a variable in an analysis without further explaining the findings or relating them to campus climates. In many other cases, race and campus climate were noted in the titles of material included in the articles' reference section. By culling these articles from the sample, I cut the total number of eligible articles for inclusion by quite a bit. Table A.3 shows that 613 articles, or 62.7 percent of the initial sample, were identified as relevant articles about race and campus climate. In the third and final stage of screening the data, I identified only the empirical articles, that is, those that documented a study. Studies could be quantitative, qualitative, or a mix of methods. Table A.4 provides an overview of the number and percentage of empirical articles were

TABLE A.3 *Journal articles included in the analysis after screening for relevant race and campus climate content*

JOURNAL	INITIAL SAMPLE	RELEVANT SAMPLE	% RETAINED
American Educational Research Journal	25	17	68.0
American Journal of Education	7	5	71.4
Community College Journal of Research and Practice	70	28	40.0
Community College Review	27	13	48.2
Educational Researcher	8	7	87.5
Equity & Excellence in Education	43	32	74.4
Journal of College Student Development	208	122	58.7
Journal of Diversity in Higher Education	147	119	81.0
Journal of Higher Education	90	61	67.8
Journal of Student Affairs Research and Practice	143	69	48.3
Research in Higher Education	96	58	60.4
Review of Higher Education	107	78	72.9
Sociology of Education	6	4	66.7
Total	977	613	62.7

found for each journal. This empirical sample, then was retained for coding and analyses. Overall, 91.0 percent of articles in the original sample of relevant race-related campus climate articles were retained for the study.

Analysis

As noted above, I used a scheme built around the MMDLE and related research on campus climates to code the articles.[12] To identify the campus climate features included in a study, I only read the methodology and results sections of the empirical articles included in the study. While it could be argued that a full reading of an article is necessary to gain a better sense of how researchers discussed their studies in relation to the larger campus climate literature, similar to higher education scholar Marc Johnston-Guerrero's ex-

TABLE A.4 *Journal articles included in the final sample after screening for empirical content*

JOURNAL	RELEVANT SAMPLE	EMPIRICAL SAMPLE	% RETAINED
American Educational Research Journal	17	16	94.1
American Journal of Education	5	5	100.0
Community College Journal of Research and Practice	28	26	92.9
Community College Review	13	12	92.3
Educational Researcher	7	1	14.3
Equity & Excellence in Education	32	28	87.5
Journal of College Student Development	122	111	90.9
Journal of Diversity in Higher Education	119	110	92.4
Journal of Higher Education	61	58	95.1
Journal of Student Affairs Research and Practice	69	65	94.2
Research in Higher Education	58	57	98.3
Review of Higher Education	78	65	83.3
Sociology of Education	4	4	100.0
Total	613	558	91.0

amination of researchers' use of race in their methodologies, I am most interested in how the researchers chose to study campus climates and what features of the climates they studied.[13] This information corresponds closely with the implications that researchers may derive from their work and what campus leaders and policy makers may use for decision-making and policy-making.

Using a method similar to that of previous studies, I used a multiple-iteration, line-by-line reading approach that allowed for constant consideration of the content within and across articles to refine coding of the campus climate items that form the dimensions at the core of the MMDLE.[14] I selected a small set of ten articles from the final sample spanning the same twenty-seven years and journals of this study to see if the coding scheme might need any changes before I coded all the articles in the sample. For example, microaggressions are an integral part of campus climate research today, but they were not studied in the early 1990s. Although the most recent iteration of the MMDLE does include a discussion of microaggressions, older iterations of the model do not. Researchers therefore need to identify any changes between versions of the model.[15] For example, I added activism as a behavioral dimension item because of the recent research on activism after the resurgence of racial justice movements on and off campus.

For each campus climate item, articles were identified as having substantively examined an item or not (1= yes; 0 = no). I took this approach rather than counting the total number of mentions in an article because of the expected repetition of some discussions around central campus climate items. Although I am the sole author and researcher of the study and am responsible for all the coding in it, I frequently discussed my approach with colleagues knowledgeable in the field of higher education and sociology, particularly those who are engaged in, or have conducted, content analyses. These conversations provided a much-needed perspective on how to clearly identify relationships among campus climate features and better interpret what those relationships mean for organizational change.

To examine how researchers studied campus climates, I coded each article according to its methodology. I identified whether the article was quantitative or qualitative or used mixed methods. I identified what populations were included as respondents in a study (e.g., undergraduate students, graduate students, faculty members, staff members, administrators, other, or multiple groups), when applicable. I coded for whether the article included anywhere in the text a definition of, or theoretical framework for, campus climates (1= yes; 0 = no). For articles that did include a definition or framework, I extracted this part of the article text for further analysis. I also documented the detailed methods that fell under each of the three main methodological approaches, the number of campuses included in the study, and the number of respondents in the study, if applicable. I did not, however, analyze this data in the current study.

In addition to the main task of examining what dimensions, forces, and related features researchers included in their studies and their methodological approach, I collected author and publication information. For each article, I included in the data set the year the article was published, the journal title, the lead author's name and institutional affiliation at the time of publication, any coauthors' names and institutional affiliations, and the article title and abstract.

Once all the coding was finalized, I calculated descriptive statistics to summarize the methodological approaches taken and campus climate dimensions, forces, and features examined in all 558 empirical articles. I created scales for each campus climate dimension by totaling the number of features under each dimension. Then, I conducted means comparisons (*t*-tests) to compare quantitative, qualitative, and mixed-methods studies for their inclusion of an explicit definition or theoretical framework of campus climates as well as the campus climate dimensions, forces, and related features. Given the multiple comparisons and chance for false positives, I applied the Bonferroni correction to provide a more conservative estimate of possible differences between each method. I also created bar graphs to plot the changes in methodological approaches to race-related campus climate research over time. I plotted a difference score between quantitative and qualitative studies for their use of each campus climate dimension over time to identify possible convergence or divergence between the methodological approaches. The difference score was calculated using the average number of dimension features included in each methodological form of study. The difference score was created by subtracting the qualitative average from the quantitative average. A score of zero would indicate that quantitative and qualitative research on race and campus climates included a dimension equally in the studies for that period. Positive scores indicate that quantitative studies focused more on a dimension than did qualitative studies, while negative scores indicate the opposite, that qualitative studies focused more on a dimension.

To explore how much race-related campus climate research incorporates the organizational dimension of the MMDLE, I ran two groups of regression analyses to examine what factors are related to the inclusion of more organizational features in a study. The organizational dimension can catalyze institutional transformation for diversity, equity, and inclusion. In the first group of regressions, the number of organizational dimension features was the dependent variable. The first model contained the other campus climate dimensions, including bridging perceptions, along with variables denoting whether the article contained an explicit definition of campus climates, whether it utilized data collected from undergraduate students, and the year of the article was published.

Two additional models were tested; they included the same variables as the first but also included interaction terms whereby two variables are multiplied together between the psychological and behavioral dimensions with bridging perceptions of campus climates, given their close relationship. The second model included the interaction term between the psychological dimension and bridging perceptions, and the third model included the interaction term between the behavioral dimension and bridging perceptions of campus climates.

The second group of multivariate analyses explored how focusing on more individual- and small group-level initiatives and outcomes that are aligned with the behavioral and psychological dimensions may pull research away from the organizational dimension of campus climates. In so doing, these focuses could curtail institutional transformation down the road. For the dependent variables in these models, I constructed two difference scores between three dimensions: organizational, behavioral, and psychological. One score compared the organizational and psychological dimensions, and the other compared the organizational and behavioral dimensions. For the first difference score, I subtracted the number of psychological dimension features from the total number of organizational dimension features for each article. A positive score suggested that an article incorporated more organizational features in the study, while a negative score means more psychological features. I used a similar process for the second score, subtracting the number of behavioral features from the number of organizational features.

The first model utilizing these two scores examined changes in each difference score with variables for the other campus climate dimensions and bridging perceptions and related article information, including the year of publication. The second model examined changes in each difference score with an interaction term with bridging perceptions included; in the organizational-psychological difference score analysis, the interaction term was between campus climate perceptions and the behavioral dimension, and in the organizational-behavioral difference score model, the interaction term was between campus climate perceptions and the psychological dimension. These interaction terms can help clarify how campus climate perceptions connect to each dimension and shift researchers' work away from the organizational dimension.

Notes

Introduction

1. Eric Hoover, "Dueling Economists: Rival Analyses of Harvard's Admissions Process Emerge at Trial," *Chronicle of Higher Education*, October 30, 2018, https://www.chronicle.com/article/Dueling-Economists-Rival/244964?cid=wcontentgrid.
2. Eric Hoover, "At Harvard Trial, Statistics Give Way to Personal Stories About Diversity," *Chronicle of Higher Education*, October 29, 2018, https://www.chronicle.com/article/At-Harvard-Trial-Statistics/244957?cid=cp229.
3. Benjamin Baez, "The 'Knowledge of Difference' and the Limits of Science," *Journal of Higher Education* 75, no. 3 (2004): 285–306; Victor E. Ray, "A Theory of Racialized Organizations," *American Sociological Review* 84, no. 1 (2019): 26–53.
4. Wendy N. Espeland, and Michael Sauder, *Engines of Anxiety: Academic Rankings, Reputation, and Accountability* (New York: Russell Sage, 2016).
5. Ray, "Theory of Racialized Organizations."
6. Roger Geiger, *The History of American Higher Education: Learning and Culture from the Founding of World War II* (Princeton, NJ: Princeton University Press, 2016); David F. Labaree, *A Perfect Mess: The Unlikely Ascendancy of American Higher Education* (Chicago: University of Chicago Press, 2016); John R. Thelin, *A History of American Higher Education*, 3rd ed. (Baltimore: Johns Hopkins University Press, 2019).
7. Leslie M. Harris, James T. Campbell, and Alfred L. Brophy, eds., *Slavery and the University: Histories and Legacies* (Athens: University of Georgia Press, 2019); Craig Steven Wilder, *Ebony & Ivy: Race, Slavery, and the Troubled History of America's Universities* (New York: Bloomsbury Press, 2013).
8. Joseph L. Graves Jr., *The Emperor's New Clothes: Biological Theories of Race at the New Millennium* (New Brunswick, NJ: Rutgers University Press, 2001); Dorothy Roberts, *Fatal Invention: How Science, Politics, and Big Business Re-create Race in the Twenty-First Century* (New York: New Press, 2011); Audrey Smedley and Brian D. Smedley, *Race in North America: Origin and Evolution of a Concept*, 4th ed. (Boulder, CO: Westview, 2011); Harriet A. Washington, *Medical Apartheid: The Dark History of Medical Experimentation on Black Americans form Colonial Times to the Present* (New York: Anchor Books, 2006); Tukufu Zuberi, *Thicker than Blood: How Racial Statistics Lie* (Minneapolis: University of Minnesota Press, 2001).
9. Thelin, *History of American Higher Education*.

10. Christi M. Smith, *Reparation and Reconciliation: The Rise and Fall of Integrated Higher Education* (Chapel Hill: University of North Carolina Press, 2016).

11. James D. Anderson, *The Education of Blacks in the South, 1860–1935* (Chapel Hill: University of North Carolina Press, 1988); Thelin, *History of American Higher Education*.

12. See Clifton Conrad and Mary Beth Gasman, *Enacting a Diverse Nation: Lessons from Minority-Serving Institutions* (Cambridge, MA: Harvard University Press, 2015).

13. William G. Bowen, Martin A. Kurzweil, and Eugene M. Tobin, *Equity and Excellence in American Higher Education* (Charlottesville: University of Virginia Press, 2005); Thelin, *History of American Higher Education*.

14. Jerome Karabel, *The Chosen: The Hidden History of Admission and Exclusion at Harvard, Yale, and Princeton* (New York: Houghton Mifflin Company, 2005); Nicholas Leman, *The Big Test: The Secret History of the American Meritocracy* (New York: Farrar, Straus, and Giroux, 1999); Joseph Soares, *The Power of Privilege: Yale and America's Elite Colleges* (Stanford, CA: Stanford University Press, 2007).

15. Graves, *The Emperor's New Clothes*; Roberts, *Fatal Invention*; Smedley and Smedley, *Race in North America*; Wilder, *Ebony & Ivy*; Zuberi, *Thicker than Blood*.

16. Sigal Alon, *Race, Class, and Affirmative Action* (New York: Russell Sage Foundation, 2015); William G. Bowen and Derek Bok, *The Shape of the River: Long-Term Consequences of Considering Race in College and University Admissions* (Princeton, NJ: Princeton University Press, 1998); Bowen, Kurzweil, and Tobin, *Equity and Excellence in American Higher Education*; Thomas J. Espenshade and Alexandria Walton Radford, *No Longer Separate, Not Yet Equal: Race and Class in Elite College Admissions and Campus Life* (Princeton, NJ: Princeton University Press, 2009); Jeffrey S. Lehman, "The Evolving Language of Diversity and Integration in Discussions of Affirmative Action from *Bakke* to *Grutter*," in *Defending Diversity: Affirmative Action at the University of Michigan*, ed. P. Gurin, J. S. Lehman, and E. Lewis (Ann Arbor: University of Michigan Press, 2004), 61–96; Lisa M. Stulberg and Anthony S. Chen, "The Origins of Race-Conscious Affirmative Action in Undergraduate Admissions: A Comparative Analysis of Institutional Change in Higher Education," *Sociology of Education* 87, no. 1 (2014): 36–52; Thelin, *History of American Higher Education*.

17. Martha Biondi, *Black Revolution on Campus* (Berkeley: University of California Press, 2012); Stefan M. Bradley, *Upending the Ivory Tower: Civil Rights, Black Power, and the Ivy League* (New York: New York University Press, 2018); Stefan M. Bradley, *Harlem vs. Columbia University: Black Student Power in the 1960s* (Urbana: University of Illinois Press, 2009); Ibram Kendi [Ibram Rogers], *The Black Campus Movement: Black Students and the Racial Reconstitution of Higher Education, 1965–1972* (New York: Palgram Macmillan, 2012); Fabio Rojas, *From Black Power to Black Studies: How a Radical Social Movement Became an Academic Discipline* (Baltimore: Johns Hopkins University Press, 2007); Joy Ann Williamson, *Black Power on Campus: The University of Illinois, 1965–1975* (Urbana: University of Illinois Press, 2003).

18. See Marvin W. Peterson, Robert T. Blackburn, Zelda F. Gamson, Carlos H. Arce, and Roselle W. Davenport, *Black Students on White Campuses: The Impacts of Increased Black Enrollments* (Ann Arbor: University of Michigan Institute for Social Research, 1978), for a case study of the University of Michigan.

19. Alon, *Race, Class, and Affirmative Action*; Bowen and Bok, *Shape of the River*; Bowen, Kurzweil, and Tobin, *Equity and Excellence in American Higher Education*; Lehman, "Evolving Language of Diversity and Integration"; Scott R. Palmer, "Diversity and Affirmative Action: Evolving Principles and Continuing Legal Battles," in *Diversity Chal-*

lenged: Evidence on the Impact of Affirmative Action., ed. G. Orfield (Cambridge, MA: The Civil Rights Project, 2001), 81–88.

20. Baez, "'Knowledge of Difference'"; Mitchell J. Chang, Daria Witt, James Jones, and Kenji Hakuta, eds., *Compelling Interest: Examining the Racial Dynamics in Colleges and Universities* (Stanford, CA: Stanford University Press, 2003); Patricia Gurin, Jeffrey S. Lehman, and Earl Lewis, *Defending Diversity: Affirmative Action at the University of Michigan* (Ann Arbor: University of Michigan Press, 2004); Patricia Gurin, Eric L. Dey, Sylvia Hurtado, and Gerald Gurin, "Diversity and Higher Education: Theory and Impact on Educational Outcomes," *Harvard Educational Review* 72, no. 3 (2002): 330–366; Sylvia Hurtado, Jeffrey Milem, Alma Clayton-Pedersen, and Walter Allen, "Enacting Diverse Learning Environments: Improving the Climate for Racial/Ethnic Diversity in Higher Education," ASHE-ERIC Higher Education Report, vol. 26, no. 8 (Washington, DC: George Washington University, 1999); Gary Orfield, ed., *Diversity Challenged: Evidence on the Impact of Affirmative Action* (Cambridge, MA: The Civil Rights Project, 2001); Daryl G. Smith, "The Diversity Imperative: Moving to the Next Generation," in *American Higher Education in the Twenty-First Century: Social, Political, and Economic Challenges*, ed. Michael N. Bastedo, P. G. Altbach, and P. J. Gumport (Baltimore: Johns Hopkins University Press, 2016), 375–400; Daryl G. Smith, *Diversity Works: The Emerging Picture of How Students Benefit* (Washington, DC: Association of American Colleges and Universities, 1997).

21. See Baez, "'Knowledge of Difference'"; Ellen Berrey, *The Enigma of Diversity: The Language and the Limits of Racial Justice* (Chicago: University of Chicago Press, 2015); W. Carson Byrd, *Poison in the Ivy: Race Relations and the Reproduction of Inequality on Elite College Campuses* (New Brunswick, NJ: Rutgers University Press, 2017); W. Carson Byrd, "College Diversity Is (but Doesn't Have to Be) for Whites," *Contexts* 14, no. 3 (2015): 74–75.

22. Bowen, Kurzweil, and Tobin, *Equity and Excellence in American Higher Education*; Soares, *Power of Privilege*; Thelin, *History of American Higher Education*; Wilder, *Ebony & Ivy*.

23. Michael Omi and Howard Winant, *Racial Formation in the United States*, 3rd ed. (New York: Routledge, 2015).

24. Ray, "Theory of Racialized Organizations."

25. Eduardo Bonilla-Silva, "The Invisible Weight of Whiteness: The Racial Grammar of Everyday Life in Contemporary America," *Ethnic & Racial Studies* 35, no. 2 (2012): 173–194.

26. Bonilla-Silva, "The Invisible Weight of Whiteness"; Ray, "Theory of Racialized Organizations."

27. Gina Garcia, *Becoming Hispanic Serving Institutions: Opportunities for Colleges and Universities* (Baltimore: Johns Hopkins University Press, 2019).

28. Joe R. Feagin, Hernan Vera, and Nikitah Imani, *The Agony of Education: Black Students at White Universities* (New York: Routledge, 1996); Wendy L. Moore, *Reproducing Racism: White Space, Elite Law Schools, and Racial Inequality* (Lanham, MD: Rowman & Littlefield 2008); Kristen A. Myers, *Racetalk: Racism Hiding in Plain Sight* (Lanham, MD: Rowman and Littlefield, 2005); Leslie H. Picca, and Joe R. Feagin, *Two-Faced Racism: Whites in the Backstage and Frontstage* (Lanham, MD: Rowman & Littlefield, 2007); Ray, "Theory of Racialized Organizations"; Melissa E. Wooten, *In the Face of Inequality: How Black Colleges Adapt* (Albany: State University of New York Press, 2015).

29. See Walter R. Allen and Joseph O. Jewell, "A Backward Glance Forward: Past, Present, and Future Perspectives of Historically Black Colleges and Universities," *Review*

of Higher Education 25, no. 3 (2002): 241–261; Anderson, *Education of Blacks in the South*; Conrad and Gasman, *Enacting a Diverse Nation*; Darrick Hamilton and William A. Darity Jr., "The Political Economy of Education, Financial Literacy, and the Racial Wealth Gap," *Federal Reserve Bank of St. Louis Review* 99, no. 1 (2017): 59–76; Aldon Morris, *The Scholar Denied: W. E. B. Du Bois and the Birth of Modern Sociology* (Berkeley: University of California Press, 2015); Wooten, *In the Face of Inequality*; Melissa E. Wooten and Lucius Couloute, "The Production of Racial Inequality Within and Among Institutions," *Sociology Compass* 11, no. 1 (2017), DOI: https://doi.org/10.1111/soc4.12446.

30. See Matthew W. Hughey, *White Bound: Nationalists, Antiracists, and the Shared Meanings of Race* (Stanford, CA: Stanford University Press, 2012); Amanda E. Lewis, "'What Group?' Studying Whites and Whiteness in the Era of 'Color-Blindness,'" *Sociological Theory* 22, no. 4 (2004): 623–646, for specific discussions of whiteness operating at an individual level.

31. Ray, "Theory of Racialized Organizations," 35.

32. Ray, 35.

33. Ray, 31; also Paul DiMaggio, "Culture and Cognition," *Annual Review of Sociology* 23 (1997): 263–287.

34. Ray, 27; William H. Sewell, "A Theory of Structure: Duality, Agency, and Transformation" *American Journal of Sociology* 98, no. 1 (1992): 1–29.

35. Cassandra M. Guarino and Victor M. H. Borden, "Faculty Service Loads and Gender: Are Women Taking Care of the Academic Family?" *Research in Higher Education* 58, no. 6 (2017): 672–694; Gabriella M. Gutiérrez, Yolanda F. Niemann, Carmen G. González, and Angela P. Harris, eds., *Presumed Incompetent: The Intersections of Race and Class for Women in Academia* (Boulder: University Press of Colorado, 2012); Audrey Williams June, "The Invisible Labor of Minority Faculty," *Chronicle of Higher Education*, November 8, 2015, https://www.chronicle.com/article/The-Invisible-Labor-of/234098; Patricia Matthew, ed., *Written/Unwritten: Diversity and the Hidden Truths of Tenure* (Chapel Hill: University of North Carolina Press, 2016); Patricia Matthew, "What Is Faculty Diversity Worth to a University?" *The Atlantic*, November 23, 2016, https://www.theatlantic.com/education/archive/2016/11/what-is-faculty-diversity-worth-to-a-university/508334; Bedelia N. Richards, "Faculty Assessments as Tools of Oppression: A Black Woman's Reflection on Colorblind Racism in the Academy," in *Intersectionality and Higher Education: Identity and Inequality on College Campuses*, ed. W. Carson Byrd, R. J. Brunn-Bevel, and S. M. Ovink (New Brunswick: Rutgers University Press, 2019), 136–151.

36. Gloria Ladson-Billings, *Beyond the Big House: African American Educators on Teacher Education* (New York: Teachers College Press, 2005).

37. Eduardo Bonilla-Silva, *Racism Without Racists: Color-Blind Racism and the Persistence of Racial Inequality in the United States*, Fifth Edition (Lanham, MD: Rowman & Littlefield, 2017); Eduardo Bonilla-Silva, "Rethinking Racism: Toward a Structural Interpretation," *American Sociological Review* 62, no. 3 (1997): 465–480; Ray, "Theory of Racialized Organizations."

38. Lawrence D. Bobo, Camille Z. Charles, Maria Krysan, and Alicia D. Simmons, "The Real Record on Racial Attitudes," in *Social Trends in American Life: Findings from the General Social Survey since 1972*, ed. P. V. Marsden (Princeton, NJ: Princeton University Press, 2012), 38–83; Matthew O. Hunt, "African American, Hispanic, and White Beliefs About Black/White Inequality, 1977–2004," *American Sociological Review* 72, no. 3

(2007): 390–415; Maria Krysan, "Prejudice, Politics, and Public Opinion: Understand the Sources of Racial Policy Attitudes," *Annual Review of Sociology* 26 (2000): 135–168; Howard Schuman, Charlotte Steeh, Lawrence Bobo, and Maria Krysan, *Racial Attitudes in America: Trends and Interpretations* (Cambridge, MA: Harvard University Press, 1997); Steven A. Tuch and Michael Hughes, "Whites' Racial Policy Attitudes in the 21st Century: The Continuing Significance of Racial Resentment," *Annals of the American Academy of Political and Social Sciences* 634 (2011): 134–152.

39. Ray, "Theory of Racialized Organizations," 33.

40. Bonilla-Silva, *Racism Without Racists*; Bonilla-Silva, "Rethinking Racism"; Ray, "Theory of Racialized Organizations."

41. Ray, "Theory of Racialized Organizations," 39; also Wendy L. Moore and Joyce M. Bell, "Maneuvers of Whiteness: 'Diversity' as a Mechanism of Retrenchment in the Affirmative Action Discourse," *Critical Sociology* 37, no. 5 (2011): 597–613.

42. Frank Samson, "Multiple Group Threat and Malleable White Attitudes Towards Academic Merit," *Du Bois Review* 10, no. 1 (2013): 233–260.

43. Ray, "Theory of Racialized Organizations," 42.

44. Sara Ahmed, *On Being Included: Racism and Diversity in Institutional Life* (Durham, NC: Duke University Press, 2012); Berrey, *Enigma of Diversity*; Frank Dobbin, *Inventing Equal Opportunity* (Princeton, NJ: Princeton University Press, 2009); Frank Dobbin, Soohan Kim, and Alexandra Kalev, "You Can't Always Get What You Need: Organizational Determinants of Diversity Programs," *American Sociological Review* 76, no. 3 (2011): 386–411; David G. Embrick, "The Diversity Ideology in the Business World: A New Oppression for a New Age," *Critical Sociology* 37, no. 5 (2011): 541–556; David G. Embrick, "The Diversity Ideology: Keeping Major Transnational Corporations White and Male in an Era of Globalization," in *Globalization and America: Race, Human Rights, and Inequality*, ed. A. J. Hattery, D. G. Embrick, and E. Smith (Lanham, MD: Rowman and Littlefield, 2008), 23–42; James M. Thomas, *Diversity Regimes: Why Talk Is Not Enough to Fix Racial Inequality at Universities* (New Brunswick, NJ: Rutgers University Press, 2020).

45. Bonilla-Silva, "The Invisible Weight of Whiteness"; David L. Brunsma, Eric S. Brown, and Peggy Placier, "Teaching Race at Historically White Colleges and Universities: Identifying and Dismantling the Walls of Whiteness," *Critical Sociology* 39, no. 5 (2013): 717–738; Moore, Reproducing Racism.

46. Byrd, *Poison in the Ivy*; Feagin, Vera, and Imani, *Agony of Education*; Moore, *Reproducing Racism*; Myers, *Racetalk*; Picca and Feagin, *Two-Faced Racism*; Ray, "Theory of Racialized Organizations."

47. T. Elon Dancy II, Kristen T. Edwards, and James Earl Davis, "Historically White Universities and Plantation Politics: Anti-Blackness and Higher Education in the Black Lives Matter Era," *Urban Education* 53, no. 2 (2018): 176–195; Harris, Campbell, and Brophy, *Slavery and the University*; Karabel, *The Chosen*; Labaree, *A Perfect Mess*; Soares, *Power of Privilege*; Thelin, *A History of American Higher Education*; Wilder, *Ebony & Ivy*.

48. Marc Parry, "A New Path to Atonement," *Chronicle of Higher Education*, January 20, 2019, https://www.chronicle.com/article/A-New-Path-to-Atonement/245511.

49. Ray, "Theory of Racialized Organizations."

50. Ray, 38; also Ibram Kendi, *Stamped from the Beginning: The Definitive History of Racist Ideas in America* (New York: Nation Books, 2016); Douglas S. Massey and Nancy A. Denton, *American Apartheid: Segregation and the Making of the Underclass* (Cambridge, MA: Harvard University Press, 1994); Wilder, *Ebony & Ivy*.

51. Berrey, *Enigma of Diversity*.

52. Byrd, *Poison in the Ivy*; Dancy, Edwards, and Davis, "Historically White Universities and Plantation Politics"; Feagin, Vera, and Imani, *Agony of Education*; Moore, *Reproducing Racism*; Myers, *Racetalk*; Julie J. Park, *Race on Campus: Debunking Myths with Data* (Cambridge, MA: Harvard Educational Press, 2018); Picca and Feagin, *Two-Faced Racism*; Jim Sidanius, Shana Levin, Colette van Laar, and David O. Sears, *The Diversity Challenge: Social Identity and Intergroup Relations on the College Campus* (New York: Russell Sage Foundation, 2008); Natasha K. Warikoo, *The Diversity Bargain: And Other Dilemmas of Race, Admissions, and Meritocracy at Elite Universities* (Chicago: University of Chicago Press, 2016).

53. See also Shaun R. Harper, "Race Without Racism: How Higher Education Researchers Minimize Racist Institutional Norms," *Review of Higher Education* 36, no. 1 (2012): 9–30.

54. See Bonilla-Silva, *Racism Without Racists*.

55. Ahmed, *On Being Included*; Thomas, *Diversity Regimes*.

56. Ahmed, *On Being Included*; Thomas, *Diversity Regimes*.

57. Ray, "Theory of Racialized Organizations," 28.

58. Espeland and Sauder, *Engines of Anxiety*; Wendy N. Espeland and Mitchell L. Stevens, "The Sociology of Quantification," *European Journal of Sociology* 49, no. 3 (2008): 401–436; Andrea Mennicken and Wendy N. Espeland, "What's New with Numbers? Sociological Approaches to the Study of Quantification," *Annual Review of Sociology* 45 (2019): 24.1–24.23.

59. Daniel Hirschman, Ellen Berrey, and Fiona Rose-Greenland, "Dequantifying Diversity: Affirmative Action at the University of Michigan," *Theory & Society* 45, no. 3 (2016): 265–301; Daniel Hirschman and Emily A. Bosk, "Standardizing Biases: Selection Devices and the Quantification of Race," *Sociology of Race and Ethnicity* (2019): DOI: https://doi.org/10.1177/2332649219844797; Espeland and Stevens, "Sociology of Quantification."

60. Espeland and Sauder, *Engines of Anxiety*; Hirschman, Berrey, and Rose-Greenland, "Dequantifying Diversity"; Hirschman and Bosk, "Standardizing Biases"; George A. Lundberg, "Contemporary Positivism in Sociology," *American Sociological Review* 4, no. 1 (1939): 42–55; Theodore M. Porter, *Trust in Numbers: The Pursuit of Objectivity in Science and Public Life* (Princeton, NJ: Princeton University Press, 1995).

61. Espeland and Sauder, *Engines of Anxiety*; Hirschman, Berrey, and Rose-Greenland, "Dequantifying Diversity."

62. Espeland and Sauder, *Engines of Anxiety*, 12.

63. Hirschman, Berrey, and Rose-Greenland "Dequantifying Diversity," 270.

64. Hirschman, Berrey, and Rose-Greenland, 270.

65. Hirschman, Berrey, and Rose-Greenland, 270.

66. Espeland and Sauder, *Engines of Anxiety*.

67. Espeland and Sauder.

68. Scott Jaschik, "College Board Overhauls 'Adversity Index,'" *Inside Higher Ed*, September 3, 2019, https://www.insidehighered.com/admissions/article/2019/09/03/college-board -overhauls-adversity-index.

69. Hirschman, Berrey, and Rose-Greenland, "Dequantifying Diversity."

70. Ahmed, *On Being Included*; Thomas, *Diversity Regimes*.

71. Bonilla-Silva, "Rethinking Racism"; Stuart Hall, "Race, Articulation, and Societies Structured in Dominance," in *Sociological Theories: Race and Colonialism* (Paris:

UNESCO), 305–345; Omi and Winant, *Racial Formation in the United States*; Ray, "Theory of Racialized Organizations."

72. Graves, *Emperor's New Clothes*; Omi and Winant, *Racial Formation in the United States*; Kenneth Prewitt, *What Is Your Race? The Census and Our Flawed to Classify Americans* (Princeton, NJ: Princeton University Press, 2016); Roberts, *Fatal Invention*; Smedley and Smedley, *Race in North America*; Zuberi, *Thicker than Blood*.

73. Ray, "Theory of Racialized Organizations"; Abigail A. Sewell, "The Racism-Race Reification Process: A Mesolevel Political Economic Framework for Understanding Racial Health Disparities," *Sociology of Race and Ethnicity* 2, no. 4 (2016): 402–432.

74. Baez, "'Knowledge of Difference.'"

75. Espeland and Sauder, *Engines of Anxiety*, 26.

76. Baez, "'Knowledge of Difference.'"

77. See W. Carson Byrd, Sandra L. Dika, and Letticia T. Ramlal, "Who's in STEM? An Exploration of Race, Ethnicity, and Citizenship Reporting in a Federal Education Dataset," *Equity and Excellence in Education* 46, no. 4 (2013): 484–501.

78. See Everett C. Hughes, "Dilemmas and Contradictions of Status," *American Journal of Sociology* 50, no. 5 (1945), 353–359.

79. See Mosi Ifatunji, "A Test of the Afro Caribbean Model Minority Hypothesis: Exploring the Roles of Cultural Attributes in Labor Market Disparities Between African American and Afro Caribbeans," *Du Bois Review* 13, no. 1 (2016): 109–138; Yasmiyn Irizarry, "Utilizing Multidimensional Measures of Race in Educational Research: The Case of Teacher Perceptions," *Sociology of Race and Ethnicity* 1, no. 4 (2015): 564–583; Jennifer Lee and Min Zhou, *The Asian American Achievement Paradox* (New York: Russell Sage Foundation, 2015); Zulema Valdez and Tanya Golash-Boza, "U.S. Racial and Ethnic Relations in the Twenty-First Century," *Ethnic & Racial Studies* 40, no. 13 (2017): 2181–2209; Mary Waters, *Black Identities: West Indian Immigrant Dreams and American Realities* (Cambridge, MA: Harvard University Press, 1999).

80. OiYan Poon, Jude M. P. Dizon, and Dian Squire, "Count Me In!: Ethnic Data Disaggregation Advocacy, Racial Mattering, and Lessons for Racial Justice Coalitions," *Journal Committed to Social Change of Race and Ethnicity* 3, no. 1 (2017): 92–124.

81. Espeland and Sauder, *Engines of Anxiety*; Hirschman and Bosk, "Standardizing Biases."

82. Baez, "'Knowledge of Difference,'" 291.

83. Baez, "'Knowledge of Difference,'" 290–291 (emphasis in original); also Ray, "Theory of Racialized Organizations"; Sewell, "Racism-Race Reification."

84. Baez, " 'Knowledge of Difference'"; Espeland and Sauder, *Engines of Anxiety*; Ray, "Theory of Racialized Organizations."

85. Baez, " 'Knowledge of Difference'"; Byrd, *Poison in the Ivy*; W. Carson Byrd, Rachelle J. Brunn-Bevel, and Parker Sexton, "'We Don't All Look Alike': The Academic Performance of Black Student Populations at Elite Colleges," *Du Bois Review* 11, no. 2 (2014): 353–385; Feagin, Vera, and Imani, *Agony of Education*; Harper, "Race Without Racism"; Moore, *Reproducing Racism*; Ray, "Theory of Racialized Organizations."

86. Baez, "'Knowledge of Difference'"; Ray, "Theory of Racialized Organizations."

87. See also Joyce A. Ladner, ed., *The Death of White Sociology: Essays on Race and Culture* (Baltimore: Black Classic Press, 1973); John H. Stanfield II, ed., *Rethinking Race and Ethnicity in Research Methods* (Walnut Creek, CA: Left Coast Press, 2011); John H. Stanfield II and Rutledge M. Dennis, eds., *Race and Ethnicity in Research Methods* (Thousand Oaks, CA: Sage, 1993); Tukufu Zuberi and Eduardo Bonilla-Silva, eds., *White Logic, White Methods: Racism and Methodology* (Lanham, MD: Rowman and Littlefield, 2008).

88. Baez, "'Knowledge of Difference.'"
89. Baez, 299.
90. Baez, "'Knowledge of Difference'"; Ray, "Theory of Racialized Organizations."
91. Espeland and Sauder, *Engines of Anxiety*.
92. Baez, "'Knowledge of Difference,'" 299; see also Pierre Bourdieu, *The State Nobility: Elite Schools in the Field of Power*, trans. Lauretta C. Clough (Stanford, CA: Stanford University Press, 1996 [French original published in 1989]); Pierre Bourdieu, *Language and Symbolic Power* (Cambridge, MA: Harvard University Press, 1991); Pierre Bourdieu, *Homo Academicus* (Stanford, CA: Stanford University Press, 1988).
93. Baez, "'Knowledge of Difference,'" 301; also Ahmed, *On Being Included*; Berrey, *Enigma of Diversity*; Bourdieu, *The State Nobility*; Byrd, *Poison in the Ivy*; Hirschman, Berrey, and Rose-Greenland, "Dequantifying Diversity"; Ray, "Theory of Racialized Organizations"; Thomas, *Diversity Regimes*.

Chapter 1

1. Sarah Brown, "8 Universities. Millions in Bribes. 10 Corrupt Coaches. What You Need to Know about the Admissions-Bribery Scandal," *Chronicle of Higher Education*, March 12, 2019, https://www.chronicle.com/article/8-Universities-Millions-in/245873; Natalie Escobar, and Amal Ahmed, "9 Revealing Moments from the College-Admissions Scandal," *The Atlantic*, March 13, 2019, https://www.theatlantic.com/education/archive/2019/03/college-admissions-scandal-9-revealing-moments/584803/; Alia Wong, "Why the College Admissions Scandal Is So Absurd," *The Atlantic*, March 12, 2019, https://www.theatlantic.com/education/archive/2019/03/college-admissions-scandal-fbi-targets-wealthy-parents/584695/; Fernanda Zamudio-Suaréz, "Photoshopped Scenes and Fake Athletic Profiles: How the Internet Is Picking Apart the College-Admission Scandal," *Chronicle of Higher Education*, March 12, 2019, https://www.chronicle.com/article/Photoshopped-ScenesFake/245868.
2. Terry Nguyen, and Zipporah Osei, "Caught in the Middle of Their Parent's Bribery Schemes, Students Stay Silent," *Chronicle of Higher Education*, March 13, 2019, https://www.chronicle.com/article/Caught-in-the-Middle-of-Their/245886; Will Stancil, "Ignorance Was Bliss for Children of the College-Admissions Scandal," *The Atlantic*, March 17, 2019, https://www.theatlantic.com/education/archive/2019/03/college-admissions-scandal-kids-didnt-need-know/585055.
3. See also Jerome Karabel, *The Chosen: The Hidden History of Admission and Exclusion at Harvard, Yale, and Princeton* (New York: Houghton Mifflin Company, 2005); Joseph Soares, *The Power of Privilege Yale and America's Elite Colleges* (Stanford, CA: Stanford University Press, 2007).
4. Scott Jaschik, "USC Blocks Registration for Students in Scandal," *InsideHigherEd*, March 20, 2019, https://www.insidehighered.com/admissions/article/2019/03/20/university-southern-california-takes-new-actions-against-students; Scott Jaschik, "Yale Revokes Admission of Student in Scandal," *InsideHigherEd*, March 26, 2019, https://www.insidehighered.com/quicktakes/2019/03/26/yale-revokes-admission-student-scandal.
5. Sabri Ben-Achour, "Wealthy Families Already Have Legal Ways of Gaming the System," *Markeplace.org*, March 13, 2019, https://www.marketplace.org/2019/03/13/education/wealthy-families-college-admissions-bribes-stanford-yale; Jessica Calarco, "When Their Kids Don't Make the Cut," *InsideHigherEd, Conditionally Accepted*, March 22, 2019, https://www.insidehighered.com/advice/2019/03/22/cheating-college-admissions-plays

-out-several-different-levels-opinion; Jessica Calarco, *Negotiating Opportunities: How the Middle Class Secures Advantages in Schools* (New York: Oxford University Press, 2018); Joe Pinsker, "A Scandal Fit for a Winner-at-All-Costs Society," *The Atlantic*, March 13, 2019, https://www.theatlantic.com/education/archive/2019/03/college-admissions -scandal-elite-anxieties/584740.

6. Daniel Golden, *The Price of Admissions: How America's Ruling Class Buys Its Way into Elite Colleges—and Who Gets Left Behind* (New York: Crown, 2009); Karabel, *The Chosen*; Soares, *Power of Privilege*; Mitchell L. Stevens, *Creating a Class: College Admissions and the Education of Elites* (Cambridge, MA: Harvard University Press, 2009); Craig Steven Wilder, *Ebony & Ivy: Race, Slavery, and the Troubled History of America's Universities* (New York: Bloomsbury Press, 2013).

7. Steven Brint, Komi T. German, Kayleigh Anderson-Natale, Zeinab F. Shuker, and Suki Wang, "Where Ivy Matters: The Educational Backgrounds of U.S. Cultural Elites," *Sociology of Education*, 93, no. 2 (2020), 153–172; Scott Carlson and Goldie Blumenstyk, "Why the College Degree Is a Signal—and Why That Should Worry You," *Chronicle of Higher Education*, March 19, 2019, https://www.chronicle.com/article /Why-the-College-Degree-Is-a/245923; Lauren A. Rivera, *Pedigree: How Elite Students Get Elite Jobs* (Princeton, NJ: Princeton University Press, 2016); Becky Supiano, "They're Already Rich. Why Were These Parents So Fixated on Elite Colleges?" *Chronicle of Higher Education*, March 13, 2019, https://www.chronicle.com/article/They-re-Already -Rich-Why/245889.

8. See prabhdeep kehal, Daniel Hirschman, and Ellen Berrey's analyses of trends in student diversity, college selectivity, and affirmative action policies (prabhdeep s. kehal, Daniel Hirschman, and Ellen Berrey, "When Colleges Drop Affirmative Action: Trends in Admissions Policies and Student Enrollment at U.S. Selective Universities, 1990–2016," *SocArXiv*, September 21, 2018, DOI: https://doi.org/10.31235/osf.io/8z629). This study highlights how white students' advantage does not deteriorate with the use of affirmative action in college admissions, while Black student enrollment shifts, depending on the level of selectivity. This study also suggests how selectivity as a proxy for academic merit does not dramatically shift with the use of affirmative action in college admissions. Other analyses (e.g., Daniel Hirschman and Ellen Berrey, "The Partial Deinstitutionalization of Affirmative Action in U.S. Higher Education, 1988 to 2014," *Sociological Science* 4 [2017]: 449–468) suggest that affirmative action is being used less frequently among colleges.

9. William A. Darity Jr., Darrick Hamilton, Mark Paul, Alan Aja, Anne Price, Antonio Moore, and Caterina Chiopris, *What We Get Wrong About Closing the Racial Wealth Gap* (Durham, NC: Duke University Samuel DuBois Cook Center on Social Equity, 2018); Darrick Hamilton and William A. Darity Jr., "Can 'Baby Bonds' Eliminate the Racial Wealth Gap in Putative Post-Racial America?" *Review of Black Political Economy* 37, no. 3–4 (2010): 207–216; Melvin L. Oliver and Thomas R. Shapiro, *Black Wealth/ White Wealth: A New Perspective on Racial Inequality*, 2nd ed. (New York: Routledge, 2006); Samuel R. Lucas, "An Archeology of Effectively Maintained Inequality Theory," *American Behavioral Scientist* 61, no. 1 (2017): 8–29; Fabian T. Pfeffer, "Growing Wealth Gaps in Education," *Demography* 55, no. 3 (2018): 1033–1068; Fabian T. Pfeffer and Alexandra Killewald, "Intergenerational Wealth Mobility and Racial Inequality," *Socius* 5 (2019): 1–2; Irene Prix and Fabian T. Pfeffer, "Does Donald Need Uncle Scrooge? Extended Family's Wealth and Children's Educational Attainment in the United States," in *Social Inequality Across Generations: The Role of Compensation and Multiplication in*

Resource Accumulation, ed. J. Erola and E. Kilpi-Jakonen (Cheltenham, UK: Edward Elga, 2017), 112–135.

10. Hubert Blumer, "Race Prejudice and a Sense of Group Positioning," *Pacific Sociological Review* 1, no. 1 (1958): 3–7; Lawrence D. Bobo, James R. Kluegel, and Ryan A. Smith, "Laissez-Faire Racism: The Crystallization of a Kinder, Gentler, Anti-Black Ideology," in *Racial Attitudes in the 1990s: Continuity and Change*, ed. S. A. Tuch and J. K. Martin (Westport, CT: Praeger, 1997), 15–42; Lawrence D. Bobo and Mia Tuan, *Prejudice in Politics: Group Position, Public Opinion, and the Wisconsin Treaty Rights Dispute* (Cambridge, MA: Harvard University Press, 2006).

11. Michael N. Bastedo, Nicholas A. Bowman, Kristen M. Glasener, and Jandi L. Kelly, "What Are We Talking About When We Talk About Holistic Review? Selective College Admissions and Its Effects on Low-SES Students," *Journal of Higher Education* 89, no. 5 (2018): 782–805; Daniel Hirschman, Ellen Berrey, and Fiona Rose-Greenland, "Dequantifying Diversity: Affirmative Action at the University of Michigan," *Theory & Society* 45, no. 3(2016): 265–301; Don Hossler, Emily Chung, Jiyhe Kwon, Jerry Lucido, Nicholas Bowman, and Michael Bastedo, "A Study of the Use of Nonacademic Factors in Holistic Undergraduate Admissions Reviews," *Journal of Higher Education* 90, no. 6 (2019): 833–859; Julie J. Park, *Race on Campus: Debunking Myths with Data* (Cambridge, MA: Harvard Educational Press, 2018).

12. Bastedo et al., "Holistic Review?"; Karabel, *The Chosen*; Nicholas Leman, *The Big Test: The Secret History of the American Meritocracy* (New York: Farrar, Straus, and Giroux, 1999); Amaka Okechukwu, *To Fulfill These Rights: Political Struggle over Affirmative Action and Open Admissions* (New York: Columbia University Press, 2019); Soares, *Power of Privilege*; Wilder, *Ebony & Ivy*.

13. Karabel, The Chosen; Lemann, *The Big Test*; Okechukwu, *To Fulfill These Rights*; Soares, *Power of Privilege*; John R. Thelin, *A History of American Higher Education*, 3rd ed. (Baltimore: Johns Hopkins University Press, 2019); Wilder, *Ebony & Ivy*.

14. Eric Hoover, "Dueling Economists: Rival Analyses of Harvard's Admissions Process Emerge at Trial," *Chronicle of Higher Education*, October 30, 2018, https://www .chronicle.com/article/Dueling-Economists-Rival/244964?cid=wcontentgrid; Eric Hoover, "At Harvard Trial, Statistics Give Way to Personal Stories About Diversity," *Chronicle of Higher Education*, October 29, 2018, https://www.chronicle.com/article /At-Harvard-Trial-Statistics/244957?cid=cp229; Scott Jaschik, "Trump Administration Endorses Appeal of Harvard Ruling," *Inside Higher Ed*, March 2, 2020, https://www .insidehighered.com/admissions/article/2020/03/02/trump-administration-files-brief -backing-appeal-harvard-ruling; Scott Jaschik, "Judge Upholds Harvard's Admissions Policy," *Inside Higher Ed*, October 7, 2019, https://www.insidehighered.com/admission s/article/2019/10/07/federal-judge-finds-harvards-policies-do-not-discriminate-against.

15. Bastedo et al., "Holistic Review?"; Hossler et al., "Nonacademic Factors in Holistic Undergraduate Admissions Reviews"; Park, *Race on Campus*; William E. Sedlacek, "Using Noncognitive Variables in Assessing Readiness for Higher Education," *Readings on Equal Education* 25 (2011): 187–205, http://web.augsburg.edu/em/UsingNCV-Sedlacek. pdf; Rebecca Zwick, *Who Gets In? Strategies for Fair and Effective College Admissions* (Cambridge, MA: Harvard University Press, 2017).

16. Bastedo et al., "Holistic Review?"; Hossler et al., "Nonacademic Factors in Holistic Undergraduate Admissions Reviews"; Stevens, *Creating a Class*.

17. Bastedo et al., "Holistic Review?"

18. Bastedo et al.; Hossler et al., "Nonacademic Factors in Holistic Undergraduate Admissions Reviews."

19. W. Carson, Byrd, "Most White Americans Will Never Be Affected by Affirmative Action. So Why Do They Hate It So Much?" *Washington Post*, October 18, 2018, https://www.washingtonpost.com/nation/2018/10/19/most-white-americans-will-never-experience-affirmative-action-so-why-do-they-hate-it-so-much/?utm_term=.2ec0cceb1d0d; W. Carson Byrd and Janelle S. Wong, "When a Test Supports Myths About Racial Inequality," *Contexts*, April 26, 2019, https://contexts.org/blog/varsity-blues-and-lawsuits-too/#wong; Hirschman and Berrey, "Partial Deinstitutionalization"; Park, *Race on Campus*.

20. Ozan Jaquette and Bradley R. Curs, "Creating the Out-of-State University: Do Public Universities Increase Nonresident Freshman Enrollment in Response to Declining State Appropriations?," *Research in Higher Education* 56, no. 6 (2015): 535–565; Ozan Jaquette, Bradley R. Curs, and Julie R. Posselt, "Tuition Rich, Mission Poor: Nonresident Enrollment Growth and the Socioeconomic and Racial Composition of Public Research Universities," *Journal of Higher Education* 87, no. 5 (2016): 635–673; Paul Tough, *The Years That Matter Most: How College Makes or Breaks Us* (Boston: Houghton Mifflin Harcourt, 2019).

21. Julie R. Posselt, Ozan Jaquette, Rob Bielby, and Michael N. Bastedo, "Access Without Equity: Longitudinal Analyses of Institutional Stratification by Race and Ethnicity, 1972–2004," *American Educational Research Journal*, 49, no. 6 (2012): 1074–1111.

22. Hirschman and Berrey, "Partial Deinstitutionalization."

23. Andrew H. Nichols, *'Segregation Forever?' The Continued Underrepresentation of Black and Latino Undergraduates at the Nation's 101 Most Selective Public Colleges and Universities* (Washington, DC: Education Trust, 2020).

24. Nicholas Hillman and Taylor Weichman, *Education Deserts: The Continuing Significance of Place in the Twenty-First Century* (Washington, DC: American Council on Education, 2016).

25. Universities considered highly selective typically admit less than a third of their applicants each year.

26. See also Byrd, "Most White Americans Will Never"; Okechukwu, *To Fulfill These Rights.*

27. Wendy N. Espeland and Michael Sauder, *Engines of Anxiety: Academic Rankings, Reputation, and Accountability* (New York: Russell Sage, 2016).

28. See Ellen Berrey, *The Enigma of Diversity: The Language and the Limits of Racial Justice* (Chicago: University of Chicago Press, 2015); Okechukwu, *To Fulfill These Rights.*

29. Hirschman, Berrey, and Rose-Greenland, "Dequantifying Diversity."

30. See Linda Darling-Hammond, "Race, Inequality, and Educational Accountability: The Irony of 'No Child Left Behind,'" *Race, Ethnicity and Education* 10, no. 3 (2007): 245–260; Linda Darling-Hammond, "The Color Line in American Education: Race, Resources, and Student Achievement," *Du Bois Review* 1, no. 2 (2004): 213–246; Angel L. Harris, *Kids Don't Want to Fail: Oppositional Culture and the Black-White Achievement Gap* (Cambridge, MA: Harvard University Press, 2011); Jonathan Kozol, *The Shame of the Nation: The Restoration of Apartheid Schooling in America* (New York: Crown Publishers, 2005); Jonathan Kozol, *Savage Inequalities: Children in America's Schools* (New York: Harper Perennial, 1991); Amanda E. Lewis and John B. Diamond, *Despite the Best Intentions: How Racial Inequality Thrives in Good Schools* (New York: Oxford University Press, 2015); R. L'Heureux Lewis-McCoy, *Inequality in the Promised Land: Race, Resources, and Suburban Schooling* (Stanford, CA: Stanford University Press, 2014); Daniel J. Losen and Tia E. Martinez, *Out of School and Off Track: The Overuse of Suspensions in American Middle and High Schools* (Los Angeles: The Civil Rights Project, 2013);

Okechukwu, *To Fulfill These Rights*; Jason A. Okonofua and Jennifer L. Eberhardt, "Two Strikes: Race and the Disciplining of Young Students," *Psychological Science* 26, no. 5 (2015): 617–624; Gary Orfield, John Kucsera, and Genevieve Siegel-Hawley, *E Pluribus . . . Separation: Deepening Double Segregation for More Students* (Los Angeles: UCLA Civil Rights Project/Proyecto Derechos Civiles, 2012); Park, *Race on Campus*; Rivera, *Pedigree*; Karolyn Tyson, *Integration Interrupted: Tracking, Black Students, and Acting White After* Brown (New York: Oxford University Press, 2011).

31. See Hirschman, Berrey, and Rose-Greenland, "Dequantifying Diversity."

32. Berrey, *Enigma of Diversity*; Jeffrey S. Lehman, "The Evolving Language of Diversity and Integration in Discussions of Affirmative Action from *Bakke* to *Grutter*," in *Defending Diversity: Affirmative Action at the University of Michigan*, ed. P. Gurin, J. S. Lehman, and E. Lewis (Ann Arbor: University of Michigan Press, 2004), 61–96; Okechukwu, *To Fulfill These Rights*; Scott R. Palmer, "Diversity and Affirmative Action: Evolving Principles and Continuing Legal Battles," in *Diversity Challenged: Evidence on the Impact of Affirmative Action.*, ed. G. Orfield (Cambridge, MA: The Civil Rights Project, 2001), 81–88.

33. Hirschman, Berrey, and Rose-Greenland, "Dequantifying Diversity," 284–287.

34. Hirschman, Berrey, and Rose-Greenland, 286.

35. Former Chief Justice William Rehnquist, quoted in Hirschman, Berrey, and Rose-Greenland, "Dequantifying Diversity," 289.

36. Hirschman, Berrey, and Rose-Greenland, 292–294.

37. Shamus Khan, *Privilege: The Making of an Adolescent Elite at St. Paul's School* (Princeton, NJ: Princeton University Press, 2011); Shamus Khan and Colin Jerolmack, "Saying Meritocracy and Doing Privilege," *Sociological Quarterly* 54, no. 1 (2013): 9–19.

38. Hirschman, Berrey, and Rose-Greenland, "Dequantifying Diversity," 293.

39. Hirschman, Berrey, and Rose-Greenland,; Daniel Hirschman and Emily A. Bosk "Standardizing Biases: Selection Devices and the Quantification of Race," *Sociology of Race and Ethnicity* (2019): DOI: https://doi.org/10.1177/2332649219844797.

40. Victor E. Ray, "A Theory of Racialized Organizations," *American Sociological Review* 84, no. 1 (2019): 26–53.

41. Okechukwu, *To Fulfill These Rights*.

42. Liliana M. Garces, Patricia Marin, and Catherine Horn, "Arguing Race in Higher Education Admissions: Examining *Amici*'s Use of Extra-Legal Sources in *Fisher*," *Journal of Diversity in Higher Education* (2019): DOI: https://doi.org/10.1037/dhe0000146.

43. J. Scott Carter, Cameron Lippard, and Andrew F. Baird, "Veiled Threats: Color-Blind Frames and Group Threat in Affirmative Action Discourse," *Social Problems* 66, no. 4 (2019), 503–518; Okechukwu, *To Fulfill These Rights*.

44. Byrd, "Most White Americans"; OiYan Poon, "How Do Colleges Use Affirmative Action? Even Some Activists Don't Understand," *The Conversation*, October 26, 2018, http://theconversation.com/how-do-colleges-use-affirmative-action-even-some-activists-dont-understand-105453; Natasha K. Warikoo and Nadirah F. Foley, "How Elite Schools Stay So White," *New York Times*, July 24, 2018, https://www.nytimes.com/2018/07/24/opinion/affirmative-action-new-york-harvard.html; Janelle Wong, "Actually, Race-Conscious Admissions Are Good for Asian Americans," *Chronicle of Higher Education*, October 4, 2018, https://www.chronicle.com/article/Actually-Race-Conscious/244727.

45. These approaches build on the work by Bastedo et al., "Holistic Review?"; and Hossler et al., "Nonacademic Factors in Holistic Undergraduate Admissions Reviews."

46. Scott Jaschik, "College Board Overhauls 'Adversity Index,'" *Inside Higher Ed*, September 3, 2019, https://www.insidehighered.com/admissions/article/2019/09/03/college-board -overhauls-adversity-index; Scott Jaschik, "College Board Pilots New Way to Measure Adversity When Considering Applications, but Some Fear Impact of Leaving Out Race," *Inside Higher Ed*, February 28, 2017, https://www.insidehighered.com/news/2017 /02/28/college-board-pilots-new-way-measure-adversity-when-considering-applications -some.

47. Espeland and Sauder, *Engines of Anxiety*.

48. College Board, "Landscape: Comprehensive Data and Methodology Summary," 2019, https://professionals.collegeboard.org/landscape.

49. Michael N. Bastedo and Nicholas A. Bowman, "Improving Admission of Low-SES Students at Selective Colleges: Results from an Experimental Simulation," *Educational Researcher* 46, no. 2 (2017): 67–77; Bastedo et al., "Holistic Review?"; Nicholas A. Bowman and Michael N. Bastedo, "What Role May Admissions Office Diversity and Practices Play in Equitable Decisions?," *Research in Higher Education* 59, no. 4 (2018): 430–447.

50. Jaschik, "College Board Overhauls 'Adversity Index.'"

51. Karl Alexander, Doris Entwisle, and Linda Olson, *The Long Shadow: Family Background, Disadvantaged Urban Youth, and the Transition to Adulthood* (New York: Russell Sage Foundation, 2014); Calarco, *Negotiating Opportunities*; Annette Lareau, *Unequal Childhoods: Class, Race, and Family Life* (Berkeley: University of California Press, 2002); Annette Lareau and Kimberly Goyette, eds., *Choosing Neighborhoods, Choosing Schools* (New York: Russell Sage Foundation, 2014); Jennifer Lee and Min Zhou, *The Asian American Achievement Paradox* (New York: Russell Sage Foundation, 2015); Lewis and Diamond, *Despite the Best Intentions*; Lewis-McCoy, *Inequality in the Promised Land*.

52. Eduardo Bonilla-Silva, *Racism Without Racists: Color-Blind Racism and the Persistence of Racial Inequality in the United States*, 5th ed. (Lanham, MD: Rowman & Littlefield, 2017); Lehman, "Evolving Language of Diversity"; Okechukwu, *To Fulfill These Rights*; Palmer, "Diversity and Affirmative Action." See Lisa M. Stulberg and Anthony S. Chen, "The Origins of Race-Conscious Affirmative Action in Undergraduate Admissions: A Comparative Analysis of Institutional Change in Higher Education," *Sociology of Education* 87, no. 1 (2014): 36–52; Thelin, *History of American Higher Education*, for an examination of the colleges and universities that desegregated their student bodies before judicial rulings and national protests.

53. Bobo and Tuan, *Prejudice in Politics*; Bonilla-Silva, *Racism Without Racists*; James R. Kluegel and Eliot R. Smith, *Beliefs About Inequality: Americans' Views of What Is and What Ought to Be* (New York: Aldine de Gruyte, 1996); Maria Krysan, "Prejudice, Politics, and Public Opinion: Understand the Sources of Racial Policy Attitudes," *Annual Review of Sociology* 26 (2000): 135–168.

54. Lawrence D. Bobo, Camille Z. Charles, Maria Krysan, and Alicia D. Simmons, "The Real Record on Racial Attitudes," in *Social Trends in American Life: Findings from the General Social Survey since 1972*, ed. P. V. Marsden (Princeton, NJ: Princeton University Press, 2012), 38–83; Bobo and Tuan, *Prejudice in Politics*; Bonilla-Silva, *Racism Without Racists*; Lani Guinier, *The Tyranny of the Meritocracy: Democratizing Higher Education in America* (Boston: Beacon, 2015); Matthew O. Hunt, "African American, Hispanic, and White Beliefs About Black/White Inequality, 1977–2004," *American Sociological Review* 72, no. 3 (2007): 390–415; Jonathan J. B. Mijs, "The Paradox of Inequality: Income Inequality and Belief in Meritocracy Go Hand in Hand," *Socio-Economic Review* (2019):

DOI: https://doi.org/10.1093/ser/mwy051; Okechukwu, *To Fulfill These Rights*; Howard
Schuman, Charlotte Steeh, Lawrence Bobo, and Maria Krysan, *Racial Attitudes in
America: Trends and Interpretations* (Cambridge, MA: Harvard University Press, 1997);
Natasha K. Warikoo, *The Diversity Bargain: And Other Dilemmas of Race, Admissions,
and Meritocracy at Elite Universities* (Chicago: University of Chicago Press, 2016).

55. W. Carson Byrd, *Poison in the Ivy: Race Relations and the Reproduction of Inequality on
Elite College Campuses* (New Brunswick, NJ: Rutgers University Press, 2017); Nolan L.
Cabrera, *White Guys on Campus: Racism, White Immunity, and the Myth of "Post-Racial"
Higher Education* (New Brunswick, NJ: Rutgers University Press, 2018); Warikoo, *The
Diversity Bargain.*

56. Ray, "Theory of Racialized Organizations."

57. Frank Samson, "Multiple Group Threat and Malleable White Attitudes Towards Academic Merit," *Du Bois Review* 10, no. 1 (2013): 233–260.

58. Mitchell J. Chang, "Amplifying Asian American Presence: Contending with Dominant
Racial Narratives in *Fisher*," in *Affirmative Action and Racial Equality: Considering the
Fisher Case to Forge the Path Ahead*, ed. U. M. Jayakumar and L. M. Garces with F. Fer-
nandez (New York: Routledge, 2015), 130–149; see also Rosalind S. Chou, and Joe R.
Feagin, *The Myth of the Model Minority: Asian Americans Facing Racism* (Boulder, CO:
Paradigm Publishers, 2008), and Lee and Zhou, *Asian American Achievement Paradox.*

59. Jennifer Lee and Van C. Tran, "The Mere Mention of Asian Americans in Affirmative
Action," *Sociological Science* 6, no. 2 (2019): 551–579.

60. Maureen A. Craig and Jennifer A. Richeson, "Information About the U.S. Racial
Demographic Shift Triggers Concerns About Anti-White Discrimination Among the
Prospective White 'Minority,'" *PLOS One* 12, no. 9 (2017): e0185389; Maureen A.
Craig and Jennifer A. Richeson, "More Diverse Yet Less Tolerant? How the Increasingly
Diverse Racial Landscape Affects White Americans' Racial Attitudes," *Personality and
Social Psychology Bulletin* 40, no. 6 (2014): 750–761; Maureen A. Craig and Jennifer A.
Richeson, "On the Precipice of a 'Majority-Minority' America: Perceived Status Threat
from the Racial Demographic Shift Affects White Americans' Political Ideology," *Psy-
chological Science* 25, no. 6 (2014): 1189–1197.

61. Guinier, *Tyranny of the Meritocracy.*

62. Espeland and Sauder, *Engines of Anxiety*; Hirschman, Berrey, and Rose-Greenland,
"Dequantifying Diversity."

63. Guinier, *Tyranny of the Meritocracy*; Leman, *The Big Test*; Karabel, *The Chosen*; Okechukwu, *To Fulfill These Rights*; Soares, *Power of Privilege*; Warikoo, *The Diversity
Bargain.*

64. Guinier, *Tyranny of the Meritocracy*; Park, *Race on Campus.*

65. There is an ongoing debate about whether an applicant's academic merits from previous
work should be given more weight than their potential should be given for admission
to a university. This debate brings to light another aspect of how strict adherence to an
ideal of meritocracy in college admissions can privilege students from well-off families
and well-resourced schools that provide more opportunities' these advantages skew
admissions toward white applicants. See Guinier, *Tyranny of the Meritocracy*, for further
discussion.

66. Darling-Hammond, "Race, Inequality, and Educational Accountability"; Darling-
Hammond, "Color Line in American Education"; Harris, *Kids Don't Want to Fail*;
Kozol, *Shame of the Nation*; Kozol, *Savage Inequalities*; Lewis and Diamond, *Despite the
Best Intentions*; Lewis-McCoy, *Inequality in the Promised Land*; Losen and Martinez, *Out*

of School and Off Track; Okechukwu, *To Fulfill These Rights*; Okonofua and Eberhardt, "Two Strikes"; Orfield et al., *E Pluribus . . . Separation*; Park, *Race on Campus*; Tyson, *Integration Interrupted.*

67. Brown, "8 Universities"; Nolan L. Cabrera, "It's All Part of the Plan," *Contexts*, April 26, 2019, https://contexts.org/blog/varsity-blues-and-lawsuits-too/#cabrera; Escobar and Ahmed, "9 Revealing Moments"; Wong, "Why the College Admissions Scandal Is So Absurd"; Zamudio-Suaréz, "Photoshopped Scenes and Fake Athletic Profiles."

68. See Elizabeth M. Lee, "Low-Income, First-Gen, Working Class Students and Left Out of Admissions Scandal (and Many Elite Colleges)," *Contexts*, April 26, 2019, https://contexts.org/blog/varsity-blues-and-lawsuits-too/#lee; Sarah M. Ovink, "Too Much Selectivity, Too Little Equity," *Contexts*, April 26, 2019, https://contexts.org/blog/varsity-blues-and-lawsuits-too/#ovink; Julie J. Park, "Inequality Beyond Varsity Blues," *Contexts*, April 26, 2019, https://contexts.org/blog/varsity-blues-and-lawsuits-too/#park; OiYan Poon, "Rethinking Institutional Priorities and Radical Change in Admissions After #AuntBeckyGate," *Contexts*, April 26, 2019, https://contexts.org/blog/varsity-blues-and-lawsuits-too/#poon.

69. In light of the recent college admissions scandals whereby affluent parents attempt to game the system to claim disadvantages such as having their children declare themselves as independents for additional financial aid opportunities, see Jodi S. Cohen and Melissa Sanchez, "Parents Are Giving Up Custody of Their Kids to Get Need-Based College Financial Aid," *Propublica Illinois*, July 29, 2019, https://www.propublica.org/article/university-of-illinois-financial-aid-fafsa-parents-guardianship-children-students. Affluent parents could arguably identify decent K-12 schools that signal disadvantage in relation to the recent creation of the "adversity index" but then buy additional opportunities to overcome such identified adversity. In admissions materials, their child could argue that they sought out better opportunities despite the social disadvantages of their school and classmates. Again, though a hypothetical situation, the recent attempts to gain advantages in college admissions to highly selective institutions suggests that affluent (white) parents will continue to attempt to identify avenues to gain further advantages for their children.

70. Benjamin Baez, "The 'Knowledge of Difference' and the Limits of Science," *Journal of Higher Education* 75, no. 3 (2004): 285–306; Berrey, *Enigma of Diversity*; Byrd, "It's Not Either-Or, It's Both-And: Or Why We Need Race and Class in College Admissions," *Contexts*, April 26, 2019, https://contexts.org/blog/varsity-blues-and-lawsuits-too/#byrd; Byrd, *Poison in the Ivy*; Byrd, "College Diversity Is (but Doesn't Have to Be) for Whites"; Okechukwu, *To Fulfill These Rights.*

71. Berrey, *Enigma of Diversity*; Okechukwu, *To Fulfill These Rights*; Warikoo, *The Diversity Bargain.*

72. Warikoo, *The Diversity Bargain*, 50.

73. Berrey, *Enigma of Diversity*; Byrd, *Poison in the Ivy*; Byrd, "College Diversity Is (But Doesn't Have to Be) For Whites"; Khan, *Privilege*; Khan and Jerolmack, "Saying Meritocracy and Doing Privilege"; Warikoo, *The Diversity Bargain.*

74. Baez, "'Knowledge of Difference'"; Berrey, *Enigma of Diversity*; Byrd, *Poison in the Ivy*; Mitchell J. Chang, Daria Witt, James Jones, and Kenji Hakuta, eds., *Compelling Interest: Examining the Racial Dynamics in Colleges and Universities* (Stanford, CA: Stanford University Press, 2003); Guinier, *Tyranny of the Meritocracy*; Gurin et al., *Defending Diversity*; Sylvia Hurtado, Jeffrey Milem, Alma Clayton-Pedersen, and Walter Allen, "Enacting Diverse Learning Environments: Improving the Climate for Racial/Ethnic

Diversity in Higher Education," ASHE-ERIC Higher Education Report, vol. 26, no. 8 (Washington, DC: George Washington University, 1999); Jeffrey F. Milem, Mitchell J. Chang, and anthony l. antonio, *Making Diversity Work on Campus: A Research-Based Perspective* (Washington, DC: Association of American Colleges & Universities, 2005); Michelle S. Moses and Mitchell J. Chang, "Toward a Deeper Understanding of the Diversity Rationale," *Educational Researcher* 35, no. 1 (2006): 6–11; Okechukwu, *To Fulfill These Rights*; Gary Orfield, ed., *Diversity Challenged: Evidence on the Impact of Affirmative Action* (Cambridge, MA: The Civil Rights Project, 2001); Park, *Race on Campus*; Julie J. Park, *When Diversity Drops: Race, Religion, and Affirmative Action in Higher Education* (New Brunswick, NJ: Rutgers University Press, 2003); Daryl G. Smith, *Diversity Works: The Emerging Picture of How Students Benefit* (Washington, DC: Association of American Colleges and Universities, 1997); Warikoo, *The Diversity Bargain*.

75. Berrey, *Enigma of Diversity*; Okechukwu, *To Fulfill These Rights*; Park, *Race on Campus*.

76. Ray, "Theory of Racialized Organizations."

77. Byrd, *Poison in the Ivy*; Park, *Race on Campus*; Warikoo, *The Diversity Bargain*.

78. Berrey, *Enigma of Diversity*; Okechukwu, *To Fulfill These Rights*.

79. Warikoo, *The Diversity Bargain*.

80. Berrey, *Enigma of Diversity*; Okechukwu, *To Fulfill These Rights*.

81. Social closure was originally developed in Max Weber, *Economy and Society: An Outline of Interpretative Sociology*, ed. G. Roth and C. Wittich (Berkeley: University of California Press, 1978), and further detailed in Frank Parkin, *Marxism and Class Theory: A Bourgeois Critique* (New York: Columbia University Press, 1979); and Kevin Stainback and Donald Tomaskovic-Devey, *Documenting Desegregation: Racial and Gender Segregation in Private Sector Employment Since the Civil Rights Act* (New York: Russell Sage Foundation, 2012), around labor markets and other aspects of the economy.

82. Sigal Alon, *Race, Class, and Affirmative Action* (New York: Russell Sage Foundation, 2015); Berrey, *The Enigma of Diversity*; Okechukwu, *To Fulfill These Rights*.

83. Okechukwu, *To Fulfill These Rights*.

84. W. Carson Byrd, "Conflating Apples and Oranges: Understanding Modern Forms of Racism," *Sociology Compass* 5, no. 11 (2011): 1005–1017.

85. Michelle Alexander, *The New Jim Crow: Mass Incarceration in the Age of Colorblindness* (New York: New Press, 2011); Richard Delgado and Jean Stefancic, *Critical Race Theory: An Introduction*, 3rd ed. (New York: New York University Press, 2017); Joe R. Feagin, *Racist America: Roots, Current Realities, and Reparations*, 4th ed. (New York: Routledge, 2018); Charles W. Mills, *The Racial Contract* (Ithaca, NY: Cornell University Press, 1997).

86. See also Bonilla-Silva, *Racism Without Racists*, which discusses how specific policies aimed at achieving more racial equality in society are viewed as forcing an issue by white people, who often prefer a more laissez-faire and gradual approach to racial progress; see also Lawrence D. Bobo, "Race and Beliefs About Affirmative Action: Assessing the Effects of Interests, Group Threat, Ideology, and Racism," in *Racialized Politics: The Debate About Racism in America*, ed. D. O. Sears, J. Sidanius, and L. D. Bobo (Chicago: University of Chicago Press, 2000), 137–164; Bobo, Smith, and Kluegel, "Laissez-Faire Racism"; Bobo and Tuan, *Prejudice in Politics*; and Krysan, "Prejudice, Politics, and Public Opinion."

87. Richard D. Kahlenberg, ed., *Affirmative Action for the Rich: Legacy Preferences in College Admissions* (Washington, DC: Century Foundation, 2010).

88. Darity et al., *Closing the Racial Wealth Gap*; Hamilton and Darity, "'Baby Bonds'"; Lucas, "Archeology of Effectively Maintained Inequality Theory"; Robert Merton, *Social*

Theory and Social Structure, rev. ed. (New York: Free Press, 1968 [1949]); Oliver and Shapiro, *Black Wealth/White Wealth*; Pfeffer, "Growing Wealth Gaps"; Pfeffer and Kille-wald, "Intergenerational Wealth Mobility"; Prix and Pfeffer, "Does Donald Need Uncle Scrooge?"

89. Shamus Khan, "The Sociology of Elites," *Annual Review of Sociology* 38 (2012): 361–377; Khan, *Privilege*; Rivera, *Pedigree*.

90. Khan, "The Sociology of Elites"; see also G. William Domhoff, *The Powers That Be: Processes of Ruling-Class Domination in America* (New York: Random House, 1978); Richard L. Zweigenhaft and G. William Domhoff, *Blacks in the White Establishment? A Study of Race and Class in America* (New Haven, CT: Yale University Press, 1991).

91. See Feagin, *Racist America*, for a concise discussion of how white elites have had substantial influence on policies and access to resources across US history.

92. Richard Kahlenberg, "Harvard Has a Choice on Diversity—and It's Not About Race," *Chronicle of Higher Education*, November 12, 2018, https://www.chronicle.com/article/Harvard-Has-a-Choice-on/245065.

93. Hirschman, Berrey, and Rose-Greenland, "Dequantifying Diversity."

94. Elizabeth A. Armstrong and Laura M. Hamilton, *Paying for the Party: How College Maintains Inequality* (Cambridge, MA: Harvard University Press, 2014); Cabrera, "It's All Part of the Plan"; Anthony A. Jack, *The Privileged Poor: How Elite Colleges Are Failing Disadvantaged Students* (Cambridge, MA: Harvard University Press, 2019); Kahlenberg, *Affirmative Action for the Rich*; Lee, "Low-Income, First-Gen, Working Class Students"; Elizabeth M. Lee, *Class and Campus Life: Managing and Experience Inequality at an Elite College* (Ithaca, NY: Cornell University Press, 2016); Ovink, "Too Much Selectivity, Too Little Equity"; Park, "Inequality Beyond Varsity Blues"; Park, *Race on Campus*; Jennifer Stuber, *Inside the College Gates: How Class and Culture Matter in Higher Education* (Lanham, MD: Rowman and Littlefield, 2011).

95. Hoover, "Dueling Economists."

96. Sean Reardon, Rachel Baker, Matt Kasman, Daniel Klasik, and Joseph B. Townsend, "What Levels of Racial Diversity Can Be Achieved with Socioeconomic-Based Affirmative Action? Evidence from a Simulation Model," *Journal of Policy Analysis and Management* 37, no. 3 (2018): 630–657; also see Julie Park's excellent and thorough discussion of research on the different forms of admissions processes as they relate to racial and socioeconomic diversity on college campuses in Park, *Race on Campus*.

97. Dominique J. Baker, "Pathways to Racial Equity in Higher Education: Modeling the Antecedents of State Affirmative Action Bans," *American Educational Research Journal* 56, no. 5 (2019): 1861–1895; Peter Hinrichs, "The Effects of Affirmative Action Bans on College Enrollment, Educational Attainment, and the Demographic Composition of Universities," *Review of Economics and Statistics* 94, no. 3 (2012): 712–722; Liliana M. Garces, "Racial Diversity, Legitimacy, and the Citizenry: The Impact of Affirmative Action Bans," *Review of Higher Education* 36, no. 1 (2012): 93–132; David Mickey-Pabello and Liliana M. Garces, "Addressing Racial Health Inequities: Understanding the Impact of Affirmative Action Bans on Applicants and Admissions in Medical Schools," *American Journal of Education* 125, no. 1 (2018): 79–108.

98. Patricia H. Collins, *Black Feminist Thought: Knowledge, Consciousness, and the Politics of Empowerment* (New York: Routledge, 2000); Patricia H. Collins and Sirma Bilge, *Intersectionality* (New York: Polity Press, 2016); Kimberlé W. Crenshaw, "Mapping the Margins: Intersectionality, Identity Politics, and Violence against Women of Color," *Stanford Law Review* 43, no. 6 (1991): 1241–1299.

 99. Park, *Race on Campus*; Reardon et al., "Socioeconomic-Based Affirmative Action."

100. Ted Thornhill, "We Want Black Students, Just Not You: How White Admissions Counselors Screen Black Prospective Students," *Sociology of Race and Ethnicity* 5, no. 4 (2019): 456–470.

101. Baker, "Pathways to Racial Equity."

102. Berrey, *Enigma of Diversity*; Okechukwu, *To Fulfill These Rights*.

103. Baez, " 'Knowledge of Difference'"; Berrey, *Enigma of Diversity*; Byrd, *Poison in the Ivy*; Okechukwu, *To Fulfill These Rights*.

104. Espeland and Sauder, *Engines of Anxiety*.

105. For an overview of how critical mass and diversity numbers were utilized before and during the *Fisher* cases, see Yuvraj Joshi, "Measuring Diversity," *Columbia Law Review Online* 117 (2017): 54–69.

106. Baez, " 'Knowledge of Difference'"; Byrd, *Poison in the Ivy*; Chang et al., *Compelling Interest*; Liliana M. Garces and Uma M. Jayakumar, "Dynamic Diversity: Toward a Contextual Understanding of Critical Mass," *Educational Researcher* 43, no. 3 (2014): 115–124; Patricia Gurin, Jeffrey S. Lehman, and Earl Lewis, *Defending Diversity: Affirmative Action at the University of Michigan* (Ann Arbor: University of Michigan Press, 2004); Sylvia Hurtado, Cynthia L. Alvarez, Chelsea Guillermo-Wann, Marcela Cuellar, and Lucy Arellano, "A Model for Diverse Learning Environments: The Scholarship on Creating and Assessing Conditions for Student Success," in *Higher Education: Handbook of Theory and Research*, vol. 27, ed. J. C. Smart and M. B. Paulsen (New York: Springer, 2012), 41–122; Sylvia Hurtado, Kimberly A. Griffin, Lucy Arellano, and Marcela Cuellar, "Assessing the Value of Climate Assessments: Progress and Future Directions," *Journal of Diversity in Higher Education* 1, no. 4 (2008): 204–221; Hurtado et al., "Enacting Diverse Learning Environments"; Milem, Chang, and antonio, *Making Diversity Work on Campus*; Moses and Chang, "Deeper Understanding of the Diversity Rationale"; Orfield, *Diversity Challenged*; Park, *Race on Campus*; Park, *When Diversity Drops*.

107. Garces and Jayakumar, "Dynamic Diversity." This point also resonates with research on intergroup contact theory (better known as the *contact hypothesis*), which is often oversimplified about the conditions needed to reduce prejudice among members of a group. For further reading on this facet of research, see Thomas Pettigrew and Linda Tropp's meta-analysis of nearly a century of research (Thomas F. Pettigrew and Linda R. Tropp, *When Groups Meet: The Dynamics of Intergroup Contact* [New York: Psychology Press, 2011]), and particularly Byrd, *Poison in the Ivy*; Park, *Race on Campus*; Park, *When Diversity Drops*; and Warikoo, *The Diversity Bargain*, for how diversity and social interactions influence students' beliefs about race, merit, policy, and inequality.

108. Calarco, *Negotiating Opportunities*; Lee and Zhou, *Asian American Academic Achievement Paradox*; Lewis and Diamond, *Despite the Best Intentions*; Lewis-McCoy, *Inequality in the Promised Land*; Losen and Martinez, *Out of School and Off Track*; Tyson, *Integration Interrupted*.

109. Hirschman, Berrey, and Rose-Greenland, "Dequantifying Diversity."

110. Bastedo and Bowman, "Improving Admission of Low-SES Students"; Bastedo et al., "Holistic Review?"; Bowman and Bastedo, "Admissions Office Diversity and Practices."

111. Don Jordan, "More than 65,000 Apply for Incoming Freshman Class," *University Record*, June 12, 2018, https://record.umich.edu/articles/more-65000-apply-incoming -freshman-class.

112. Espeland and Sauder, *Engines of Anxiety*; Hirschman, Berrey, and Rose-Greenland, "Dequantifying Diversity."

113. Espeland and Sauder, *Engines of Anxiety*; Golden, *Price of Admissions*; Karabel, *The Chosen*; Soares, *Power of Privilege*; Stevens, *Creating a Class*.

114. Scott Jaschik, "Research Universities Join the Test-Optional Movement," *InsideHigherEd*, June 15, 2020, https://www.insidehighered.com/admissions/article/2020/06/15/research-universities-join-test-optional-movement-least-year; Scott Jaschik, "Harvard, Princeton, and Stanford Join Test-Optional Colleges, for a Year," *InsideHigherEd*, June 22, 2020, https://www.insidehighered.com/admissions/article/2020/06/22/harvard-princeton-and-stanford-go-test-optional.

115. Andrew S. Belasco, Kelly O. Rosinger, and James C. Hearn, "The Test-Optional Movement at America's Selective Liberal Arts Colleges: A Boon for Equity or Something Else?," *Educational Evaluation and Policy Analysis* 37, no. 2 (2015): 206–223; Steven T. Syverson, Valerie W. Franks, and William C. Hiss, *Defining Access: How Test Optional Works* (Arlington, VA: National Association of College Admissions Counseling, 2018).

Chapter 2

1. Paul Tough, *The Years That Matter Most: How College Makes or Breaks Us* (Boston: Houghton Mifflin Harcourt, 2019).

2. Benjamin Baez, "The 'Knowledge of Difference' and the Limits of Science," *Journal of Higher Education* 75, no. 3 (2004): 285–306; W. Carson Byrd, *Poison in the Ivy: Race Relations and the Reproduction of Inequality on Elite College Campuses* (New Brunswick, NJ: Rutgers University Press, 2017); Mitchell J. Chang, Daria Witt, James Jones, and Kenji Hakuta, eds., *Compelling Interest: Examining the Racial Dynamics in Colleges and Universities* (Stanford, CA: Stanford University Press, 2003); Liliana M. Garces and Uma M. Jayakumar, "Dynamic Diversity: Toward a Contextual Understanding of Critical Mass," *Educational Researcher* 43, no. 3 (2014): 115–124; Patricia Gurin, Jeffrey S. Lehman, and Earl Lewis, *Defending Diversity: Affirmative Action at the University of Michigan* (Ann Arbor: University of Michigan Press, 2004); Hurtado et al., "A Model for Diverse Learning Environments"; Sylvia Hurtado, Kimberly A. Griffin, Lucy Arellano, and Marcela Cuellar, "Assessing the Value of Climate Assessments: Progress and Future Directions," *Journal of Diversity in Higher Education* 1, no. 4 (2008): 204–221; Sylvia Hurtado, Jeffrey Milem, Alma Clayton-Pedersen, and Walter Allen, "Enacting Diverse Learning Environments: Improving the Climate for Racial/Ethnic Diversity in Higher Education," ASHE-ERIC Higher Education Report, vol. 26, no. 8 (Washington, DC: George Washington University, 1999); Jeffrey F. Milem, Mitchell J. Chang, and anthony antonio, *Making Diversity Work on Campus: A Research-Based Perspective* (Washington, DC: Association of American Colleges & Universities, 2005); Michelle S. Moses and Mitchell J. Chang, "Toward a Deeper Understanding of the Diversity Rationale," *Educational Researcher* 35, no. 1 (2006): 6–11; Orfield, *Diversity Challenged*; Park, *Race on Campus*; Park, *When Diversity Drops*.

3. Yuvraj Joshi, "Measuring Diversity," *Columbia Law Review Online* 117 (2017): 54–69.

4. Liliana M. Garces and Uma M. Jayakumar, "Dynamic Diversity: Toward a Contextual Understanding of Critical Mass," *Educational Researcher* 43, no. 3 (2014): 115–124.

5. Wendy N. Espeland, and Michael Sauder, *Engines of Anxiety: Academic Rankings, Reputation, and Accountability* (New York: Russell Sage, 2016); Victor E. Ray, "A Theory of Racialized Organizations," *American Sociological Review* 84, no. 1 (2019): 26–53."

6. See William Ryan and Carol Stack's work, among many other studies, about the deleterious effects of victim blaming (William Ryan, *Blaming the Victim* [New York: Vintage, 1976]; Carol Stack, *All Our Kin: Strategies for Survival in a Black Community* [New York: Basic Books, 1974]).

7. Byrd, *Poison in the Ivy*; W. Carson Byrd, Rachelle J. Brunn-Bevel, and Sarah M. Ovink, eds., *Intersectionality and Higher Education: Identity and Inequality on College Campuses* (New Brunswick, NJ: Rutgers University Press, 2019); and Anthony A. Jack, *The Privileged Poor: How Elite Colleges Are Failing Disadvantaged Students* (Cambridge, MA: Harvard University Press, 2019), and a wide range of other research highlights the power and privilege afforded to white students, particularly those of higher socioeconomic positions, on college campuses across the United States, which marginalized and minoritized students must navigate.

8. W. E. B. Du Bois, *The Philadelphia Negro: A Social Study* (Philadelphia: University of Pennsylvania, 1899); Nicole M. Garcia, Nancy López, and Verónica Vélez, "QuantCrit: Rectifying Quantitative Methods Through Critical Race Theory," *Race Ethnicity and Education* 21, no. 2 (2018): 149–157; Aldon Morris, *The Scholar Denied: W. E. B. Du Bois and the Birth of Modern Sociology* (Berkeley: University of California Press, 2015); Tukufu Zuberi, *Thicker than Blood: How Racial Statistics Lie* (Minneapolis: University of Minnesota Press, 2001).

9. See José Itzigsohn, and Karida Brown, *The Sociology of W. E. B. Du Bois: Racialized Modernity and the Global Color Line* (New York: New York University Press, 2020); Morris, *The Scholar Denied*; and Earl Wright II, *The First American School of Sociology: W. E. B. Du Bois and the Atlanta Sociological Laboratory* (New York: Ashgate, 2018), for additional discussions of W. E. B. Du Bois's groundbreaking work.

10. Garcia, López, and Vélez, "QuantCrit"; Daniel G. Solórzano, Octavio Villalpando, and Leticia Oseguera, "Educational Inequities and Latina/o Undergraduate Students in the United States: A Critical Race Analysis of Their Educational Progress," *Journal of Hispanic Higher Education* 4, no. 3 (2005): 272–294; Daniel G. Solórzano and Tara J. Yosso, "Critical Race Methodology: Counter-Storytelling as an Analytical Framework for Education Research," *Qualitative Inquiry* 8, no. 1 (2002): 23–44; Daniel G. Solórzano and Tara J. Yosso, "Toward a Critical Race Theory of Chicana and Chicano Education," in *Charting New Terrains of Chicana (o)/Latina(o) Education: Themes of Urban and Inner City Education*, ed. C. Tejeda, C. Martinez, and Z. Leonardo (Cresskill, NJ: Hampton Press, 2002), 35–65.

11. Critical race theory allows researchers to identify how power, policies, and processes cause racial inequalities. Built as an interdisciplinary project, the theory has several central tenets, including these: (1) racism is a systemic reality influencing life chances and intersecting with other forms of oppression; (2) race-conscious approaches are needed to analyze inequality; (3) race is foundational to organizations' structure, language, policies, and everyday operations or processes, all of which influence outcomes (i.e., structural determinism); (4) economic factors can shift relationships between racial and ethnic groups (i.e., material determinism); (5) racial progress results when dominant and subordinate groups in society variously overlap; it often serves the interests of white people (i.e., interest convergence); and (6) counter-storytelling elaborates on how culture and structure shape marginalized community members' experiences navigating an unequal society (Derrick Bell, *Faces at the Bottom of the Well: The Permanence of Racism* (New York: Basic Books, 1992); Derrick Bell, *And We Are Not Saved: The Elusive Quest for Racial Justice* (New York: Basic Books, 1987); Kimberlé W. Crenshaw, "Critical Race

Studies, the First Decade: Critical Reflections, or 'A Foot in the Closing Door,'" *UCLA Law Review* 49 (2002): 1343–137; Richard Delgado and Jean Stefancic, *Critical Race Theory: An Introduction*, 3rd ed. (New York: New York University Press, 2017); Garcia, López, and Vélez, "QuantCrit"; Nicole M. Garcia and Oscar J. Mayorga, "The Threat of Unexamined Secondary Data: A Critical Race Transformative Convergent Mixed Methods," *Race Ethnicity and Education* 21, no. 2 (2018): 231–252; Mari J. Matsuda, Charles R. Lawrence III, Richard Delgado, Kimberlé W. Crenshaw, *Words That Wound: Critical Race Theory, Assaultive Speech, and the First Amendment* (Boulder, CO: Westview, 1993); Ray, "Theory of Racialized Organizations"). The theoretical framework of intersectionality simultaneously developed with critical race theory to examine how multiple identities and positions (e.g., race, ethnicity, gender, socioeconomic status, sexual orientation, citizenship, and disability) intersect in relation to systems of power such as racism, capitalism, sexism, and ableism. For examples of early intersectional works, see the Combahee River Collective, "A Black Feminist Statement," in *All the Women Are White, All the Blacks Are Men, But Some of Us Are Brave: Black Women's Studies*, ed. G. Hull, P. Bell-Scott, and B. Smith (New York: Feminist Press at the City University of New York, 1982), 13–22; Angela Y. Davis, *Women, Race, & Class* (New York: Random House, 1981); Audra Lorde, *Sister Outsider* (Berkeley, CA: Crossing Press, 1984); and the writings of Sojourner Truth, among others. See also Lisa Bowleg, "When Black + Lesbian + Woman ≠ Black Lesbian Woman: The Methodological Challenges of Qualitative and Quantitative Intersectionality Research," *Sex Roles* 59 (2008): 312–325; Patricia H. Collins, *Black Feminist Thought: Knowledge, Consciousness, and the Politics of Empowerment* (New York: Routledge, 2000); Patricia H. Collins and Sirma Bilge, *Intersectionality* (New York: Polity Press, 2016); Kimberlé W. Crenshaw, "Mapping the Margins: Intersectionality, Identity Politics, and Violence against Women of Color," *Stanford Law Review* 43, no. 6 (1991): 1241–1299. Given the fluidity of people's identities in relation to different situations in their communities, the connections between identity and inequality can shift under different circumstances. Intersectionality also makes us consider inequality as a continuum of experiences rather than as a binary (yes-no) condition. For example, different students on a college campus experience differing levels of support as it relates to student services (Rachelle J. Brunn-Bevel, Sarah M. Ovink, W. Carson Byrd, and Antron D. Mahoney, "Always Crossing Boundaries, Always Existing in Multiple Bubbles: Intersected Positions and Experiences on College Campuses," in *Intersectionality and Higher Education: Identity and Inequality on College Campuses*, ed. W. C. Byrd, R. J. Brunn-Bevel, and S. M. Ovink (New Brunswick, NJ: Rutgers University Press, 2019), 3–24; Collins, *Black Feminist Thought*; Collins and Bilge, *Intersectionality*). Furthermore, aligning with the perspective of universities operating as racialized organizations whose underlying norms, processes, and policies can shape resources, opportunities, and how people navigate these organizations, intersectionality elaborates on how multiple domains of power can shape the "matrix of domination" resulting from intersecting inequalities (Brunn-Bevel et al., "Always Crossing Boundaries"; Collins, *Black Feminist Thought*; Ray, "Theory of Racialized Organizations").

12. See Margaret Anderson and Patricia H. Collins, "Why Race, Class, and Gender Still Matter," in *Race, Class, and Gender: An Anthology*, 8th ed., ed. M. Anderson and P. Hill Collins (Boston: Cengage, 2013), 1–14; see p. 8.

13. There exist numerous references for scholarship utilizing critical race theory and intersectionality in the study of education. Examples include Byrd, Brunn-Bevel, and Ovink, *Intersectionality and Higher Education*; and Donald Mitchell Jr., Jakia Marie, and Tiffany

Steele, eds., *Intersectionality and Higher Education: Theory, Research, and Praxis*, 2nd ed. (New York: Peter Lang, 2019) for extended conversations about intersectional analyses of higher education, and Taylor, Gillborn, and Ladson-Billing's influential volume on critical race theory in education (Edward Taylor, Robert Gillborn, and Gloria Ladson-Billings, eds., *Foundations of Critical Race Theory in Education*, 2nd ed. [New York: Routledge, 2015]).

14. Jessica C. Harris and Lori D. Patton, "Un/Doing Intersectionality Through Higher Education Research," *Journal of Higher Education*, 90, no. 3 (2019): 347–372.

15. See Byrd, *Poison in the Ivy*; W. Carson Byrd, Sandra L. Dika, and Letticia T. Ramlal, "Who's in STEM? An Exploration of Race, Ethnicity, and Citizenship Reporting in a Federal Education Dataset," *Equity and Excellence in Education* 46, no. 4 (2013): 484–501; Yasmiyn Irizarry, "Utilizing Multidimensional Measures of Race in Educational Research: The Case of Teacher Perceptions," *Sociology of Race and Ethnicity* 1, no. 4 (2015): 564–583; Angela James, "Making Sense of Race and Racial Classification," in *White Logic White Methods: Racism and Methodology*, ed. Tukufu Zuberi and Eduardo Bonilla-Silva (Lanham, MD: Rowman & Littlefield, 2008), 31–46; Nancy López, Christopher Erwin, Melissa Binder, and Mario J. Chavez, "Making the Invisible Visible: Advancing Quantitative Methods in Higher Education Using Critical Race Theory and Intersectionality," *Race Ethnicity and Education* 21, no. 2 (2018): 180–207; Abigail A. Sewell, "The Racism-Race Reification Process: A Mesolevel Political Economic Framework for Understanding Racial Health Disparities," *Sociology of Race and Ethnicity* 2, no. 4 (2016): 402–432; Zuberi and Bonilla-Silva, *White Logic, White Methods*.

16. This quantitative approach builds on an early iteration of quantitative criticalism that encourages researchers to "consciously [choose] questions that seek to challenge, illuminate, conflict, and develop critique through quantitative methods to move theory, knowledge, and policy to a higher plane" (Frances K. Stage, "Answering Critical Questions with Quantitative Data," *New Directions for Institutional Research* 133 [2007]: 5–16; see p. 8). See also Benjamin Baez, "Thinking Critically About the 'Critical': Quantitative Research as Social Critique," *New Directions for Institutional Research* 133 (2007): 17–23; Joe L. Kincheloe and Peter L. McLaren, "Rethinking Critical Theory and Qualitative Research," in *Handbook of Qualitative Research*, ed. N. K. Denzin and Y. S. Lincoln (Thousand Oaks, CA: Sage, 1994), 138–157; Robert T. Teranishi, "Race, Ethnicity, and Higher Education Policy: The Use of Critical Quantitative Research," *New Directions for Institutional Research* 133 (2007): 37–49; and Robert T. Teranishi, Bach Mai Dolly Nguyen, Cynthia M. Alcantar, and Edward R. Curammeng, eds., *Measuring Race: Why Disaggregating Data Matters for Addressing Educational Inequality* (New York: Teachers College Press, 2020), for a critical examination of racial and ethnic data in educational inequality research.

17. Alejandro Covarrubias and Verónica N. Vélez, "Critical Race Quantitative Intersectionality: An Anti-Racist Research Paradigm That Refuses to 'Let the Numbers Speak for Themselves,'" in *Handbook of Critical Race Theory in Education*, ed. M. Lynn and A. D. Dixson (New York: Routledge, 2013), 270–285; Garcia, López, and Vélez, "QuantCrit"; David Gillborn, Paul Warmington, and Sean Demack, "QuantCrit: Education, Policy, 'Big Data,' and Principles for a Critical Race Theory of Statistics," *Race Ethnicity and Education* 21, no. 2 (2018): 158–179.

18. Espeland and Sauder, *Engines of Anxiety*.

19. Espeland and Sauder.

20. Garcia, López, and Vélez, "QuantCrit"; Gillborn, Warmington, and Demack, "QuantCrit."

21. Espeland and Sauder, *Engines of Anxiety*; Garcia, López, and Vélez, "QuantCrit"; Gillborn, Warmington, and Demack, "QuantCrit"; see also Ann Swidler, "Culture in Action: Symbols and Strategies," *American Sociological Review* 51, no. 2 (1986): 273–286, for additional discussions of how quantitative methods and related methodological and epistemological perspectives can fit in people's broader cultural toolkits in society.

22. Gillborn, Warmington, and Demack, "QuantCrit."

23. Espeland and Sauder, *Engines of Anxiety*.

24. Eduardo Bonilla-Silva, "Rethinking Racism: Toward a Structural Interpretation," *American Sociological Review* 62, no. 3 (1997): 465–480; Stuart Hall, "Race, Articulation, and Societies Structured in Dominance," in *Sociological Theories: Race and Colonialism* (Paris: UNESCO), 305–345; Michael Omi and Howard Winant, *Racial Formation in the United States*, 3rd ed. (New York: Routledge, 2015); Ray, "Theory of Racialized Organizations."

25. Joseph L. Graves Jr., *The Emperor's New Clothes: Biological Theories of Race at the New Millennium* (New Brunswick, NJ: Rutgers University Press, 2001); Omi and Winant, *Racial Formation in the United States*; Kenneth Prewitt, *What Is Your Race? The Census and Our Flawed to Classify Americans* (Princeton, NJ: Princeton University Press, 2016); Dorothy Roberts, *Fatal Invention: How Science, Politics, and Big Business Re-create Race in the Twenty-First Century* (New York: New Press, 2011); Audrey Smedley and Brian D. Smedley, *Race in North America: Origin and Evolution of a Concept*, 4th ed. (Boulder, CO: Westview, 2011); Zuberi, *Thicker than Blood*.

26. Ray, "Theory of Racialized Organizations"; Sewell, "The Racism-Race Reification Process."

27. Ray, "Theory of Racialized Organizations."

28. Karly S. Ford and Ashley N. Patterson, "'Cosmetic Diversity': University Websites and the Transformation of Race Categories," *Journal of Diversity in Higher Education* 12, no. 2 (2019): 99–114.

29. Baez, " 'Knowledge of Difference'."

30. Kerrianne Rockquemore, David L. Brunsma, and Daniel Delgado, "Racing to Theory or Retheorizing Race? Understanding the Struggle to Build a Multiracial Identity Theory," *Journal of Social Issues* 65, no. 1 (2009): 13–34.

31. Espeland and Sauder, *Engines of Anxiety*; Robert Kelchen, *Higher Education and Accountability* (Baltimore: Johns Hopkins University Press, 2018); Gary Orfield and Nicholas Hillman, eds., *Accountability and Opportunity in Higher Education: The Civil Rights Dimension* (Cambridge, MA: Harvard Education Press, 2018); Gary Orfield, Patricia Marin, and Catherine L. Horn, eds., *Higher Education and the Color Line: College Access, Racial Equity, and Social Change* (Cambridge, MA: Harvard Education Press, 2005).

32. Baez, " 'Knowledge of Difference'"; Espeland and Sauder, *Engines of Anxiety*; Hirschman, Berrey, and Rose-Greenland, "Dequantifying Diversity"; see also the conversations in Garces and Jayakumar, "Dynamic Diversity"; Uma M. Jayakumar, and Liliana M. Garces, eds., *Affirmative Action and Racial Equity: Considering the Fisher Case to Forge the Path Ahead* (New York: Routledge, 2015).

33. Baez, "'Knowledge of Difference'"; Garcia, López, and Vélez, "QuantCrit"; Gillborn, Warmington, and Demack, "QuantCrit."

34. Rockquemore, Brunsma, and Delgado, "Racing to Theory or Retheorizing Race?"

35. James, "Making Sense of Race and Racial Classification"; Omi and Winant, *Racial Formation in the United States*; Prewitt, *What Is Your Race?*

36. See also Samantha Viano, and Dominique J. Baker, "How Administrative Data Collection and Analysis Can Better Reflect Racial and Ethnic Identities," *Review of Educational Research* 44 (2020): 301–331.

37. Espeland and Sauder, *Engines of Anxiety.*

38. See Valdez and Golash-Boza, "U.S. Racial and Ethnic Relations in the Twenty-First Century," for an in-depth exploration of how processes of race and ethnicity are intertwined and must be discussed in relation to one another to shed light on different experiences of racialization in society.

39. National Center for Education Statistics, "IPEDS: Collecting Race and Ethnicity Data from Students and Staff Using the New Categories," (2020), https://nces.ed.gov/ipeds /report-your-data/race-ethnicity-collecting-data-for-reporting-purposes.

40. Ray, "A Theory of Racialized Organizations."

41. See Garcia and Mayorga, "The Threat of Unexamined Secondary Data."

42. Samantha Viano and Dominique J. Baker, "How Administrative Data Collection and Analysis Can Better Reflect Racial and Ethnic Identities," *Review of Research in Education*, 44 (2020): 301–331.

43. See the available disaggregated race and ethnicity data for the University of California system (https://www.universityofcalifornia.edu/infocenter/disaggregated-data) and the overview of categories used for student enrollment reporting in relation to federal reporting instructions (https://www.universityofcalifornia.edu/sites/default/files/Race-Eth%20 Data%20Collection.pdf).

44. D'vera Cohn, "Federal Officials May Revamp How Americans Identify Race, Ethnicity on Census and Other Forms." Pew Research Center (2016), http://www.pewresearch .org/fact-tank/2016/10/04/federal-officials-may-revamp-how-americans-identify-race -ethnicity-on-census-and-other-forms; Jennifer Lee and Karthick Ramakrishnan, "Who Counts as Asian?," *Ethnic and Racial Studies* (2019): DOI: https://doi.org/10.1080/01419 870.2019.1671600.

45. See my brief description of how the shifting connections between race and ethnicity in relation to US Census categories can influence interpretations of group member experiences in Byrd, *Poison in the Ivy.*

46. Covarrubias and Vélez, "Critical Race Quantitative Intersectionality"; Garcia, López, and Vélez, "QuantCrit"; Gillborn, Warmington, and Demack, "QuantCrit"; López et al., "Making the Invisible Visible"; Teranishi et al., *Measuring Race.*

47. See Jennifer Lee and Min Zhou, *The Asian American Achievement Paradox* (New York: Russell Sage Foundation, 2015), for an example.

48. See Derrick Brooms, *Being Black, Being Male on Campus: Understanding and Confronting Black Male Collegiate Experiences* (Albany, NY: State University of New York Press, 2017), Byrd, Brunn-Bevel, and Sexton 2014, Chou and Feagin, *The Myth of the Model Minority*, Eric R. Felix, and Ray Ramirez, "Counterstories of Policy Implementation: Using Reform to Address Latinx Student Equity," *Journal of Latinos and Education* (2020) DOI: https://doi.org/10.1080/15348431.2020.1782205, Shaun R. Harper, "An Anti-deficit Achievement Framework for Research on Students of Color in STEM," *New Directions for Institutional Research* 148 (2010): 63–74; Lee and Zhou, *Asian American Achievement Paradox*; Park, *Race on Campus*, and Robert T. Teranishi, *Asians in the Ivory Tower: Dilemmas of Racial Inequality in American Higher Education* (New York: Teachers College Press, 2010), among others, for research debunking stereotypes and deficit perspectives informing knowledge of and policy to support students of color in higher education.

49. Irizarry, "Utilizing Multidimensional Measures of Race in Educational Research." See also the use of "street race" by Nancy López (Nancy López, "Killing Two Birds With One Stone? Why We Need Two Separate Questions on Race and Ethnicity in 2020

Census and Beyond," *Latino Studies Journal* 11, no. 3 (2013): 428–438; Nancy López, Edward Vargas, Melina Juarez, Lisa Cacari-Stone, and Sonia Bettez, "What's Your "Street Race"? Leveraging Multidimensional Measures of Race and Intersectionality for Examining Physical and Mental Health Status Among Latinxs," *Sociology of Race and Ethnicity* 4, no. 1 (2018): 49–66).

50. Espeland and Sauder, *Engines of Anxiety*; Hirschman, Berrey, and Rose-Greenland, "Dequantifying Diversity"; Omi and Winant, *Racial Formation in the United States*; Ray, "A Theory of Racialized Organizations."

51. Byrd, Dika, and Ramlal, "Who's in STEM?"; Hughes, "Dilemmas and Contradictions of Status."

52. Graves, *The Emperor's New Clothes*; Omi and Winant, *Racial Formation in the United States*; Prewitt, *What is Your Race?*; Roberts, *Fatal Invention*; Smedley and Smedley, *Race in North America*; Zuberi, *Thicker than Blood*.

53. Poon, Dizon, and Squire, "Count Me In!"

54. Espeland and Sauder, *Engines of Anxiety*; Daniel Hirschman and Emily A. Bosk "Standardizing Biases: Selection Devices and the Quantification of Race," *Sociology of Race and Ethnicity* (2019): DOI: https://doi.org/10.1177/2332649219844797.

55. Baez, "'Knowledge of Difference'," 291.

56. Baez, 290–291 (emphasis in original); also Ray, "Theory of Racialized Organizations"; Sewell, "Racism-Race Reification Process."

57. Baez, "'Knowledge of Difference'"; Espeland and Sauder, *Engines of Anxiety*; Ray, "Theory of Racialized Organizations."

58. Baez, "'Knowledge of Difference'"; Byrd, *Poison in the Ivy*; W. Carson Byrd, Rachelle J. Brunn-Bevel, and Parker Sexton, "'We Don't All Look Alike': The Academic Performance of Black Student Populations at Elite Colleges," *Du Bois Review* 11, no. 2 (2014): 353–385; Joe R. Feagin, Hernan Vera, and Nikitah Imani, *The Agony of Education: Black Students at White Universities* (New York: Routledge, 1996); Shaun R. Harper, "Race without Racism: How Higher Education Researchers Minimize Racist Institutional Norms," *Review of Higher Education* 36, no. 1 (2012): 9–30; Wendy L. Moore, *Reproducing Racism: White Space, Elite Law Schools, and Racial Inequality* (Lanham, MD: Rowman & Littlefield 2008); Ray, "Theory of Racialized Organizations."

59. Sylvia Hurtado, Cynthia L. Alvarez, Chelsea Guillermo-Wann, Marcela Cuellar, and Lucy Arellano, "A Model for Diverse Learning Environments: The Scholarship on Creating and Assessing Conditions for Student Success," in *Higher Education: Handbook of Theory and Research*, vol. 27, ed. J. C. Smart and M. B. Paulsen (New York: Springer, 2012), 41–122; Hurtado et al., "Assessing the Value of Climate Assessments"; Hurtado et al., "Enacting Diverse Learning Environments."

60. National Center for Education Statistics (NCES), *Digest of Educational Statistics* (Washington, DC: US Department of Education, 2019), https://nces.ed.gov/programs/digest, table 303.10. Much of this growth occurred across higher education, driven by a burgeoning for-profit sector, which is now significantly shrinking.

61. NCES, table 302.20. The three-year moving average considers the two previous years of data in relation to the specific target year of interest. For example, data for 2010 will average data for 2008, 2009, and 2010 to adjust for any possible changes and smooth the averages across years.

62. NCES, table 302.20.

63. Karl Alexander, Doris Entwisle, and Linda Olson, *The Long Shadow: Family Background, Disadvantaged Urban Youth, and the Transition to Adulthood* (New York: Russell Sage

Foundation, 2014; Jessica Calarco, *Negotiating Opportunities: How the Middle Class Secures Advantages in Schools* (New York: Oxford University Press, 2018); Linda Darling-Hammond, "Race, Inequality, and Educational Accountability: The Irony of 'No Child Left Behind,'" *Race, Ethnicity and Education* 10, no. 3 (2007): 245–260; Linda Darling-Hammond, "The Color Line in American Education: Race, Resources, and Student Achievement," *Du Bois Review* 1, no. 2 (2004): 213–246; Angel L. Harris, *Kids Don't Want to Fail: Oppositional Culture and the Black-White Achievement Gap* (Cambridge, MA: Harvard University Press, 2011); Jonathan Kozol, *The Shame of the Nation: The Restoration of Apartheid Schooling in America* (New York: Crown Publishers, 2005); Jonathan Kozol, *Savage Inequalities: Children in America's Schools* (New York: Harper Perennial, 1991); Amanda E. Lewis and John B. Diamond, *Despite the Best Intentions: How Racial Inequality Thrives in Good Schools* (New York: Oxford University Press, 2015); R. L'Heureux Lewis-McCoy, *Inequality in the Promised Land: Race, Resources, and Suburban Schooling* (Stanford, CA: Stanford University Press, 2014); Daniel J. Losen and Tia E. Martinez, *Out of School and Off Track: The Overuse of Suspensions in American Middle and High Schools* (Los Angeles: The Civil Rights Project, 2013); Amaka Okechukwu, *To Fulfill These Rights: Political Struggle over Affirmative Action and Open Admissions* (New York: Columbia University Press, 2019); Jason A. Okonofua and Jennifer L. Eberhardt, "Two Strikes: Race and the Disciplining of Young Students," *Psychological Science* 26, no. 5 (2015): 617–624; Gary Orfield, John Kucsera, and Genevieve Siegel-Hawley, *E Pluribus . . . Separation: Deepening Double Segregation for More Students* (Los Angeles: UCLA Civil Rights Project/Proyecto Derechos Civiles, 2012); Julie J. Park, *Race on Campus: Debunking Myths with Data* (Cambridge, MA: Harvard Educational Press, 2018); Karolyn Tyson, *Integration Interrupted: Tracking, Black Students, and Acting White After* Brown (New York: Oxford University Press, 2011).

64. Tanya Golash-Boza, *Deported: Immigrant Policing, Disposable Labor and Global Capitalism* (New York: New York University Press, 2015); Lee and Ramakrishnan, "Who Counts as Asian?"; Jennifer Lee and Van C. Tran, "The Mere Mention of Asian Americans," *Sociological Science* 6 (2019): 551–579; Lee and Zhou, *Asian American Achievement Paradox*.

65. Lorelle Espinosa, Jonathan M. Turk, Morgan Taylor, and Hollie M. Chessman, *Race and Ethnicity in Higher Education: A Status Report* (Washington, DC: American Council on Education, 2019), figure 3.1.

66. NCES, *Digest of Education Statistics*, table 306.20.

67. Espinosa et al., *Race and Ethnicity in Higher Education*, figure 3.11.

68. Espinosa et al., table 3.1.

69. See Jason C. Garvey, Sydnee Viray, Katie Stango, Claire Estep, and Jae Jaeger, "Emergence of Third Spaces: Exploring Trans Students' Campus Climate Perceptions Within Collegiate Environments," *Sociology of Education* 92, no. 3 (2019): 229–246; Megan Nanney, "Making Room for Gendered Possibilities: Using Intersectionality to Discover Transnormative Inequalities in the Women's College Admissions Process," in *Intersectionality and Higher Education: Identity and Inequality on College Campuses*, ed. W. Carson Byrd, R. J. Brunn-Bevel, and S. M. Ovink (New Brunswick, NJ: Rutgers University Press, 2019), 227–241; and Z. Nicolazzo, *Trans* in College: Transgender Students' Strategies for Navigating Campus Life and Institutional Politics of Inclusion* (Sterling, VA: Stylus, 2017), for examples of discussions concerning the changing policies about, and experiences of, nonbinary students on college campuses.

70. Espinosa et al., *Race and Ethnicity in Higher Education*, figures 3.9 and 3.10.

71. Espinosa et al., figure 3.12 and table 3.2.

72. See Tressie M. Cottom, *Lower Ed: The Troubling Rise of For-Profit Colleges in the New Economy* (New York: New Press, 2017).

73. See Wilder's *Ebony and Ivy* for additional historical insight into early colonial college efforts to control Native American communities.

74. Ray, " Theory of Racialized Organizations."

75. See Barrett J. Taylor and Brendan Cantwell, *Unequal Higher Education: Wealth, Status, and Student Opportunity* (New Brunswick, NJ: Rutgers University Press, 2019), for an examination of socioeconomic inequality in higher education. See also William G. Bowen, Martin A. Kurzweil, and Eugene M. Tobin, *Equity and Excellence in American Higher Education* (Charlottesville: University of Virginia Press, 2005), for additional historical discussion of these inequalities.

76. Espinosa et al., figure 3.13.

77. Espinosa et al., table 3.5.

78. Mark Huelsman, *Social Exclusion: The State of State U for Black Students* (Washington, DC: Demos, 2018).

79. Anthony P. Carnevale, Martin Van Der Werf, Michael C. Quinn, Jeff Strohl, and Dmitri Reprikov, *Our Separate & Unequal Public Colleges: How Public Colleges Reinforce White Racial Privilege and Marginalize Black and Latino Students* (Washington, DC: Georgetown University Center for Education and the Workforce, 2018); Espinosa et al., *Race and Ethnicity in Higher Education*; Jason N. Houle and Fenaba R. Addo, "Racial Disparities in Student Debt and the Reproduction of the Fragile Black Middle Class," *Sociology of Race and Ethnicity* 5, no. 4 (2019): 562–577; Huelsman, *Social Exclusion*; Benjamin Miller, "Graduate School Debt: Ideas for Reducing the $37 Billion in Annual Student Loans That No One Is Talking About," Center for American Progress, January 13, 2020, https://www.americanprogress.org/issues/education-postsecondary/reports /2020/01/13/479220/graduate-school-debt/; Laura Sullivan, Tatjana Meschede, Thomas Shapiro, and Fernanda Escobar, *Stalling Dreams: How Student Debt Is Disrupting Life Chances and Widening the Racial Wealth Gap* (Waltham, MA: Brandies University Institute on Assets and Social Policy, 2019).

80. See Lewis and Diamond, *Despite the Best Intentions*; Jeannie Oakes, *Keeping Track: How Schools Structure Inequality* (New Haven, CT: Yale University Press, 2005); Tyson, *Integration Interrupted*.

81. Espinosa et al., *Race and Ethnicity in Higher Education*, tables 3.8 and 3.9.

82. See Espinosa et al. for further discussion of differences in completion rates in higher education, particularly chapter 5.

83. Espinosa et al., figure 4.2.

84. Espinosa et al., figure 4.4.

85. Espinosa et al., figure 4.10 and table 4.2. See also Cottom, *Lower Ed*, for an in-depth conversation about the predatory practices of for-profit institutions and questionable degree programs.

86. Espinosa et al., *Race and Ethnicity in Higher Education*, figure 4.11.

87. Espinosa et al., table 4.6.

88. See Espinosa et al., chapter 6, report for further discussion.

89. Espinosa et al., figure 10.1.

90. Espinosa et al., figure 10.2.

91. Espinosa et al., figures 10.4–10.11 and tables 10.1–10.4.

92. Espinosa et al., figures 10.15–10.19.

93. Espinosa et al., figure 10.12.

94. Espinosa et al., figure 10.13.
95. Ray, "Theory of Racialized Organizations"; see also Eddie R. Cole, *The Campus Color Line: College Presidents and the Struggle for Black Freedom* (Princeton, NJ: Princeton University Press, 2020), an exceptional discussion of race and college presidents.
96. Espinosa et al., *Race and Ethnicity in Higher Education*, figure 10.14.
97. W. Carson Byrd, Sarah M. Ovink, and Rachelle J. Brunn-Bevel, "Tips of Icebergs in the Ocean: Reflections on Future Research Embracing Intersectionality in Higher Education," in *Intersectionality and Higher Education: Identity and Inequality on College Campuses*, ed. W. Carson Byrd, R. J. Brunn-Bevel, and S. M. Ovink (New Brunswick, NJ: Rutgers University Press, 2019), 263–267.
98. Baez, "'Knowledge of Difference.'" See also Ruth Burke and Grace Kao, "Bearing the Burden of Whiteness: The Implication of Racial Self-identification for Multiracial Adolescents' School Belonging and Academic Achievement," *Ethnic & Racial Studies* 36, no. 5 (2013): 747–773, Jamie M. Doyle and Grace Kao, "Are Racial Identities of Multiracials Stable? Changing Self-Identification Among Single and Multiple Race Individuals," *Social Psychology Quarterly* 70, no. 4 (2007): 405–423; David R. Harris and Jeremiah J. Sim, "Who Is Multiracial? Assessing the Complexity of Lived Race," *American Sociological Review* 67, no. 4 (2002): 614–627; Eileen O'Brien, *The Racial Middle: Latinos and Asian Americans Living Beyond the Racial Divide* (New York: New York University Press, 2008); Rockquemore, Brunsma, and Delgado, "Racing to Theory or Retheorizing Race?; Aliya Saperstein and Andrew M. Penner, "Racial Fluidity and Inequality in the United States," *American Journal of Sociology* 118, no. 3 (2012): 676–727; and Mary Waters, *Black Identities: West Indian Immigrant Dreams and American Realities* (Cambridge, MA: Harvard University Press, 1999), among others, for examples of how racial identity can shift depending on contexts, particularly for multiracial individuals.
99. López et al., "Making the Invisible Visible"; Jenna Sablan, "Can You Really Measure That? Critical Race Theory and Quantitative Methods," *American Educational Research Journal* 56, no. 1 (2019): 178–203.
100. Garcia and Mayorga, "The Threat of Unexamined Secondary Data"; James, "Making Sense of Race and Racial Classification"; Sewell, "Racism-Race Reification Process"; Zuberi, *Thicker than Blood*.
101. Addressing the question of controlling for race in studies and constructing comparisons in quantitative data, a study I completed with Rachelle Brunn-Bevel and Parker Sexton ("'We Don't All Look Alike'") shows why running separate models for Black student groups rather than including a set of dichotomous variables can pinpoint what campus experiences and barriers influence Black students' degree pursuits. For example, separate models can better show which students are more likely to experience stereotype threat. African American students were particularly likely to experience these situations on college campuses, but our common approaches to creating a homogenized Black student group can influence our interpretations of the analyses. In other research, I considered how aspects of colorism can influence students' social experiences and perceptions of the campus racial climate and the persistence of racial inequality in society (Byrd, *Poison in the Ivy*). For example, Black and Latinx students with darker skin complexions had fewer friendships with white students in college but more friendships with Black students. These are examples of exploring intracategorical intersectionality quantitatively, allowing for fuller interpretations that do not readily rely on deficit perspectives or stereotypes of groups (Leslie McCall, "The Complexity of Intersectionality," *Signs* 30, no. 3 (2005): 1771–1800). See also Nicole M. Else-Quest and Janet S. Hyde, "In-

tersectionality in Quantitative Psychological Research: II. Methods and Techniques," *Psychology of Women Quarterly* 40, no. 3 (2016): 319–336.

102. Irizarry, "Multidimensional Measures of Race."

103. See Byrd, Dika, and Ramlal, "Who's in STEM?"

104. Bowleg, "Black + Lesbian + Woman."

105. Ange-Marie Hancock, "Empirical Intersectionality: A Tale of Two Approaches," *UC Irvine Law Review* (2013) 3, no. 2: 259–296. See also Nicole M. Else-Quest and Janet S. Hyde, "Intersectionality in Quantitative Psychological Research: I. Theoretical and Epistemological Issues," *Psychology of Women Quarterly* 40, no. 2 (2016): 155–170.

106. Lauren Schudde, "Heterogeneous Effects in Education: The Promise and Challenge of Incorporating Intersectionality into Quantitative Methodological Approaches," *Review of Research in Education*, 42 (2018): 72–92. see also Else-Quest and Hyde, "Intersectionality in Quantitative Psychological Research: II."

107. López et al., "Making the Invisible Visible."

108. Schudde, "Heterogeneous Effects in Education," 82–87.

109. Alejandro Covarrubias, "Quantitative Intersectionality: A Critical Race Analysis of the Chicana/o Educational Pipeline," *Journal of Latinos and Education* 10, no. 2 (2011): 86–105; Alejandro Covarrubias, Pedro E. Nava, Argelia Lara, Rebeca Burciaga, Verónica N. Vélez, and Daniel G. Solórzano, "Critical Race Quantitative Intersections: A *Testimonio* Analysis," *Race Ethnicity and Education* 21, no. 2 (2018): 253–273.

110. See, for example, Sung T. Jang, "The Implications of Intersectionality on Southeast Asian Female Students' Educational Outcomes in the United States: A Critical Quantitative Intersectionality Analysis," *American Educational Research Journal* 55, no. 6 (2018): 1268–1306.

111. Sewell, "Racism-Race Reification Process."

112. Sablan, "Can You Really Measure That?"

113. Byrd, Brunn-Bevel, and Ovink, *Intersectionality and Higher Education*; Covarrubias et al., "Critical Race Quantitative Intersections"; Garcia, López, and Vélez, "QuantCrit"; Garcia and Mayorga, "The Threat of Unexamined Secondary Data."

114. Covarrubias et al. 2018, "Critical Race Quantitative Intersections."

115. Garcia, López, and Vélez, "QuantCrit"; Gillborn, Warmington, and Demack, "QuantCrit."

116. Park, *Race on Campus*.

117. Park, *Race on Campus*; see also Byrd, *Poison in the Ivy*.

118. Park, *Race on Campus*; Park, *When Diversity Drops*.

119. Natasha K. Warikoo, *The Diversity Bargain: And Other Dilemmas of Race, Admissions, and Meritocracy at Elite Universities* (Chicago: University of Chicago Press, 2016).

120. See Whitney E. H. Bortz, David B. Knight, Chelsea H. Lyles, Timothy Kinoshita, Nathan H. Choe, Maya Denton, and Maura Borrego, "A Competitive System: Graduate Student Recruitment in STEM and Why Money May Not be the Answer, " *Journal of Higher Education* (2019): DOI: https://doi.org/10.1080/00221546.2019.1706017.

121. See Byrd, Ovink, and Brunn-Bevel, "Tips of Icebergs."

122. See Christa J. Porter, Candace M. Moore, Ginny J. Boss, Tiffany J. Davis, and Dave A. Louis, "To Be Black Women and Contingent Faculty: Four Scholarly Personal Narratives," *Journal of Higher Education* 91, no. 5 (2020): 674–697; Covarrubias, "Quantitative Intersectionality"; Covarrubias et al., "Critical Race Quantitative Intersections"; Collins, *Black Feminist Thought*; Collins and Bilge, *Intersectionality*; Delgado and Stefancic, *Critical Race Theory*. Also, consider Meera Deo's recent intersectional examination of women

of color in law schools for another critical example of the power of counternarratives that are missed behind heavily quantitative approaches that do not uncover climate issues that plague faculty career endeavors (Meera Deo, *Unequal Profession: Race and Gender in Legal Academia* [Stanford, CA: Stanford University Press, 2019]).

123. Espeland and Sauder, *Engines of Anxiety.*

124. Sara Ahmed, *On Being Included: Racism and Diversity in Institutional Life* (Durham, NC: Duke University Press, 2012); Baez, "'Knowledge of Difference'"; Eduardo Bonilla-Silva, "The Invisible Weight of Whiteness: The Racial Grammar of Everyday Life in Contemporary America," *Ethnic & Racial Studies* 35, no. 2 (2012): 173–194; David L. Brunsma, Eric S. Brown, and Peggy Placier, "Teaching Race at Historically White Colleges and Universities: Identifying and Dismantling the Walls of Whiteness," *Critical Sociology* 39, no. 5 (2013): 717–738; Byrd, *Poison in the Ivy*; Nolan L. Cabrera, *White Guys on Campus: Racism, White Immunity, and the Myth of "Post-Racial" Higher Education* (New Brunswick, NJ: Rutgers University Press, 2018); Feagin, Vera, and Imani, *Agony of Education*; Moore, *Reproducing Racism*; Ray, "Theory of Racialized Organizations"; James M. Thomas, *Diversity Regimes: Why Talk Is Not Enough to Fix Racial Inequality at Universities* (New Brunswick, NJ: Rutgers University Press, 2020).

125. See Baez, "'Knowledge of Difference'"; Byrd, *Poison in the Ivy*; Chang et al., *Compelling Interest*; Garces and Jayakumar, "Dynamic Diversity"; Gurin et al., *Defending Diversity*; Hurtado et al., "A Model for Diverse Learning Environments"; Hurtado et al., "Assessing the Value of Climate Assessments"; Hurtado et al., "Enacting Diverse Learning Environments"; Milem, Chang, and antonio, *Making Diversity Work on Campus*; Moses and Chang, "Deeper Understanding of the Diversity Rationale"; Orfield, *Diversity Challenged*; Park, *Race on Campus*; Park, *When Diversity Drops.*

126. Baez, "'Knowledge of Difference'."

127. Baez; Garces and Jayakumar, "Dynamic Diversity."

128. Baez, " 'Knowledge of Difference'; Garces and Jayakumar, "Dynamic Diversity"; Gurin et al., *Defending Diversity*; Hurtado et al., "Model for Diverse Learning Environments"; Hurtado et al., "Value of Climate Assessments"; Hurtado et al., "Enacting Diverse Learning Environments"; Milem, Chang, and antonio, *Making Diversity Work on Campus*; Moses and Chang, "Deeper Understanding of the Diversity Rationale"; Orfield, *Diversity Challenged*; Park, *Race on Campus*; Park, *When Diversity Drops.*

129. Covarrubias et al., "Critical Race Quantitative Intersections"; Garces and Jayakumar, "Dynamic Diversity"; López et al., "Making the Invisible Visible"; Ray, "Theory of Racialized Organizations."

130. Espeland and Sauder, *Engines of Anxiety.*

131. Ahmed, *On Being Included*; Byrd, *Poison in the Ivy*; Gurin et al., *Defending Diversity*; Hurtado et al., "Model for Diverse Learning Environments"; Hurtado et al., "Value of Climate Assessments"; Hurtado et al., "Enacting Diverse Learning Environments"; Ray, "Theory of Racialized Organizations"; Warikoo, *The Diversity Bargain.*

132. Byrd, *Poison in the Ivy*; Cabrera, *White Guys on Campus*; Thomas, *Diversity Regimes.*

133. Baez, "'Knowledge of Difference'"; Gurin et al., *Defending Diversity*; Shaun R. Harper and Sylvia Hurtado, "Nine Themes in Campus Racial Climates and Implications for Institutional Transformation," *New Directions for Student Services* 120 (2007): 7–24; Sylvia Hurtado, "The Campus Racial Climate: Contexts of Conflict," *Journal of Higher Education* 63, no. 5 (1992): 539–569; Hurtado et al., "Enacting Diverse Learning Environments"; Milem, Chang, and antonio, *Making Diversity Work on Campus*; Moses

and Chang, "Deeper Understanding of the Diversity Rationale"; Smith, *Diversity Work*; Smith, "The Diversity Imperative."

134. Baez, "'Knowledge of Difference'."

Chapter 3

1. Benjamin Baez, "The 'Knowledge of Difference' and the Limits of Science," *Journal of Higher Education* 75, no. 3 (2004): 285–306; Ellen Berrey, *The Enigma of Diversity: The Language and the Limits of Racial Justice* (Chicago: University of Chicago Press, 2015); W. Carson Byrd, *Poison in the Ivy: Race Relations and the Reproduction of Inequality on Elite College Campuses* (New Brunswick, NJ: Rutgers University Press, 2017); Liliana M. Garces and Uma M. Jayakumar, "Dynamic Diversity: Toward a Contextual Understanding of Critical Mass," *Educational Researcher* 43, no. 3 (2014): 115–12; Patricia Gurin, Jeffrey S. Lehman, and Earl Lewis, *Defending Diversity: Affirmative Action at the University of Michigan* (Ann Arbor: University of Michigan Press, 2004); Sylvia Hurtado, Cynthia L. Alvarez, Chelsea Guillermo-Wann, Marcela Cuellar, and Lucy Arellano, "A Model for Diverse Learning Environments: The Scholarship on Creating and Assessing Conditions for Student Success," in *Higher Education: Handbook of Theory and Research*, vol. 27, ed. J. C. Smart and M. B. Paulsen (New York: Springer, 2012), 41–122; Sylvia Hurtado, Jeffrey Milem, Alma Clayton-Pedersen, and Walter Allen, "Enacting Diverse Learning Environments: Improving the Climate for Racial/Ethnic Diversity in Higher Education," ASHE-ERIC Higher Education Report, vol. 26, no. 8 (Washington, DC: George Washington University, 1999); Jeffrey F. Milem, Mitchell J. Chang, and anthony l. antonio, *Making Diversity Work on Campus: A Research-Based Perspective* (Washington, DC: Association of American Colleges & Universities, 2005); Amaka Okechukwu, *To Fulfill These Rights: Political Struggle over Affirmative Action and Open Admissions* (New York: Columbia University Press, 2019); Julie J. Park, *Race on Campus: Debunking Myths with Data* (Cambridge, MA: Harvard Educational Press, 2018); Daryl G. Smith, "The Diversity Imperative: Moving to the Next Generation," in *American Higher Education in the Twenty-First Century: Social, Political, and Economic Challenges*, ed. Michael N. Bastedo, P. G. Altbach, and P. J. Gumport (Baltimore: Johns Hopkins University Press, 2016), 375–400; Daryl G. Smith, *Diversity Works: The Emerging Picture of How Students Benefit* (Washington, DC: Association of American Colleges and Universities, 1997).

2. See Garces and Jayakumar, "Dynamic Diversity."

3. See David L. Brunsma, David G. Embrick, and James M. Thomas, "College Leaders Often Deny Racial Tensions at Their Own Institutions," *InsideHigherEd*, August 25, 2016 https://www.insidehighered.com/views/2016/08/25/college-leaders-often-deny -racial-tensions-theirown-institutions-essay; W. Carson Byrd, LeAnna Luney, Jakia Marie, and Kimberly N. Sanders, "Demanding Attention: An Exploration of Institutional Characteristics of Recent Student Demands," *Journal of Diversity in Higher Education*, (2019): DOI: https/doi.org/10.1037/dhe0000133.

4. Roberta M. Hall and Bernice R. Sandler, *Out of the Classroom: A Chilly Campus Climate for Women?* Project on the Status and Education of Women (Washington, DC: Association of American Colleges, 1984); Bernice R. Sandler and Roberta M. Hall, *The Campus Climate Revisited: Chilly for Women, Administrators, and Graduate Students*, Project on the Status and Education of Women (Washington, DC: Association of American Colleges, 1986).

5. Baez, "'Knowledge of Difference'"; Mitchell J. Chang, Daria Witt, James Jones, and Kenji Hakuta, eds., *Compelling Interest: Examining the Racial Dynamics in Colleges and Universities* (Stanford, CA: Stanford University Press, 2003); Patricia Gurin, Eric L. Dey, Sylvia Hurtado, and Gerald Gurin, "Diversity and Higher Education: Theory and Impact on Educational Outcomes," *Harvard Educational Review* 72, no. 3 (2002): 330–366; Hurtado et al., "Enacting Diverse Learning Environments"; Milem, Chang, and antonio, *Making Diversity Work on Campus*; Okechukwu, *To Fulfill These Rights*; Smith, *Diversity Works*.

6. Google Books has digitized over 25 million books across many languages. The current analyses focus only on books published in American English.

7. Google Ngram only analyzes books digitized up to 2008.

8. Eduardo Bonilla-Silva, *Racism Without Racists: Color-Blind Racism and the Persistence of Racial Inequality in the United States*, 5th ed. (Lanham, MD: Rowman & Littlefield, 2017); Patricia H. Collins, *Black Feminist Thought: Knowledge, Consciousness, and the Politics of Empowerment* (New York: Routledge, 2000); T. Elon Dancy II, Kristen T. Edwards, and James Earl Davis, "Historically White Universities and Plantation Politics: Anti-Blackness and Higher Education in the Black Lives Matter Era," *Urban Education* 53, no. 2 (2018): 176–195; Ray, "A Theory of Racialized Organizations."

9. Ray, "Theory of Racialized Organizations."

10. Baez, "'Knowledge of Difference'"; Berrey, *Enigma of Diversity*; Byrd, *Poison in the Ivy*; Garces and Jayakumar, "Dynamic Diversity"; Gurin et al., *Defending Diversity*; Hurtado et al., "Model for Diverse Learning Environments"; Hurtado et al., "Value of Climate Assessments"; Hurtado et al., "Enacting Diverse Learning Environments"; Uma M. Jayakumar and Liliana M. Garces, *Affirmative Action and Racial Equity: Considering the Fisher Case to Forge the Path Ahead* (New York: Routledge, 2015); Milem, Chang, and antonio, *Making Diversity Work on Campus*; Okechukwu, *To Fulfill These Rights*; Park, *Race on Campus*; Smith, "Diversity Imperative"; Smith, *Diversity Works*.

11. Patricia Gurin, Eric L. Dey, Sylvia Hurtado, and Gerald Gurin, "Diversity and Higher Education: Theory and Impact on Educational Outcomes," *Harvard Educational Review* 72, no. 3 (2002): 330–366; Sylvia Hurtado, "The Campus Racial Climate: Contexts of Conflict," *Journal of Higher Education* 63, no. 5 (1992): 539–569"; Hurtado et al., "Enacting Diverse Learning Environments"; Milem, Chang, and antonio, *Making Diversity Work on Campus*; Smith, *Diversity Works*.

12. Hurtado et al., "Enacting Diverse Learning Environments"; Ray, "Theory of Racialized Organizations."

13. Hurtado, "Campus Racial Climate." This study was part of a larger set of analyses further developing the connection between campus climates and student learning and social outcomes (see Sylvia Hurtado, *Campus Racial Climates and Educational Outcomes* [PhD diss., University of California, Los Angeles, 1990]).

14. See Ernest T. Pascarella and Patrick T. Terenzini, *How College Affects Students: A Third Decade of Research.*, vol. 2 (San Francisco: Jossey-Bass, 2005); Ernest T. Pascarella and Patrick T. Terenzini, *How College Affects Students: Findings and Insights from Twenty Years of Research* (San Francisco: Jossey-Bass, 1991); Matthew J. Mayhew, Alyssa N. Rockenbach, Nicholas A. Bowman, Tricia A. D. Seifert, Gregory C. Wolniak, Ernest T. Pascarella, and Patrick T. Terenzini, *How College Affects Students: 21st Century Evidence That Higher Education Works*, vol. 3 (San Francisco: Jossey-Bass, 2016).

15. Hurtado, "Campus Racial Climate."

16. Hurtado et al., "Model for Diverse Learning Environments."

17. Hurtado et al., "Enacting Diverse Learning Environments."

18. Hurtado et al., "Enacting Diverse Learning Environments."

19. Milem, Chang, and antonio, *Making Diversity Work on Campus*, 18–19.

20. Hurtado et al., "Model for Diverse Learning Environments," 45; Also, Milem, Chang, and antonio, *Making Diversity Work on Campus*.

21. Hurtado et al., "Enacting Diverse Learning Environments;" Milem, Chang, and antonio, *Making Diversity Work on Campus*.

22. Hurtado et al., "A Model for Diverse Learning Environments," 44–45.

23. Hurtado et al., "A Model for Diverse Learning Environments"; Milem, Chang, and antonio, *Making Diversity Work on Campus*.

24. Alexander W. Astin, *What Matters in College? Four Critical Years Revisited* (San Francisco, CA: Jossey-Bass, 1993); Alexander W. Astin, *Four Critical Years: Effects of College on Beliefs, Attitudes, and Knowledge* (San Francisco: Jossey-Bass, 1977); Kenneth A. Feldman, ed., *College & Student: Selected Readings in the Social Psychology of Higher Education* (Oxford, UK: Pergamon, 1972); Kenneth A. Feldman and Theodore M. Newcomb, *The Impact of College on Students* (San Francisco: Jossey-Bass, 1970).

25. Hurtado et al., "Model for Diverse Learning Environments," 46.

26. Hurtado et al., 47–49.

27. Hurtado et al.; Ray, "Theory of Racialized Organizations."

28. Stephen D. Bruning, Shea McGrew, and Mark Cooper, "Town-Gown Relationships: Exploring University-Community Engagement from the Perspective Community Members," *Public Relations Review* 32, no. 2 (2006): 125–130.

29. Hurtado et al., "Model for Diverse Learning Environments," 93–99; Robert Kelchen, *Higher Education and Accountability* (Baltimore: Johns Hopkins University Press, 2018); Barrett J. Taylor and Brendan Cantwell, *Unequal Higher Education: Wealth, Status, and Student Opportunity* (New Brunswick, NJ: Rutgers University Press, 2019).

30. Hurtado et al., "Model for Diverse Learning Environments," 60; Milem, Chang, and antonio, *Making Diversity Work on Campus*; Ray, "Theory of Racialized Organizations."

31. Each of these features is derived from Hurtado et al., "A Model for Diverse Learning Environments"; Hurtado et al., "Value of Climate Assessments"; Hurtado et al., "Enacting Diverse Learning Environments"; Shaun R. Harper and Sylvia Hurtado, "Nine Themes in Campus Racial Climates and Implications for Institutional Transformation," *New Directions for Student Services* 120 (2007): 7–24; *New Directions for Student Services* 120 (2007): 7–24; and Milem, Chang, and antonio, *Making Diversity Work on Campus*.

32. Hurtado et al., "Model for Diverse Learning Environments," 59; Hurtado et al., "Value of Climate Assessments"; Hurtado et al., "Enacting Diverse Learning Environments."

33. Gina Garcia, *Becoming Hispanic Serving Institutions: Opportunities for Colleges and Universities* (Baltimore: Johns Hopkins University Press, 2019).

34. Charles W. Mills, *Racial Contract* (Ithaca, NY: Cornell University Press, 1997); Jennifer C. Mueller, "Racial Ideology or Racial Ignorance? An Alternative Theory of Racial Cognition," *Sociological Theory* 38, no. 2 (2020): 142–169; Ray, "Theory of Racialized Organizations."

35. Hurtado et al., "Model for Diverse Learning Environments"; Hurtado et al., "Enacting Diverse Learning Environments."

36. anthony l. antonio, Mitchell J. Chang, Kenji Hakuta, David A. Kenny, and Jeffrey F. Milem, "Effects of Racial Diversity on Complex Thinking in College Students," *Psychological Science* 15, no. 8 (2004): 507–510; Nicholas A. Bowman, "College Diversity Experiences and Cognitive Development: A Meta-Analysis," *Review of Educational*

Research 80, no. 1 (2010): 4–33; Byrd, *Poison in the Ivy*; Mitchell J. Chang, Alexander W. Astin, and Dongbin Kim, "Cross-Racial Interaction among Undergraduates: Some Consequences, Causes, and Patterns," *Research in Higher Education* 45, no. 5 (2004): 529–553; Mitchell J. Chang, Nida Denson, Victor Saenz, and Kimberly Misa, "The Educational Benefits of Sustaining Cross-Race Interaction Among Undergraduates," *Journal of Higher Education* 77, no. 3 (2006): 430–455; Nida Denson, "Do Curricular and Cocurricular Diversity Activities Influence Racial Bias? A Meta-Analysis," *Review of Educational Research* 79, no. 2 (2009): 805–838; Garces and Jayakumar, "Dynamic Diversity"; Gurin et al., "Diversity and Higher Education"; Hurtado et al., "Model for Diverse Learning Environments."

37. Angela M. Locks, Sylvia Hurtado, Nicholas A. Bowman, and Leticia Oseguera, "Extending Notions of Campus Climate and Diversity to Students' Transition to College," *Review of Higher Education* 31, no. 3 (2008): 257–285; Claude M. Steele, *Whistling Vivaldi: How Stereotypes Affect Us and What We Can Do* (New York: W. W. Norton, 2010); Claude M. Steele, "A Threat in the Air: How Stereotypes Shape Intellectual Identity and Performance," *American Psychologist* 52, no. 6 (1997): 613–629; Claude M. Steele, "Stereotype Threat Does Not Live by Steele and Aronson (1995) Alone," *American Psychologist* 59, no. 1 (2004): 47–48; Claude M. Steele and Joshua Aronson, "Stereotype Threat and Intellectual Performance of African Americans," *Journal of Personality and Social Psychology* 69, no. 5 (1995): 797–811.

38. Garces and Jayakumar, "Dynamic Diversity"; Hurtado et al., "Model for Diverse Learning Environments."

39. Hurtado et al., "Model for Diverse Learning Environments," 66; see also Sylvia Hurtado "The Next Generation of Diversity and Intergroup Contact Research," *Journal of Social Issues* 61, no. 3 (2005): 595–610; Hurtado et al., "Value of Climate Assessments."

40. Gurin et al., *Defending Diversity*; Gurin et al., "Diversity and Higher Education"; Hurtado et al., "Model for Diverse Learning Environments"; Sylvia Hurtado, Eric L. Dey, Patricia Y. Gurin, and Gerald Gurin, "College Environments, Diversity, and Student Learning," in *Higher Education: Handbook of Theory and Research*, ed. J. C. Smart (New York: Springer, 2003), 145–189.

41. Daniel G. Solórzano and Tara J. Yosso, "Critical Race Methodology: Counter-Storytelling as an Analytical Framework for Education Research," *Qualitative Inquiry* 8, no. 1 (2002): 23–44; Derald W. Sue, Christina M. Capodilupo, Gina C. Torino, Jennifer M. Bucceri, Aisha M. B. Holder, Kevin L. Nadal, and Marta Esquilin, "Racial Microaggressions in Everyday Life: Implications for Clinical Practice," *American Psychologist*. 62, no. 4 (2007): 271–286; Hurtado et al., "Model for Diverse Learning Environments."

42. Hurtado et al., "Model for Diverse Learning Environments"; Hurtado et al., "Enacting Diverse Learning Environments."

43. Bowman, "College Diversity Experiences and Cognitive Development"; Byrd, *Poison in the Ivy*; Denson, "Curricular and Cocurricular Diversity Activities"; Hurtado et al., "Model for Diverse Learning Environments"; Hurtado et al., "Enacting Diverse Learning Environments"; Park, *Race on Campus*; Julie J. Park, *When Diversity Drops: Race, Religion, and Affirmative Action in Higher Education* (New Brunswick, NJ: Rutgers University Press, 2003); Jim Sidanius, Shana Levin, Colette van Laar, and David O. Sears, *The Diversity Challenge: Social Identity and Intergroup Relations on the College Campus* (New York: Russell Sage Foundation, 2008).

44. Hurtado et al., "Model for Diverse Learning Environments," 70; see also Hurtado et al., "Enacting Diverse Learning Environments."

45. Kenneth A. Bollen and Rick H. Hoyle, "Perceived Cohesion: A Conceptual and Empirical Examination," *Social Forces* 69, no. 2 (1990): 479–504; Kimberly A. Griffin, Wilfredo del Pilar, Kadian McIntosh, and Autumn Griffin, "'Oh, of Course I'm Going to Go to College': Understanding How Habitus Shapes the College Choice Process of Black Immigrant Students," *Journal of Diversity in Higher Education.* 5, no. 2 (2012): 96–111; Sylvia Hurtado and Deborah F. Carter, "Effects of College Transition and Perceptions of the Campus Racial Climate on Latino College Students' Sense of Belonging," *Sociology of Education* 70, no. 4 (1997): 324–345; Locks et al., "Students' Transition to College"; Laura I. Rendón, "Validating Culturally Diverse Students: Toward a New Model of Learning and Student Development," *Innovative Higher Education* 19, no. 1 (1994): 33–51. See W. Carson Byrd, Rachelle J. Brunn-Bevel, and Sarah M. Ovink, eds., *Intersectionality and Higher Education: Identity and Inequality on College Campuses* (New Brunswick, NJ: Rutgers University Press, 2019), for examples of how intersectionality can reveal more information on the experiences of students, faculty, and staff on college campuses.

46. Kristen A. Clayton, "Biracial College Students' Racial Identity Work: How Black-White Biracial Students Navigate Racism and Privilege at Historically Black and Historical White Institutions," in *Intersectionality and Higher Education: Identity and Inequality on College Campuses*, ed. W. Carson Byrd, R. J. Brunn-Bevel, and S. M. Ovink (New Brunswick, NJ: Rutgers University Press, 2019), 73–87; Kimberly A. Griffin, Jessica C. Bennett, and Jessica Harris, "Marginalizing Merit? Gender Differences in Black Faculty D/discourses on Tenure, Advancement, and Professional Success," *Review of Higher Education* 36, no. 4 (2013): 489–512; Kimberly A. Griffin, Marcela M. Muñiz, and Lorelle Espinosa, "The Influence of Campus Racial Climate on Diversity in Graduate Education," *Review of Higher Education* 35, no. 4 (2011): 535–566; Kimberly A. Giffin, Jessica C. Bennett, and Jessica Harris, "Analyzing Gender Differences in Black Faculty Marginalization Through a Sequential Mixed-Methods Design," *New Directions for Institutional Research* 151 (2011): 45–61; Kimberly A. Griffin, Meghan J. Pifer, Jordan R. Humphrey, and Ashley M. Hazelwood, "(Re)Defining Departure: Exploring Black Professors' Experiences with and Responses to Racism and Racial Climate," *American Journal of Education* 117, no. 4 (2011): 495–526; Hurtado et al., "Model for Diverse Learning Environments"; Locks et al., "Students' Transition to College"; Samuel D. Museus and Kimberly A. Griffin, "Mapping the Margins in Higher Education: On the Promise of Intersectionality Frameworks in Research and Discourse," *New Directions for Institutional Research* 151 (2012): 5–13; Samuel D. Museus and Dina C. Maramba, "The Impact of Culture on Filipino American Students' Sense of Belonging," *Review of Higher Education* 34, no. 2 (2011): 231–258; Samuel D. Museus, Andrew H. Nichols, and Amber D. Lambert, "Racial Differences in the Effects of Campus Racial Climate on Degree Completion: A Structural Equation Model," *Review of Higher Education* 32, no. 1 (2008): 107–134.

47. Steele, *Whistling Vivaldi*; Steele, "Stereotype Threat"; Steele, "A Threat in the Air"; Steele and Aronson, "Stereotype Threat and Intellectual Performance."

48. Nolan L. Cabrera, *White Guys on Campus: Racism, White Immunity, and the Myth of "Post-Racial" Higher Education* (New Brunswick, NJ: Rutgers University Press, 2018); Byrd, *Poison in the Ivy*; Park, *Race on Campus*; Park, *When Diversity Drops*; Natasha K. Warikoo, *The Diversity Bargain: And Other Dilemmas of Race, Admissions, and Meritocracy at Elite Universities* (Chicago: University of Chicago Press, 2016).

49. Hurtado et al., "Model for Diverse Learning Environments," 69–70.

50. Linda Darling-Hammond, "Race, Inequality, and Educational Accountability: The Irony of 'No Child Left Behind,'" *Race, Ethnicity and Education* 10, no. 3 (2007): 245–260; Wendy N. Espeland and Michael Sauder, *Engines of Anxiety: Academic Rankings, Reputation, and Accountability* (New York: Russell Sage, 2016); Hurtado et al., "Model for Diverse Learning Environments"; Amanda E. Lewis and John B. Diamond, *Despite the Best Intentions: How Racial Inequality Thrives in Good Schools* (New York: Oxford University Press, 2015); Diane Ravitch, *The Reign of Error: The Hoax of the Privatization Movement and the Danger to America's Public Schools* (New York: Vintage, 2013); Diane Ravitch, *The Death and Life of the Great American School System: How Testing and Choice Are Undermining Education* (New York: Basic Books, 2010).

51. Nicholas A. Bowman, "Promoting Sustained Engagement with Diversity: The Reciprocal Relationships Between Informal and Formal College Diversity Experiences," *Review of Higher Education* 36, no. 1 (2012): 1–24; Bowman, "College Diversity Experiences and Cognitive Development"; Denson, "Curricular and Cocurricular Diversity Activities"; Harper and Hurtado, "Nine Themes in Campus Racial Climates"; Jenni Hart and Jennifer Fellabaum, "Analyzing Campus Climate Studies: Seeking to Define and Understand," *Journal of Diversity in Higher Education* 1, no. 4 (2008): 222–234; Hurtado et al., "Value of Climate Assessments."

52. Hurtado et al., "Model for Diverse Learning Environments"; Hurtado et al., "Value of Climate Assessments"; Hurtado et al., "Enacting Diverse Learning Environments."

53. Hurtado et al., "Model for Diverse Learning Environments"; Hurtado et al., "Value of Climate Assessments"; Hurtado et al., "Enacting Diverse Learning Environments"; Milem, Chang, and antonio, *Making Diversity Work on Campus.*

54. Espeland and Sauder, *Engines of Anxiety*; Hirschman, Berrey, and Rose-Greenland, "Dequantifying Diversity."

55. Bowman, "College Diversity Experiences and Cognitive Development"; Denson, "Curricular and Cocurricular Diversity Activities"; Hurtado et al., "Model for Diverse Learning Environments"; Hurtado et al., "Value of Climate Assessments"; Hurtado et al., "Enacting Diverse Learning Environments"; Milem, Chang, and antonio, *Making Diversity Work on Campus.*

56. Gurin et al., *Defending Diversity*; Gurin et al., "Diversity and Higher Education"; Hurtado et al., "Model for Diverse Learning Environments"; Hurtado et al., "College Environments, Diversity, and Student Learning"; Hurtado et al., "Enacting Diverse Learning Environments."

57. A possibility that a connection between organizational and behavioral dimensions of campus climates was tested with similar models but was not supported by the analyses.

58. Espeland and Sauder, *Engines of Anxiety*; Nicole M. Garcia, Nancy López, and Verónica Vélez, "QuantCrit: Rectifying Quantitative Methods Through Critical Race Theory," *Race Ethnicity and Education* 21, no. 2 (2018): 149–157; David Gillborn, Paul Warmington, and Sean Demack, "QuantCrit: Education, Policy, 'Big Data,' and Principles for a Critical Race Theory of Statistics," *Race Ethnicity and Education* 21, no. 2 (2018): 158–179; Hirschman, Berrey, and Rose-Greenland, "Dequantifying Diversity"; Daniel Hirschman and Emily A. Bosk "Standardizing Biases: Selection Devices and the Quantification of Race," *Sociology of Race and Ethnicity* (2019): DOI: https://doi.org /10.1177/2332649219844797; Nancy López, Christopher Erwin, Melissa Binder, and Mario J. Chavez, "Making the Invisible Visible: Advancing Quantitative Methods in Higher Education Using Critical Race Theory and Intersectionality," *Race Ethnicity and Education* 21, no. 2 (2018): 180–207.

59. Espeland and Sauder, *Engines of Anxiety*.
60. Garcia, López, and Vélez, "QuantCrit"; Gillborn, Warmington, and Demack, "Quant-Crit"; López et al., "Making the Invisible Visible"; Jenna Sablan, "Can You Really Measure That? Critical Race Theory and Quantitative Methods," *American Educational Research Journal* 56, no. 1 (2019): 178–203.
61. Hurtado et al., "Model for Diverse Learning Environments"; Hurtado et al., "Enacting Diverse Learning Environments"; Ray, "Theory of Racialized Organizations."
62. James M. Thomas, *Diversity Regimes: Why Talk Is Not Enough to Fix Racial Inequality at Universities* (New Brunswick, NJ: Rutgers University Press, 2020); see also Berrey, *Enigma of Diversity*.
63. Espeland and Sauder, *Engines of Anxiety*.
64. Ray, "Theory of Racialized Organizations."
65. Ray.
66. Warikoo, *Diversity Bargain*; See also Byrd, *Poison in the Ivy*, for related discussion of students' individualization of racial inequality.
67. Garcia, *Becoming Hispanic Serving Institutions*.
68. Garcia; see also Cabrera, *White Guys on Campus*; Nolan L. Cabrera, Jeremy D. Franklin, and Jesse S. Watson, *Whiteness in Higher Education: The Missing Link in Diversity and Racial Analyses* (Hoboken, NJ: Wiley, 2017), for more on how whiteness is embedded in universities.
69. Thomas, *Diversity Regimes*.
70. Martha Ackelsberg, Jeni Hart, Naomi J. Miller, Kate Queeny, and Susan Van Dyne, "Faculty Microclimate Change at Smith College," in *Doing Diversity in Higher Education: Faculty Leaders Share Challenges and Strategies*, ed. W. Brown-Glaude (New Brunswick, NJ: Rutgers University Press, 2009), 83–102, especially p. 84.
71. Garcia, *Becoming Hispanic Serving Institutions*; Gina A. Garcia, "Exploring Student Affairs Professionals' Experiences with the Campus Racial Climate at a Hispanic Serving Institution (HSI)," *Journal of Diversity in Higher Education* 9, no. 1 (2016): 20–33.
72. Kimberly A. Griffin, *Achieving Diversity and the Intersection of STEM Culture and Campus Climate* (Washington, DC: American Council on Education, 2019).
73. Annemarie Vaccaro, "Campus Microclimates for LGBT Faculty, Staff, and Students: An Exploration of the Intersections of Social Identities and Campus Roles," *Journal of Student Affairs Research and Practice* 49, no. 4 (2012): 429–446.
74. Baez, "'Knowledge of Difference'"; Berrey, *Enigma of Diversity*; Chang et al., *Compelling Interest*; Garces and Jayakumar, "Dynamic Diversity"; Gurin et al., *Defending Diversity*; Gurin et al., "Diversity and Higher Education"; Jayakumar and Garces, *Affirmative Action and Racial Equity*; Jeffrey S. Lehman, "The Evolving Language of Diversity and Integration in Discussions of Affirmative Action from *Bakke* to *Grutter*," in *Defending Diversity: Affirmative Action at the University of Michigan*, ed. P. Gurin, J. S. Lehman, and E. Lewis (Ann Arbor: University of Michigan Press, 2004), 61–96"; Milem, Chang, and antonio, *Making Diversity Work on Campus*; Okechukwu, *To Fulfill These Rights*; Scott R. Palmer, "Diversity and Affirmative Action: Evolving Principles and Continuing Legal Battles," in *Diversity Challenged: Evidence on the Impact of Affirmative Action*, ed. G. Orfield (Cambridge, MA: The Civil Rights Project, 2001), 81–88; Park, *Race on Campus*.
75. Also noted by Hurtado et al., "Model for Diverse Learning Environments," 99–100.
76. Dominique J. Baker, "Pathways to Racial Equity in Higher Education: Modeling the Antecedents of State Affirmative Action Bans," *American Educational Research Journal*

56, no. 5 (2019): 1861–1895; Susan K. Brown, and Charles Hirschman, "The End of Affirmative Action in Washington State and Its Impact on the Transition from High School to College," *Sociology of Education* 79, no. 2 (2006): 106–130; Mark C. Long and Nicole A. Bateman, "Long-Run Changes in Underrepresentation After Affirmative Action Bans in Public Universities," *Educational Evaluation and Policy Analysis* 42, no. 2 (2020): 188–207.

77. Baker, "Pathways to Racial Equity."

78. Hurtado et al., "Model for Diverse Learning Environments," 88–101.

79. For more on the social structure and personality framework, see James S. House, "Social Support and Social Structure," *Sociological Forum* 2, no. 2 (1987): 135–146; James S. House, "The Three Faces of Social Psychology," *Sociometry* 40, no. 2 (1977): 161–177; James S. House, Deborah J. Umberson, and Karl R. Landers, "Structures and Processes of Social Support," *Annual Review of Sociology* 14 (1988): 293–318; and Jane McLeod and Kathryn J. Lively, "Social Structure and Personality," in *Handbook of Social Psychology*, ed. J. Delamater (New York: Springer, 2006), 77–102.

80. Brunsma, Embrick, and Thomas, "College Leaders Often Deny Racial Tensions."

81. Eddie R. Cole, "Colleges Have a Lot to Answer For—Beyond Racists' Names on Their Buildings," *Los Angeles Times*, July 8, 2020, https://www.latimes.com/opinion/story/2020-07-08/colleges-racists-woodrow-wilson-history; Cole, *Campus Color Line*; Eddie R. Cole and Shaun R. Harper, "Race and Rhetoric: An Analysis of College Presidents' Statements on Campus Racial Incidents," *Journal of Diversity in Higher Education* 10, no. 4 (2017): 318–333.

82. Garcia, *Becoming Hispanic Serving Institutions*; Ray, "Theory of Racialized Organizations"; Thomas, *Diversity Regimes*.

Chapter 4

1. See Whitney N. L. Pirtle, "Racial Capitalism: A Fundamental Cause of Novel Coronavirus (COVID-19) Pandemic Inequities in the United States," *Health Education & Behavior* 47, no. 4 (2020), DOI: https://doi.org/10.1177/1090198120922942, for discussion about the role of racial capitalism in COVID-19 health disparities. For the role of universities in broader racial health disparities over the years, see Alondra Nelson, *Body and Soul: The Black Panther Party and the Fight Against Medical Discrimination* (Minneapolis: University of Minnesota Press, 2013); Harriet A. Washington, *Medical Apartheid: The Dark History of Medical Experimentation on Black Americans form Colonial Times to the Present* (New York: Anchor Books, 2006); and Craig Steven Wilder, *Ebony & Ivy: Race, Slavery, and the Troubled History of America's Universities* (New York: Bloomsbury Press, 2013), among others.

2. W. E. B. Du Bois, *Dusk of Dawn: An Essay Toward an Autobiography of a Race Concept, The Oxford W. E. B. Du Bois*, ed. H. L. Gates (New York: Oxford University Press, 2007[1940]), 24.

3. Rashawn Ray, "George Floyd's Murder Is the Twenty-First Century Emmett Till Moment: How Sociological Research Informs Police Reform," *ASA Footnotes* 48, no. 4 (2020): 3–5, page 5.

4. W. Carson Byrd and William D. Lopez, "College Students Will Bring Racial Economic Disparities of the Pandemic Back with Them to Campus," *Washington Post*, July 20, 2020, https://www.washingtonpost.com/nation/2020/07/20/college-students-will-bring-racial-economic-disparities-pandemic-back-campus-are-universities-ready.

5. For more about the consequences of the happy talk of diversity, see Joyce M. Bell and Douglas Hartmann, "Diversity in Everyday Discourse: The Cultural Ambiguities and Consequences of 'Happy Talk,'" *American Sociological Review* 72, no. 6 (2007): 895–914; see also Sara Ahmed, *On Being Included: Racism and Diversity in Institutional Life* (Durham, NC: Duke University Press, 2012); T. Elon Dancy II, Kristen T. Edwards, and James Earl Davis, "Historically White Universities and Plantation Politics: Anti-Blackness and Higher Education in the Black Lives Matter Era," *Urban Education* 53, no. 2 (2018): 176–195; Gina Garcia, *Becoming Hispanic Serving Institutions: Opportunities for Colleges and Universities* (Baltimore: Johns Hopkins University Press, 2019); James M. Thomas, *Diversity Regimes: Why Talk Is Not Enough to Fix Racial Inequality at Universities* (New Brunswick, NJ: Rutgers University Press, 2020).

6. Victor E. Ray, "A Theory of Racialized Organizations," *American Sociological Review* 84, no. 1 (2019): 26–53.

7. See Wendy N. Espeland, and Michael Sauder, *Engines of Anxiety: Academic Rankings, Reputation, and Accountability* (New York: Russell Sage, 2016); Daniel Hirschman, Ellen Berrey, and Fiona Rose-Greenland, "Dequantifying Diversity: Affirmative Action at the University of Michigan," *Theory & Society* 45, no. 3 (2016): 265–301.

8. Ray, "Theory of Racialized Organizations"; see also Eduardo Bonilla-Silva, *Racism Without Racists: Color-Blind Racism and the Persistence of Racial Inequality in the United States*, 5th ed. (Lanham, MD: Rowman & Littlefield, 2017).

9. Hirschman, Berrey, and Rose-Greenland, "Dequantifying Diversity."

10. Hurtado et al., "Model for Diverse Learning Environments"; Hurtado et al., "Enacting Diverse Learning Environments"; Garces and Jayakumar, "Dynamic Diversity"; Julie J. Park, *Race on Campus: Debunking Myths with Data* (Cambridge, MA: Harvard Educational Press, 2018).

11. Ahmed, *On Being Included*; Bell and Hartmann, "Diversity in Everyday Discourse"; Garcia, *Becoming Hispanic Serving Institutions*; Thomas, *Diversity Regimes*.

12. Ahmed, *On Being Included*; Bell and Hartmann, "Diversity in Everyday Discourse"; Thomas, *Diversity Regimes*.

13. US Department of Justice, "Justice Department Finds Yale Illegally Discriminates Against Asians and Whites in Undergraduate Admissions in Violation of Federal Civil-Rights Laws," *Justine News*, August 13, 2020, https://www.justice.gov/opa/pr/justice-department-finds-yale-illegally-discriminates-against-asians-and-whites-undergraduate.

14. See also Sigal Alon, *Race, Class, and Affirmative Action* (New York: Russell Sage Foundation, 2015); Berrey, *Enigma of Diversity*; and Amaka Okechukwu, *To Fulfill these Rights: Political Struggle over Affirmative Action and Open Admissions* (New York: Columbia University Press, 2019), for further discussion of the political battle around the University of Texas admissions policies and the implementation and effectiveness of the percentage-plan admissions approach.

15. US Department of Justice, "Yale Illegally Discriminates."

16. Garces and Jayakumar, "Dynamic Diversity"; Park, *Race on Campus*; see also Yuvraj Joshi, "Measuring Diversity," *Columbia Law Review Online* 117 (2017): 54–69.

17. Ray, "Theory of Racialized Organizations."

18. Baez, "'Knowledge of Difference'"; Robert T. Teranishi, Bach Mai Dolly Nguyen, Cynthia M. Alcantar, and Edward R. Curammeng, eds., *Measuring Race: Why Disaggregating Data Matters for Addressing Educational Inequality* (New York: Teachers College Press, 2020).

19. José Itzigsohn, and Karida Brown, *The Sociology of W. E. B. Du Bois: Racialized Modernity and the Global Color Line* (New York: New York University Press, 2020); Aldon Morris, *The Scholar Denied: W. E. B. Du Bois and the Birth of Modern Sociology* (Berkeley: University of California Press, 2015); Earl Wright II, *First American School of Sociology: W. E. B. Du Bois and the Atlanta Sociological Laboratory* (New York: Ashgate, 2018).

20. Sara Goldrick-Rab, *Paying the Price: College Costs, Financial Aid, and the Betrayal of the American Dream* (Chicago: University of Chicago Press, 2020); Robert Kelchen, Sara Goldrick-Rab, and Braden Hosch. "The Costs of College Attendance: Examining Variation and Consistency in Institutional Living Cost Allowances," *Journal of Higher Education* 88, no. 6 (2018): 947–971.

21. Espeland and Sauder, *Engines of Anxiety*.

22. Espeland and Sauder.

23. Espeland and Sauder; Hirschman, Berrey, and Rose-Greenland, "Dequantifying Diversity"; Theodore M. Porter, *Trust in Numbers: The Pursuit of Objectivity in Science and Public Life* (Princeton, NJ: Princeton University Press, 1995).

24. William G. Bowen, Matthew M. Chingos, and Michael S. McPherson, *Crossing the Finish Line: Completing Colleges at America's Public Universities* (Princeton, NJ: Princeton University Press 2009); Thomas J. Espenshade and Alexandria Walton Radford, *No Longer Separate, Not Yet Equal: Race and Class in Elite College Admissions and Campus Life* (Princeton, NJ: Princeton University Press, 2009).

25. Espenshade and Radford, *No Longer Separate, Not Yet Equal*, 249 and 261, note academic mismatch can produce "frog pond" effects whereby students with high grades and test scores may attend less selective institutions and perform better than they may have at a more selective institution. Also, although selectivity is considered important in a variety of analyses, it does not indicate how much students learn in college (see Ernest T. Pascarella and Patrick T. Terenzini, *How College Affects Students: A Third Decade of Research.*, vol. 2 [San Francisco: Jossey-Bass, 2005]).

26. W. Carson Byrd, *Poison in the Ivy: Race Relations and the Reproduction of Inequality on Elite College Campuses* (New Brunswick, NJ: Rutgers University Press, 2017); Ray, "Theory of Racialized Organizations."

27. See Julie Park's important discussion in Park, *Race on Campus*, chapter 6.

28. Barrett J. Taylor and Brendan Cantwell, *Unequal Higher Education: Wealth, Status, and Student Opportunity* (New Brunswick, NJ: Rutgers University Press, 2019).

29. See Ben Hofstra, Vivek V. Kulkarni, Sebastian Munoz-Najar Galvez, Bryan He, Dan Jurafsky, and Daniel A. McFarland, "The Diversity-Innovation Paradox in Science," *Proceedings of the National Academy of Science* 117, no. 17 (2020): 9284–9291, for a discussion of how scholars of color are not rewarded at the same rate as white scholars are for their research.

30. See, for example, William G. Bowen and Derek Bok, *The Shape of the River: Long-Term Consequences of Considering Race in College and University Admissions* (Princeton, NJ: Princeton University Press, 1998); William G. Bowen, Martin A. Kurzweil, and Eugene M. Tobin, *Equity and Excellence in American Higher Education* (Charlottesville: University of Virginia Press, 2005); Steven Brint, *Two Cheers for Higher Education: Why American Universities are Stronger than Ever—and How to Meet Challenges They Face* (Princeton, NJ: Princeton University Press, 2019), Adrianna J. Kezar, Tony C. Chambers, and John C. Burkhardt, eds., *Higher Education for the Public Good: Emerging Voices of a National Movement* (San Francisco: Jossey-Bass, 2005).

31. Kezar, Chambers, and Burkhardt, *Higher Education for the Public Good*, xii–xvi.

32. Berrey, *Enigma of Diversity*; Martha Biondi, *Black Revolution on Campus* (Berkeley: University of California Press, 2012); Bradley, *Upending the Ivory Tower*; Bradley, *Harlem vs. Columbia University*; W. Carson Byrd, LeAnna Luney, Jakia Marie, and Kimberly N. Sanders, "Demanding Attention: An Exploration of Institutional Characteristics of Recent Student Demands," *Journal of Diversity in Higher Education*, (2019): DOI: https/doi.org/10.1037/dhe0000133; Cole, *Campus Color Line*; Ibram Kendi [Ibram Rogers], *Black Campus Movement: Black Students and the Racial Reconstitution of Higher Education, 1965–1972* (New York: Palgram Macmillan, 2012); Demetri L. Morgan, and Charles H. F. Davis, eds., *Student Activism, Politics, and Campus Climate in Higher Education* (New York: Routledge, 2019); Fabio Rojas, *From Black Power to Black Studies: How a Radical Social Movement Became an Academic Discipline* (Baltimore: Johns Hopkins University Press, 2007); Katherine I. E. Wheatle and Felecia Commodore, "Reaching Back to Move Forward: The Historic and Contemporary Role of Student Activism in the Development and Implementation of Higher Education Policy," *Review of Higher Education* 42, supplement (2019): 5–35.

33. Rahsaan Mahadeo, "As Campuses Cut Ties to Police, Sociology Departments Must Do the Same," *Truthout*, July 21, 2020, https://truthout.org/articles/as-campuses-cut-ties-to-police-sociology-departments-must-do-the-same; University of Minnesota Department of Sociology, "George Floyd and the Minneapolis Uprising: A Statement from the University of Minnesota Department of Sociology," June 2, 2020, https://cla.umn.edu/sociology/news-events/news/george-floyd-and-minneapolis-uprising-statement-university-minnesota-sociology-department-faculty.

34. John J. Sloan III, "Race, Violence, Justice, and Campus Police," *ASA Footnotes* 48, no. 4 (2020): 9–11.

35. W. Carson Byrd and Jacob Rugh, "Town-Gown Segregation: How Colleges Influence Residential Segregation," paper presentation, American Sociological Association annual conference, New York City, August 2019.

36. For example, Duke University recently blocked the creation of a light-rail public transportation option in Durham, which can impact employment, housing, and overall community-university relations and possible election results (see Jeffrey C. Billman, "We Spent 20 Years and $130 Million Dollars on Light Rail. Then Duke Decided It Was Inconvenient," *Indy Week*, March 5, 2019, https://indyweek.com/news/northcarolina/duke-light-rail-gotriangle-durham; Richard Faussett, "Durham Dreamed of a Transit Line. Duke All but Killed it," *New York Time*, March 18, 2019, https://www.nytimes.com/2019/03/18/us/duke-durham-light-rail-chapel-hill.html; Jane Stancill, "Thanks to Duke, Durham's Light Rail Dream Is All but Dead," *CityLab*, March 14, 2019, https://www.citylab.com/transportation/2019/03/durham-light-rail-duke-gotriangle-transit-research-triangle/584839). Additionally, the history of higher education includes many episodes of confrontation with communities—confrontations that have racial inequality implications (see Ellen Berrey, *The Enigma of Diversity: The Language and the Limits of Racial Justice* [Chicago: University of Chicago Press, 2015]; Dancy et al., "Historically White Universities and Plantation Politics"; Roger Geiger, *The History of American Higher Education: Learning and Culture from the Founding of World War II* (Princeton, NJ: Princeton University Press, 2016); David F. Labaree, *A Perfect Mess: The Unlikely Ascendancy of American Higher Education* (Chicago: University of Chicago Press, 2016); Nelson, *Body and Soul*; Okechukwu, *To Fulfill these Rights*; John R. Thelin, *A History of American Higher Education*, 3rd ed. (Baltimore: Johns Hopkins University Press, 2019); Washington, *Medical Apartheid*; Wilder, *Ebony and Ivy*.

37. Amalia Dache, "Ferguson's Radical Imagination and the Scyborgs of Community-Student Resistance," *Review of Higher Education* 42, supplement (2019): 63–84.

38. Ahmed, *On Being Included*; derria byrd, "The Diversity Distraction: A Critical Comparative Analysis of Discourse in Higher Education Scholarship," *Review of Higher Education* 42, supplement (2019): 135–172; Veronica Lerma, Laura T. Hamilton, and Kelly Nielsen, "Racialized Equity Labor, University Appropriation, and Student Resistance," *Social Problems* 67, no. 2 (2020): 286–303; Chris Linder, Stephen J. Quaye, Alex C. Lange, Ricky E. Roberts, Marvette C. Lacy, and Wilson K. Okello, "'A Student Should Have the Privilege of Just Being a Student': Student Activism as Labor," *Review of Higher Education* 42, supplement (2019): 37–62; Lori D. Patton, Berenice Sánchez, and D-L Stewart, "An Inconvenient Truth About 'Progress': An Analysis of the Promises and Perils of Campus Diversity Initiatives," *Review of Higher Education* 42, supplement (2019): 173–198; Kelly E. Slay, Kimberly A. Reyes, and Julie R. Posselt, "Bait and Switch: Representation, Climate, and Tensions of Diversity Work in Graduate Education," *Review of Higher Education* 42, supplement (2019): 255–286; Thomas, *Diversity Regimes*.

39. See Byrd et al., "Demanding Attention."

40. Espeland and Sauder, *Engines of Anxiety*; Park, *Race on Campus*; Louise Seamster and Victor E. Ray "Against Teleology in the Study of Race: Toward the Abolition of Progress Paradigm," *Sociological Theory* 36, no. 4 (2018): 315–342.

41. Ibram X Kendi, *How to Be an Antiracist* (New York: One World, 2019); Victor E. Ray "Antiracism Is a Constant Struggle," *Contexts* (2020), https://contexts.org/articles/antiracism-is-a-constant-struggle; Ray, "Theory of Racialized Organizations."

Appendix

1. Nolan L. Cabrera, "Where Is the Racial Theory in Critical Race Theory? A Constructive Criticism of the Crits," *Review of Higher Education* 42, no. 1 (2018): 209–233; Maria Ledesma, "California Sunset: O'Conner's Post-Affirmative Action Ideal Comes of Age in California," *Review of Higher Education* 42, no. supplement (2019): 227–254.

2. Sylvia Hurtado, "The Campus Racial Climate: Contexts of Conflict," *Journal of Higher Education* 63, no. 5 (1992): 539–569; Sylvia Hurtado, Cynthia L. Alvarez, Chelsea Guillermo-Wann, Marcela Cuellar, and Lucy Arellano, "A Model for Diverse Learning Environments: The Scholarship on Creating and Assessing Conditions for Student Success," in *Higher Education: Handbook of Theory and Research*, vol. 27, ed. J. C. Smart and M. B. Paulsen (New York: Springer, 2012), 41–122; Sylvia Hurtado, Jeffrey Milem, Alma Clayton-Pedersen, and Walter Allen, "Enacting Diverse Learning Environments: Improving the Climate for Racial/Ethnic Diversity in Higher Education," ASHE-ERIC Higher Education Report, vol. 26, no. 8 (Washington, DC: George Washington University, 1999).

3. Hurtado et al., "Model for Diverse Learning Environments"; Jeffrey F. Milem, Mitchell J. Chang, and anthony l. antonio, *Making Diversity Work on Campus: A Research-Based Perspective* (Washington, DC: Association of American Colleges & Universities, 2005).

4. Hurtado et al., "Model for Diverse Learning Environments"; Hurtado et al., "Enacting Diverse Learning Environments."

5. Nicholas A. Bowman, "College Diversity Experiences and Cognitive Development: A Meta-Analysis," *Review of Educational Research* 80, no. 1 (2010): 4–33"; Nida Denson, "Do Curricular and Cocurricular Diversity Activities Influence Racial Bias? A Meta-Analysis," *Review of Educational Research* 79, no. 2 (2009): 805–838"; Shaun R. Harper and Sylvia Hurtado, "Nine Themes in Campus Racial Climates and Implications for

Institutional Transformation," *New Directions for Student Services* 120 (2007): 7–24; Sylvia Hurtado, Kimberly A. Griffin, Lucy Arellano, and Marcela Cuellar, "Assessing the Value of Climate Assessments: Progress and Future Directions," *Journal of Diversity in Higher Education* 1, no. 4 (2008): 204–221."

6. See also Hurtado et al., "Model for Diverse Learning Environments," 69–70.

7. Hurtado, "Campus Racial Climate."

8. Roberta M. Hall and Bernice R. Sandler, *Out of the Classroom: A Chilly Campus Climate for Women?* Project on the Status and Education of Women (Washington, DC: Association of American Colleges, 1984); Bernice R. Sandler and Roberta M. Hall, *The Campus Climate Revisited: Chilly for Women, Administrators, and Graduate Students*, Project on the Status and Education of Women (Washington, DC: Association of American Colleges, 1986).

9. Hurtado et al., "Model for Diverse Learning Environments"; Hurtado et al., "Enacting Diverse Learning Environments."

10. Shaun R. Harper, "Race Without Racism: How Higher Education Researchers Minimize Racist Institutional Norms," *Review of Higher Education* 36, no. 1 (2012): 9–30.

11. Fabio Rojas, W. Carson Byrd, and Sanjay Saint, "Institutional Origins of Health Care Associated Infection Knowledge: Lessons from an Analysis of Articles About Methicillin-Resistant Staphylococcus Aureus Published in Leading Biomedical Journals from 1960–2009," *American Journal of Infection Control* 43, no. 2 (2015): 121–126.

12. Bowman, "College Diversity Experiences and Cognitive Development"; Denson, "Curricular and Cocurricular Diversity Activities"; Harper and Hurtado, "Nine Themes in Campus Racial Climates"; Hurtado et al., "Model for Diverse Learning Environments"; Hurtado et al., "Value of Climate Assessments"; Hurtado et al., "Enacting Diverse Learning Environments."

13. Marc P. Johnston-Guerrero, "The (Mis)Uses of Race in Research on College Students: A Systematic Review," *Journal Committed to Social Change on Race and Ethnicity* 3, no. 1 (2017): 6–41.

14. Cabrera, "Where Is the Racial Theory in Critical Race Theory?"; Harper, "Race Without Racism"; Klaus Krippendorff, *Content Analysis: An Introduction to Its Methodology*, 3rd ed. (Newbury Park, CA: Sage, 2013); Ledesma, "California Sunset"; Matthew B. Miles and A. Michael Huberman, *Qualitative Data Analysis*, 2nd ed. (Thousand Oaks, CA: Sage, 1994).

15. Bowman, "College Diversity Experiences and Cognitive Development"; Denson, "Curricular and Cocurricular Diversity Activities"; Harper and Hurtado, "Nine Themes in Campus Racial Climates"; Hurtado et al., "Model for Diverse Learning Environments"; Hurtado et al., "Value of Climate Assessments"; Hurtado et al., "Enacting Diverse Learning Environments."

Acknowledgments

I told myself that I was not going to write another book. After all, for my first book, it took me over five years to dust off my dissertation and turn it into something people may want to read. Yet, while I examined race and racism in higher education and how social inequalities evolved, the outside world, too, was grappling with these issues. The seeming deluge of attacks on both race-conscious admissions policies and diversity initiatives, and the questioning generally floating through the ether of society about whether race mattered in higher education and life, prompted me to weigh in on these issues. I wanted to explore how we can better study and talk about racial inequality to produce racial equity, inclusivity, and justice on college campuses. This was not an easy task, but I had a wonderful group of friends and colleagues behind me. Without them, this book would still be scribbles in a moleskin notebook.

Thank you, Jayne Fargnoli, for shepherding this project along at Harvard Education Press. When the world was falling apart and my writing was suffering from it, you always encouraged me to craft a conversation that would speak to more than just fellow researchers. Thank you to Anne Noonan for working with me throughout the production process, and Patricia Boyd for your excellent editing pen. Thanks are also owed to David Brunsma, David Embrick, Oliver Rollins, Joshua Brown, Jessica Buckley, Melanie Gast, and Sarah Ovink for the feedback on earlier iterations of this book's ideas. Thank you, Elizabeth Popp Berman, Ellen Berrey, Nolan Cabrera, Karly Ford, Daniel Hirschman, and prabhdeep kehal, for taking the time to read over chapter drafts and pointing out where arguments did not align or where I needed to dive deeper into ideas for stronger takeaways. If there is one person who was always willing to provide feedback, tell me bluntly that I needed to do more, or chat about the writing process and the many headaches it causes, especially while living through an era where it seemed as if the whole world were on fire and that the uncertainty would continue forever, it was Victor Ray. Thank you for your continued friendship.

Encouragement from a (social) distance was also a necessity throughout this writing process. Kind words, support, and inspiration along the way came from many people, including Elizabeth Armstrong, Dominique Baker, Latrica Best, Jenni Brady, Sara Brownell, Rachelle Brunn-Bevel, Tabbye Chavous, Susan Cheng, Ryon Cobb, Dan Collier, Paul Courant, Charles Davis, Pawan Dhingra, Allyson Flaster, Raúl Gámez, Neil Gong, Ellington Graves, James Hammond, Tony Jack, Yuvraj Joshi, Nita Kedharnath, Ben Koester, Ji-won Lee, Steve Lonn, Bill Lopez, Juniar Lucien, Chris Marsicano, David Martinez, Tim McKay, Becky Wai-Ling Packard, Julie Park, Meaghan Pearson, OiYan Poon, Rashawn Ray, Fabio Rojas, Louise Seamster, Megan Segoshi, Jarell Skinner-Roy, Kevin Stange, J. T. Thomas, Marie Ting, Paulette Vincent-Ruz, Aya Waller-Bey, Natasha Warikoo, Maiya Whiteside, Cobretti Williams, Janelle Wong, and Al Young. Most of this book was written while I was a Scholar in Residence at the National Center for Institutional Diversity and the Department of Sociology at the University of Michigan. This opportunity would not have existed or been as fruitful without the generous support from Tabbye Chavous, Karin Martin, Ching-Yune Sylvester, Marie Ting, Dana Brown, Laura Sánchez-Parkinson, and Charlotte Ezzo. I was also supported while writing this book by my gracious colleagues in the Department of Sociology at the University of Louisville.

The last acknowledgment is saved for the person who is loving, supportive, and, above all, brilliant. Thank you to my partner in life, Kat. Despite the many struggles we have faced, which includes a global pandemic now, we have faced them together. As always, here's to the many pages we continue to write together in life after this book.

About the Author

W. Carson Byrd, Faculty Director of Diversity and Equity Research Initiatives for the National Center for Institutional Diversity at the University of Michigan and associate professor of sociology at the University of Louisville, examines higher education inequality with a particular focus on race and racism. He is the author of *Poison in the Ivy: Race Relations and the Reproduction of Inequality on Elite College Campuses* (Rutgers University Press, 2017), which explores college students' beliefs about race and racial inequality and how their social interactions during college can shape these beliefs. He is also the coeditor of *Intersectionality and Higher Education: Identity and Inequality on College Campuses* (Rutgers University Press, 2019), a compilation of scholarship on how students, faculty, and staff navigate unequal campuses and understand the inequality around them as they live, work, and study. His work has also appeared beyond academic journals in forums such as the *Washington Post, InsideHigherEd*, and the *Chronicle of Higher Education*, among others.

Index